Crime Reduction and Community Safety

Crime Reduction and Community Safety
Labour and the politics of local crime control

Daniel Gilling

WILLAN
PUBLISHING

Published by

Willan Publishing
Culmcott House
Mill Street, Uffculme
Cullompton, Devon
EX15 3AT, UK
Tel: +44(0)1884 840337
Fax: +44(0)1884 840251
e-mail: info@willanpublishing.co.uk
website: www.willanpublishing.co.uk

Published simultaneously in the USA and Canada by

Willan Publishing
c/o ISBS, 920 NE 58th Ave, Suite 300,
Portland, Oregon 97213-3786, USA
Tel: +001(0)503 287 3093
Fax: +001(0)503 280 8832
e-mail: info@isbs.com
website: www.isbs.com

First published 2007

ISBN   978-1-84392-251-3 paperback
       978-1-84392-252-0 hardback

British Library Cataloguing-in-Publication Data

A catalogue record for this book is available from the British Library.

Typeset by GCS, Leighton Buzzard, Bedfordshire
Printed and bound by T.J. International Ltd, Padstow, Cornwall

For Karen, Jack and Alfie

Contents

List of abbreviations

ABC	acceptable behaviour contract
ABI	area-based initiative
ACPO	Association of Chief Police Officers
ASB	anti-social behaviour
ASBO	anti-social behaviour order
ASBU	Anti-Social Behaviour Unit
BCS	British Crime Survey
BCU	basic command unit
BSC	Building Safer Communities
BVPI	Best Value Performance Indicator
CAD	Communities Against Drugs
CCT	compulsory competitive tendering
CCTV	closed-circuit television
CDP	Community Development Project
CDRP	Crime and Disorder Reduction Partnership
CLP	community liaison panel
CND	Campaign for Nuclear Disarmament
CPA	comprehensive performance assessment
CRASBO	anti-social behaviour order on conviction
CSO	community safety officer
DAT	Drug Action Team
DCLG	Department for Communities and Local Government
DETR	Department of the Environment, Transport and the Regions
DTLR	Department for Transport, Local Government and the Regions

FPN	fixed penalty notice
GIS	geographical information system
HAT	Housing Action Trust
HMIC	Her Majesty's Inspectorate of Constabulary
IPPR	Institute for Public Policy Research
ISO	individual support order
LAA	local area agreement
LGA	Local Government Association
LGMB	Local Government Management Board
LSP	Local Strategic Partnership
MINC	mixed income and tenure community
MUD	moral underclass discourse
NACRO	National Association for the Care and Resettlement of Offenders
NDC	New Deal for Communities
NIM	National Intelligence Model
NOMS	National Offender Management System
NRF	Neighbourhood Renewal Fund
NRU	Neighbourhood Renewal Unit
NSNR	National Strategy for Neighbourhood Renewal
ODPM	Office of the Deputy Prime Minister
OECD	Organisation for Economic Co-operation and Development
PAT	Policy Action Team
PCSO	police community support officer
PCT	primary care trust
PDF	Partnership Development Fund
PND	penalty notice for disorder
PPO	prolific and other priority offender
PSA	public service agreement
PSU	Police Standards Unit
RED	redistributivist discourse
SARA	scan, analyse, respond and assess
SCI	Safer Communities Initiative
SEU	Social Exclusion Unit
SID	social integrationist discourse
SLCNG	Social Landlords' Crime and Nuisance Group
SRB	single regeneration budget
SSCF	Stronger and Safer Communities Fund
TMO	Tenant Management Organisation
UDC	Urban Development Corporation
YOT	Youth Offending Team

Preface

It was a dark and stormy night that preceded the day I first started working at an academic institution. I remember then reading a short document prepared by a colleague who had proposed, in anticipation of the impending research assessment exercise, that every member of staff should be producing at least a book every five years, along with a specified number of journal articles, book chapters, and so forth. I am sure his prescriptive views were not exceptional, and I am sure, having just 'Googled' him, that he would not be the first academic not to have practised what he preached. While I fail to be impressed by this way of measuring academic 'performance', and by the way such a mentality is transforming the academy into a forum for competitive entrepreneurial spirits whose existence attest to the 'successes' of the neo-liberal project, by his reckoning I am at least a couple of books down on my contribution. This book has been a long time coming, but it is time to make amends, and to pay my dues.

Between taking shape in my head, and appearing on the virtual paper of my computer screen, the ideas behind the book have suffered, but hopefully also benefited from, a number of translations. I had intended to offer an account of the domain that was much closer to the ground, focusing, for example, upon the auditing practices of local community safety practitioners; their efforts to put into effect something that amounted to evidence-based practice; their struggles in seeking to hold together Crime and Disorder Reduction Partnerships (CDRPs) going through very turbulent times; and so forth. I also wanted to explore the different ways in which crime and disorder reduction was translated, for example between urban and rural areas; or between neighbourhoods within the same local authority area. Furthermore, I wanted to examine what they did, in terms of the balance between situational and social crime prevention; the emphasis given to volume and low-level crimes; and the space accorded to less conventionally defined local crime problems, such as homophobic violence, or local corporate crime. But it didn't work out that way, in part because the evidence to write such a book is still a bit thin, and in part because I have been distracted by a felt need to understand the bigger picture of the New Labour project, and its place in the reproduction and governance of late-modern social relations. This bigger picture certainly speaks to the things that are happening closer to the ground, but for various reasons that are explored in this book, it is not reducible to them.

I would like to think that in the decade since I produced my last book I have grown up, that my analysis is more sophisticated, and my observations more incisive. Yet while I think I know more, I hope this book does not reveal that in a decade's ageing I understand less. Since my last book I have added to my family, and my family has added to the reasons the book has taken so long. The nappy days are behind us, but target-training can still be a bit of an issue. My family remains a beautiful distraction that I wouldn't and couldn't be without, and I would like to thank them all for enduring a sometimes stressed and short-tempered father and partner. They know by now that finishing the book won't eliminate that, though I continue to kid them that, like the First World War, it'll all be over by Christmas. Though the errors are all of my own making, I would also like to thank those people who have helped me along the way. We're a long way out of the loop down here in Devon, but I have nevertheless managed to benefit from contact 'abroad' with colleagues that include Gordon Hughes, Adam Edwards, Kevin Stenson, Tim Hope, Mike Maguire and Barry Loveday. Thanks also to those, such as Steve Savage, Ken Pease and Rob Mawby, who have helped me at various times along the path I have followed for most of my working life, except for the bits spent cleaning toilets and polishing brass cannons at Southsea Castle, although not at the same time. Thanks are also due to Lesley Simmonds, who helped me collect some of the source material on anti-social behaviour, to those who helped prepare the ground for a short sabbatical to write up much of this book, and to those at Willan, especially Emma Gubb, for putting together the finished item.

Chapter 1

Introduction

Crime prevention, community safety, crime reduction and the New Labour project

I regret that the concept in the subtitle of this book – *local crime control* – is somewhat vague, and does not help the prospective reader to map out the terrain that the book is intended to cover. Yet the choice of a vague subtitle is deliberate, because it reflects the essential ambiguity of the New Labour project in this particular area, as in many others. When New Labour came to power in 1997 after nearly two decades of Conservative government, they set out their stall with the 1998 Crime and Disorder Act, which amongst its omnibus provisions laid out a set of statutory requirements for what, after the Act, came to be called *crime and disorder reduction*. Hence localities in England and Wales, based on district council or unitary authority boundaries, were required to establish Crime and Disorder Reduction Partnerships (CDRPs), complete with three-yearly crime and disorder reduction strategies (Home Office 1998). For some of these 376 localities, mostly urban, Labour-controlled ones, this requirement for crime and disorder reduction came to be overlain on existing structures and practices that had, following the popularisation of the term in the 1991 Morgan Report (Home Office 1991), come to be known as *community safety*. Many of these localities preferred the term community safety as a description of their activities, and thus referred to their partnerships, even after 1998, as community safety partnerships, and referred to their strategies as community safety strategies. Indeed, in Wales, even in official discourse, the term Community Safety Partnership is the

1

preferred one for describing the statutory bodies established in the wake of the 1998 Act.

If crime and disorder reduction became, after 1998, the preferred official discourse for practices that had previously been conceived in terms of community safety, there was some great irony in this, because community safety itself had been a replacement discourse (van Swaaningen 2002) for *crime prevention*, a preferred term of the previous Conservative government. The Morgan Report (Home Office 1991) had been set up as a Home Office inquiry into the reasons behind the apparent slow local take-up of the crime prevention partnership approach which had been heavily promoted by the Conservatives since at least the inter-departmental *Circular 8/84* (Home Office 1984). Amongst its other recommendations the Morgan Report had suggested that this partnership approach would obtain broader appeal if the term community safety was used in preference to crime prevention. Crime prevention, the report argued, was too narrow a term which came with strong situational connotations which made it appear irrelevant to many agencies, particularly social ones, whose field of operations did not touch upon situational aspects of local crime problems, linked in the main as they were to issues of design, surveillance and target-hardening. Community safety, by contrast, was more inclusive, and more attractive to a broad church of interests, and thus it would be a better descriptor of the domain, and a more effective call-to-arms. Although this was not necessarily the most contentious of the Morgan Report's recommendations, all of its main recommendations, including this one, were nevertheless rejected by the Conservative government of the time, although as noted above some urban local authorities started to describe their work in such terms, quite possibly in deliberate opposition to the government's increasingly unpopular position. Many had expected New Labour, who in opposition had been far more supportive of Morgan's recommendations, to implement these recommendations when they assumed power in 1997, but as events transpired, New Labour preferred the nomenclature of crime and disorder reduction.

What's in a name?, as Shakespeare's Juliet puts to her familial arch-rival Romeo. My argument in this book is that the name matters. Since community safety came to be used by many in preference to crime prevention, and since crime and disorder reduction has in turn come to be used by the Home Office as its preferred term of use, we are left in a position of some uncertainty – hence the book's ambiguous subtitle of *local crime control*. What shape has this local crime control taken under Labour's political leadership and direction? And why should this matter?

Names matter because their use infers the existence of approaches to controlling crime that differ in terms of what the problem is to be addressed, who does it, how it is done, and with what consequences beyond the obvious one of controlling crime. Inevitably, it is important to point out that the names refer to social constructions, the contours of which defy precise topographical description because their existence is intrinsically incomplete and contested. Consequently, in what follows we are drawing attention to tendencies and ideal typical characteristics that help us, for analytic purposes, to separate one from the other, rather than providing definitive accounts of each. The three variants of local crime control with which we are interested are crime prevention, community safety, and crime and disorder reduction. At this point it is possible to elaborate upon the core elements of crime prevention and community safety, because both are relatively well established. In order to establish the nature of crime and disorder reduction, however, we first need to explore the unfolding of New Labour's political project for this area of governmental activity, and since this is what much of the rest of the book is about, we will leave our discussion of it to the final chapter.

Crime prevention is most closely associated in the UK with the practices of local crime control that developed under the Conservatives from the 1980s onwards. Dominant as a theme amongst such practices was that of responsibilisation (Garland 2001), an attempt to disperse the responsibility for crime control beyond the narrow confines of the criminal justice system, where it has traditionally lain, and on to others, notably those within civil society who have been obliged to adopt a certain *privatised prudentialism* (O'Malley 1992) in their approach to crime, reflected in such practices as neighbourhood watch, and the private consumption of security goods and advice. This accords roughly with the primary model of crime prevention identified by Brantingham and Faust (1976), in which crime prevention is embedded in the routine activities of the general population, thereby addressing that part of 'the crime problem' that lay beneath the tip of the iceberg of detected crimes, which form the routine focus of the conventional criminal justice system's activities. This capacity of crime prevention, to address the vast majority of crime that lay beyond the reaches of the criminal justice system, was a major justification for the promotion of such an approach to crime control, and one that fitted the neo-liberal understanding of the limitations of state action, to which the Conservatives at this time subscribed.

Responsibilisation also disperses the responsibility for crime control onto those agencies whose interests and activities touch upon the causes of crime in one way or another. This recognises the centrality of the multi-agency approach to crime prevention, albeit imagined in a particular way which is best represented by the situational model devised by Home Office researchers in the 1970s (Gladstone 1980). This model valorised a problem-oriented approach to crime prevention which, in analysing the situation of the offence, inevitably led to the adoption of opportunity-reducing or target-hardening measures that sought to change criminogenic situations, often by means of 'technical fixes' that designed out crime, and that drew heavily upon a practical application of rational choice and routine activity theories. This is not to suggest that this aspirational vision of crime prevention was what the Conservatives always got in practice, but it was certainly their preference, and it fitted an ideological disinterest in social causation, even though local practitioners frequently found a way of working 'social' crime prevention back in (Sutton 1996).

In summary, then, crime prevention is taken to represent an approach to crime control that is based mainly upon responsibilisation that extends beyond the reaches of the traditional criminal justice system, and that draws upon situational measures that seek to block criminal opportunities and reduce risks either through problem-oriented partnership approaches, or through the efforts of private citizens.

Community safety comprises a much more expansive notion of local crime control. It accommodates situational crime prevention, but also moves beyond it to include social crime prevention, thereby recognising the need for a more holistic approach that may well block criminal opportunities, as situational crime prevention can do, but also addresses the criminal motivations that are likely to be frustrated by such opportunity reduction and that, without a complementary social approach, would probably lead to crime displacement. In this sense, community safety may best be seen as a welfare liberal critique of situational crime prevention, just as penal welfarism represents a leftist critique of retributive penality. The aetiological focus of community safety, however, is not so much the individual of the rehabilitative ideal, but rather the local social context, emphasising in particular the family and parenting as sites of 'developmental' crime prevention for young people, and the neighbourhood as the site of 'community' crime prevention.

The holism of community safety extends beyond the combination of the situational and social 'sides' of the crime prevention political divide, because it also drags crime into the broader domain of what might be referred to as 'unsafety'. As an ideal, community safety is potentially pan-hazard, incorporating a panoply of threats to safety, from traffic to waste management, from pollution to workplace safety, and more radically, from discrimination to disadvantage brought about by social inequalities. While some might subscribe to such a pan-hazard view, seeing community safety as the overarching social good of all social goods, such a pan-hazard domain remains a virtual one residing in the imagination of its idealistic proponents, because community safety has been born into and largely remains a creature of the crime control domain, and this has endowed it with a certain path-dependency that narrows the scope of its greater potential. Thus, while some may still hold out for the hope that community safety provides a means of 'socialising' the discourse of crime control in multifarious ways, in practice community safety has tended to restrict its understanding of unsafety to crime-related matters, notably the fear of crime, disorder and anti-social behaviour.

The focus upon the fear of crime, and upon disorder, takes community safety into left realist terrain, and perhaps it is no coincidence that those local authorities that most trumpeted the cause of community safety in the 1990s were also those that drew heavily upon left realist crime survey methodology. In anchoring itself to left realist crime survey methodology, community safety ends up positioning the fear of crime as a 'rational' response to the everyday risks of crime, disorder and anti-social behaviour that attach themselves to contemporary urban living, particularly in deprived areas. And in so far as this approach opens itself up to support for measures of law enforcement that address such disorder issues, then community safety also countenances an enforcement orientation that can steer it into the right realist path trodden by the likes of James Q. Wilson, whose 'broken windows' approach (Wilson and Kelling 1982) strongly supports a law enforcement approach targeted at minor disorders and nuisances, under the premise of 'nipping crime in the bud' and helping the 'respectable majority' to regain control of the streets.

Like crime prevention, community safety also places considerable faith in the potential of a multi-agency or partnership approach, although this may be seen less as a means of realising a problem-oriented approach (as it is under situational crime prevention), and more as a means of addressing the reality of crime through the left realist analytic device of *the square of crime*, which requires a comprehensive approach towards both understanding and

5

responding to crime, through a combination of formal and informal social controls, and measures to address victim vulnerabilities as well as offender motivations, which include the distinctly welfare liberal idea of relative deprivation. This brings us back to the combination of situational and social crime prevention, but it is important to note also that the left realist justification for partnership also acknowledges the capacity of such partnerships to exercise more in the way of democratic control over the activities of law enforcement agencies than opportunities provided by existing mechanisms of accountability. Particular prominence is attached here to the role of local government.

In summary, then, community safety is taken here to represent a progressive approach to local crime control that calls upon a partnership approach to provide a more holistic and democratic response to crime that combines situational and social crime prevention, and that, along with local crime problems, directs attention to the fear of crime and disorder as problems in their own right. For some critics this dilutes the practical and indeed the scientific purity of situational crime prevention, while for others it opens up the scope for a more comprehensive approach to the problem of crime.

There are particular and personal reasons for my interest in the development of local crime control under New Labour. Firstly, for me, as an adult, a Labour government has been something of a novelty, now an enduring one. After nearly two decades of Thatcherism and the build up of a socially injurious but never complete neo-liberal hegemonic project, I was more than a little interested in the capacity of an apparently left-of-centre political party to turn back the tide in favour of a more progressive politics of local crime control. Aware that New Labour's status as a left-of-centre political party is itself the subject of debate, and that there are many who would see Tony Blair's governments as little more than a mark II version of Thatcherism, I was nevertheless interested to see what New Labour's vision would inscribe upon the practical field of local crime control.

Secondly, my previous book (Gilling 1997), written over a decade ago, was completed at a time when the sun was setting over John Major's conflict-ridden and beleaguered government, just as it is in 2007 over Tony Blair's government, and over the New Labour project more generally, although its fate at the time of writing still hangs in the balance. That book charted the development of crime prevention policy under the Conservatives, as crime prevention moved, not only in the UK, from the very margins of crime control policy to the mainstream. Where, in the 1960s, crime prevention had failed to take a hold because it was 'swimming against the tide' (Heal 1987) of dominant paradigms of crime control, by the end of the 1980s it was confidently surfing the waves of the newly established neo-liberal hegemonic project. Yet in the 1990s crime prevention policy in the UK stagnated under Conservative governments that were unprepared to accept the recommendations of the Morgan Report, and that preferred to fall back on a populist punitive discourse, epitomised in Michael Howard's unsubstantiated claim that 'prison works'. They may well have been pushed to adopt such a position in a vain attempt to keep New Labour's office-seeking hounds at bay, but the relative lack of attention given to local crime control, beyond initiating the closed-circuit television (CCTV) explosion that began in the mid-1990s, left a lot of unanswered questions about the future direction of local crime control. Would crime prevention be left behind as government turned increasingly to reassert its punitive sovereign authority through the prison, and a national objectives-led police service? Or would New Labour come to claim the local as the rightful domain of community safety? New Labour's preference for the term crime and disorder reduction obscures the picture, and necessitates the kind of enquiry engaged in over the following pages.

Another book, written by Gordon Hughes (1998) at much the same time as my first offering, but benefiting from an exposure to more of the then unfolding New Labour project, provided an insightful prognosis of three different future scenarios that potentially lay ahead for local crime control. The first of these was a model of 'privatism and exclusion', which effectively takes the privatised prudentialism of crime prevention to its logical limits, giving to those who have the resources and the property interests, including not just private citizens but also the proprietors of mass private property spaces such as shopping malls, the power to defend their interests, through exclusionary risk management techniques, against those 'others' who are perceived in one way or another to threaten them. If New Labour's crime and disorder reduction policy is characterised by such a dystopian model, and is realised in practice, then it will be achieved largely through the pursuit of a discourse of crime prevention: crime and disorder reduction will be little more than the unfolding of the Conservatives' model of neo-liberal local crime control.

The other two scenarios identified by Hughes reflect different tendencies within, and possibly readings of, community safety. The second scenario, that of 'high-trust authoritarian communitarian societies' is one of strong moral communities combined with, and supported by, a strong authoritarian state. This is the model that Hughes discerns through the obfuscating mists of third way rhetoric, and this makes it, therefore, the front-runner in predicting the likely course of New Labour's policy of crime and disorder reduction. Unlike neo-liberal crime prevention, such a model recognises the social, but only in a neo-conservative way, where the state projects a normative view of a socially unequal moral community, and civil society is coerced and cajoled into performing as such a community. This reflects core elements of community safety such as the apparently progressive rebalancing of situational crime prevention with social crime prevention (albeit of a particular kind), and an emphasis upon law enforcement targeted at disorders and other problems that have a disintegrative impact upon communities.

The third and final scenario is that of 'inclusive civic safe cities', which offers a more radical reading of the potential of community safety. This particularly emphasises the democratic potential of the partnership approach, which as noted above is an important ideal typical feature of community safety. The democratic potential is not only construed 'negatively', in terms of holding state agencies – and particularly the police – to account, but also 'positively', in terms of building pressure to address crime problems through more expansive political, social and economic strategies. In other words, this speaks to the pan-hazard potential of community safety, and particularly to its potential role in socialising the discourse of criminal justice. Hughes may not discern strong whiffs of this scenario in New Labour's third way rhetoric, but as he would probably agree nor is it entirely absent from some of the associated discourses of social inclusion, civil renewal and community cohesion which emanate from other parts of New Labour's political programme, but which alight at various times on the domain of crime control, and which are explored in later parts of this book. Moreover, given the potential of community safety to be steered as much from below as from above, nor would he and Adam Edwards rule out the possibility of local advocacy coalitions being able to push local crime control more in this radical direction (Edwards and Hughes 2005).

To summarise this section, then, we have a New Labour approach to local crime control which has been conceived as crime and disorder reduction, thereby providing a terminological break with the past, where the Conservatives spoke mainly in terms of crime prevention, and their critics, and particularly those from a more progressive local government constituency, spoke more of community safety. The trajectory of crime and disorder reduction is consequently uncertain.

It may be crime prevention or community safety by another name, or perhaps some amalgam, or something entirely different. Rhetorically, it comes closest to a conservative reading of community safety, but this is only rhetoric, and whilst it may be important as a guide to action, it does not necessarily have a determining force. My exploration of the unfolding of New Labour's local crime control project over subsequent chapters of this book will hopefully put us in a better position to understand exactly where it is heading.

Constraints on the New Labour project

In this section of the chapter I want to examine the constraints that act upon the New Labour project, which have a role in shaping the form of that project, and in shaping the translation of that project into practice. With regard to the former, we are interested here in macro-level social changes that provide structural conditions that influence the New Labour project generally, and that are in turn reinforced and influenced by that project. We are particularly interested in the way such conditions influence the enterprise of local crime control, as interpreted by a number of key writers in the field. With regard to the translation of the New Labour project into practice, the focus is more upon the constraints of policy-making, where central authority is constrained by the influence of others on the policy process, and by its dependence upon various others to implement its political programme. But first let us focus on the broader macro-level social changes.

Structural constraints

In aiming to understand the structural conditions that help to influence and shape the direction of the New Labour project it is important that we do not give them too much explanatory power, or too determining an influence, because to do so would be to deny New Labour, and others, agency in the social world in which they operate, and which their activities help to shape. That is to say that the governmental activities of New Labour entail processes that help to shape the structures, that in turn impose some constraint over the operation of social processes: this is the reflexivity of social action. Thus, for example, as we shall see in Chapter 2, while New Labour's third way is frequently 'sold' as a response to the structural forces of globalisation, this is only a half-truth, because the third way itself contributes to the creation and sustenance of such globalising forces. What is conceived by New Labour as a powerful constraint is nevertheless a constrained choice, an exercise in self-denial that limits the ambitions of a centre-left political project (Hirst and Thompson 1996; Hirst 2000). Consequently, structural conditions do not simply 'act on' political projects such as New Labour's, but rather such political projects help to constitute these conditions, and could potentially constitute others. To adapt a Marxist adage, New Labour makes its own history, albeit not entirely in a manner of its own choosing.

Hughes (2006) is mindful of the capacity of the local to contribute to the constitution of structural conditions when he calls for analysts of crime control to be sensitive to specific 'geo-historical contexts', although he goes on to argue that this does not necessitate going to the other extreme and adopting an 'ideographic relativism' which assumes that every context is uniquely different. Rather, common structural conditions are constituted and responded to differently in different contexts, according to the political activities of different local interests. Hughes's particular focus here is on crime control at the very local level, and while this is very important for our understanding of whether and how the New Labour project is translated into local practice, and for our understanding of commonalties and differences between different local contexts, our particular focus is on the 'geo-historical context' occupied and shaped by New Labour, both for itself and for those operating at a more local level.

The structural conditions in which we are interested are those that commentators have a habit of presenting or clothing in epochal terms, as represented by concepts such as late-modernity, advanced liberalism (as opposed to welfare liberalism or neo-liberalism [Rose 1999]), or the risk society (Beck 1992). When applied specifically to crime control, such epochal terms as *the exclusive society* (Young 1999), *the culture of control* (Garland 2001) or *the new penology* (Feeley and Simon 1994) are deployed. These epochal concepts capture a sense of significant change and transformation, and of paradigmatic shifts in which the old has declined and the new has arrived. Sometimes the newness of the new may be exaggerated, as may the extent of the disappearance of the old, and it may be better to see many of these stories as revealing newer tendencies that come to be overlain on existing ones. Particularly because there is much common ground in many of these accounts, my preference in what follows is to select from them, magpie-like, rather than to deal with each systematically in turn – I leave that to others who may feel better qualified.

When one encounters new tendencies, there is probably a natural inclination to trace such tendencies back to a cause, and particularly to some material cause, although as Rose (1999) points out, what may be important is not some real event so much as a change in patterns of thought, and the social impact that such a change has on social practices such as governing. Nevertheless, even if what is important is the thought rather than the event, it is generally agreed that the source lies somewhere in the 1970s. It could have been the 1973 oil crisis, the 'monetarist turn' of the Labour government under James Callaghan, or perhaps the excessively flared trousers and tank-tops of questionable design in the decade that style forgot. Whatever, prior to the 1970s the advance of modernity coincided with the 'governmentalisation' of the state, as the state assumed a major if not the principal responsibility for governing a space largely conceived in terms of 'the social', occupied by 'the population' whose health, morality and so forth could be plotted and measured in a myriad ways including, for example, the crime rate as measured by police crime statistics. This was the era of welfare liberalism, represented particularly by the soft social democracy of the post-war welfare state, and in the case of crime control by penal welfarism and the rehabilitative ideal (Garland 2001). Somewhere in the melting pot of the 1970s it became abundantly clear that the progressive aspirations of social government had not been realised, and the legitimacy and competence of the state as a governmental authority were called into question by critics from both the right and the left, though the right's attacks evidently carried more political weight. Consequently, welfare liberalism fell into decline as a political orthodoxy, supplanted by a neo-liberalism that valorised individual freedom and the free market as the best arbiter of our wants and needs, and of social progress more generally. Neo-liberalism set capital free from its 'unnecessary' regulatory chains and fiscal burden, thus creating the 'nomadic capital' (Bauman 2000) that set in motion what many regard as the unstoppable force of economic globalisation, further assisted by technological changes that have helped to shrink both space and time. The decline of welfare liberalism brought with it a loss of support for social solidarity and integration as political objectives, and a tolerance of widening social inequalities: the resultant market society (Taylor 1999) is also an exclusive society (Young 1999).

The new neo-liberal globalised hegemony requires a very different governmental form from that pertaining to the governmentalised state of welfare liberalism. On one level it requires *less* government by the state: a 'rolling back' of the frontiers of the state and its withdrawal from spaces now deemed to be more appropriate as spaces for enterprise, whether that be former public utilities, or welfare or even crime control functions from which it is possible for the state to withdraw under the banner of responsibilisation (Garland 2001). The withdrawal or reduction of the role of the state from the business of governing opens up space for other governmental agents, and for the emergent phenomenon of governance (Stoker 2004), in which the state's role is apparently decentred, although debate remains (Pierre and Peters 2000) over the extent to which the state is best regarded as one interest among many, or as the dominant interest that remains more or less in charge, albeit as a backseat driver, or as a steerer rather than a rower, to utilise the analogy popularised by Osborne and Gaebler (1992). In all probability, the relative power of state interests over other governmental interests in relations of governance is an empirical question that may vary from sector to sector (Pierre and Peters 2000). In the case of crime control, there are those (Garland 2001; Johnston and Shearing 2003) who welcome the potential of governance to deliver more democratic solutions to problems such as crime, even though governance often muddies the waters between public and private interests (Johnston and Shearing 2003), and provides spaces in which state interests can colonise private interests, as well as vice versa.

However, while on one level neo-liberalism appears to require less government by the state, it is an important paradox of neo-liberalism that on another level it requires *more* government, albeit to a different orientation. Although freedom is deployed in rhetorical neo-liberal critiques of too much government, as both Rose (1999) and O'Malley (2004) make plain, freedom is imagined in a particular way that often requires governmental action to be 'made'. The freedom that neo-liberalism seeks is the freedom of the responsibilised, self-actualised citizen-as-consumer, and this by no means comes naturally. Thus, this is a freedom that may need to be enforced through social authoritarian neo-conservatism, a contradiction that was noted by several commentators of Thatcherism as it was practised in the 1980s and 1990s (Hall 1985). Freedom may be enforced by inducement, or by coercion, through punishments that may be designed to secure compliance, or that may simply be exclusionary for those unwilling or unable to become the responsible individuals of neo-liberal doctrine. There are obvious implications for crime control here: not just penal policies, but also the local crime control policies and practices that concern us in later chapters of this book. The question is to what extent have New Labour's policies of local crime control reflected this neo-liberal agenda of 'enforcing' and thus governing through freedom?

Freedom may require enforcement, but it also comes with other 'baggage'. Welfare liberal modernity effectively traded freedom for security, but neo-liberalism has done the reverse (Bauman 2000), and in this zero-sum conception this leaves neo-liberalism's individuals free, yet nevertheless insecure. Ploughing a similar furrow to Bauman, O'Malley (2004) charts a shift from the socialisation of risk under welfare liberalism, to the individualisation of risk under neo-liberalism, specifically in the form of privatised prudentialism. In order for individuals to be prudential, they require the 'motivation' of uncertainty – conceptually similar to insecurity – to identify and take action against perceived risks. Uncertainty also unleashes an enterprising soul that too much security and socialised risk makes inert through dependency, as the well-established neo-liberal critique of welfarism often contends. Yet there is a down side to this, because as many observers note, risk generates its own dynamic, and an associated anxiety in the never-ending pursuit of freedom from risk, which is easily projected on to manifest 'bads' such as crime and disorder, particularly in a context where high crime rates have become a 'normal' feature of late-modern societies (Garland 2001). The relatively recent 'discovery' of problems such as the fear of crime and anti-social behaviour can be seen in this light, as the inevitable flip sides to the more 'productive' side of uncertainty and risk that neo-liberalism so valorises.

So, to summarise, New Labour finds itself sitting under an hegemonic neo-liberal cloud, which has unleashed the forces of economic globalisation, and which valorises freedom, which, despite its use as a normative critique of too much government, is in fact an object of neo-liberal government, to be achieved if necessary by enforcement. This freedom co-exists with a certain insecurity and uncertainty that can be productive, but that can also manifest as an unpleasant 'side effect', evidenced particularly in a fear of crime, and a neo-liberal cultural inclination to demonise, essentialise and 'other' (Young 1999) those who may be the objects of our fears, whether they be members of a putative 'underclass', asylum-seekers, immigrants and minority ethnic groups, or 'anti-social' young people more generally. The cultural inclination is not, as it might have been under welfare liberalism, one that gives expression to an inclusive society, but rather an exclusive one (ibid.). Again, then, the question is to what extent New Labour bows to, and in so doing reinforces, the pressure of these structural conditions, or to what extent does it challenge them with an alternative, more progressive vision?

What are the crime control implications that flow from these structural conditions of late-modernity? One indication has been provided by Feeley and Simon (1994) in their characterisation of a new penology of actuarial justice, based upon a mainly exclusionary form of risk management that is evidenced particularly in the mass incarcerations of penal policy in the USA, but that also underpins the governance of spaces of mass private property by private interests, as well as the practices of neighbourhood watch groups upon which are inscribed the logic of privatised prudentialism. This new penology forms a part of the 'privatism and exclusion' model of one future scenario mapped out by Hughes (1998) and referred to above. But as O'Malley (2004) points out, it is quite possible for actuarial justice to follow more inclusionary lines, where risky groups and populations are identified through the risk factors they display, and 'worked upon' with a view to producing more responsibilised, self-actualising consumers, and it may be that such an inclusionary logic would appeal more to a centre left constituency such as that apparently represented by New Labour. This conditional inclusionary vision more closely matches Hughes's 'high trust authoritarian communitarian society' future scenario, demonstrating that actuarialism per se does not necessitate exclusionary responses.

Another indication of the direction of crime control under the structural conditions of neo-liberalism is provided in Garland's (2001) reading of the culture of control. Such a culture, for Garland, is characterised by a sovereignty predicament in which, on the one hand, there is a strategy of responsibilisation, which Garland, like Johnston and Shearing (2003), sees as a potentially positive opening up of space for more progressive community-based approaches to crime control. But on the other hand Garland sees a penal populism, geared towards penal exclusion, marshalled by a tough sovereign state. Perhaps this predicament is no more than the manifestation of 'the powers of freedom' (Rose 1999), where freedom is governed through a dual strategy of responsibilisation, and tough enforcement, geared towards responsibilised inclusion for *those who will*, and exclusion for *those who will not*. Thus the culture of control combines elements of the two future scenarios mapped out by Hughes (1998), as discussed above.

Policy-making constraints

If the structural conditions of neo-liberal late-modernity provide one kind of constraint upon the New Labour project, another is provided by its limited capacity to control the policy process at the meso- and micro-levels of analysis. This book focuses upon the New Labour project as a project that unfolds from the centre, and particularly from the Home Office, outwards and downwards. A danger of such a focus is that it privileges or lends weight to a fallacious view of the policy process, which presumes that policy is 'made' or formulated at the centre, amongst the New Labour political elite and its political advisors both within and outside of the civil service, and then unfolded, through a succession of stages, into implemented action at the 'bottom', through practitioners who find themselves at the 'delivery end' of the policy process. This 'stagist' model has a certain longevity as an heuristic device (Parsons 1995), having been deeply ingrained upon the intellects of generations of students of public administration, but it does not reflect the socially constructed reality of policy as a more fluid and contingent phenomenon, that looks very different depending upon the angle, not to mention the period of time, from which it is probed. Particularly in the age of networked or *nodal governance* (Johnston and Shearing 2003), when government interests are decentred from the analysis, it is unwise to cling too firmly to this stagist model, and to associated concepts such as the 'implementation gap', that privilege a particular source of policy that may in fact be unwarranted.

Particular problems arise when, as is often the case, the stagist model is allied to a 'top-down' view that tends to operate with the assumption that policy is all about putting into effect the will of those with legitimate political authority and power. This top-down view is a fiction of the Westminster model of ministerial accountability (Rhodes 1997), a normative model that is still 'sold' to the public, still animates party politics, and probably also reflects the normative expectations of those with a will to power. I do not subscribe to such a 'top-down' view myself, and it should not therefore be assumed that, because my focus is on the New Labour project, and particularly the unfolding of this project once the reins of political power were grabbed in 1997, there is any implication that the dreams of the likes of Tony Blair, Jack Straw, David Blunkett, Charles Clarke and John Reid have become reality. These protagonists probably wish that like Captain Jean-Luc Picard in *Star Trek* they can issue commands to 'make it so', but as advocates of an alternative 'bottom-up' perspective point out, there are plenty of others in the policy process, from civil service bureaucrats to bureau-professional 'street-level bureaucrats' who are there to thwart the ambitions of those at the centre. In the context of the shift from government to governance, moreover, the picture has been rendered even less certain by the involvement of those from other private, voluntary and community sectors who may lie beyond the reach of the rational-legal authority of the centre, and who bring their own particularistic interests to the policy process, and whose presence obfuscates, through an inevitable blurring of boundaries, the distinction between public and private interests.

The top-down/bottom-up refrain provides an interests-based account of policy that does to some extent animate the chapters that follow. Thus for example, the tools of new public management have been deployed by New Labour as an art form, to control the actions of 'provider interests' about whom New Labour's political elite have remained deeply mistrustful. Sometimes these 'provider interests' have manifested themselves, for example, in the bureaucratic risk-aversion (Hughes 2003) of civil servants that played its part in scuppering the progressively experimental plans of the Crime Reduction Programme (see Chapter 4); or the bureaucratic process focus (Hughes 2003) which has tended to de-couple (Power 1997) auditing and accounting from their ends-orientation, to become ends in themselves; or the political resistance of local practitioners to elements of crime and disorder reduction policy that do not accord with their more progressive visions of community safety. But we should not think of policy only in terms of interests, because to do so neglects the importance of policy as a discursive accomplishment, which is closer to Barrett and Fudge's (1981) view of policy as action framed around particular negotiated orders, which does not privilege any particular set of interests. Thus policy is not only a thing that is 'fought over' by competing interests, but it is also a thing that is differentially constructed and acted upon, according to different logics of, in this case, local crime control. Power, therefore, does not just exist in the position, authority and behaviour of these interests, but in their capacity to shape and act upon the domain through discourses.

Writing in critical realist terms, Edwards and Hughes (2005) identify power-dependence as a relational constant or necessity of the local governance of crime. Within complex networks, there is always a requirement for those with a desire to govern to bargain and negotiate with others to 'get things done'. Power-dependence, then, is an important constraint on the New Labour project, and one that requires us to pay heed to those others, aside from New Labour's political elite, who may be involved in the business of governing through crime (Simon 1997), who may have different ideas about which problems local crime control should be addressing, and how they should be addressed. Yet while the power-dependence of local governance may decentre governments from our analytic 'hotspots', it is nevertheless important to acknowledge, as indeed Edwards and Hughes (2005) do, that, compared to other European states, Britain does appear to invest the centre with more power, particularly in terms of its constitutional 'right' to direct local government, and in terms of its informational resources, which endow it with an ability to more effectively monitor and audit the activities of local practitioners.

The benefits of a comparative, geo-historical approach are manifest and well argued in the work of Edwards and Hughes (2005), but the peculiarities of the British context equally warrant the kind of focus that is adopted in this book. Despite the advent of governance, considerable power and authority reside with the centre, both in its ability to make legislation and to impose obligations upon other statutory bodies in this area, and in its ability to commit public funds and its obligation to account for the probity and effectiveness of their usage. Thus, while policy may not be 'made' at the centre, an authoritative, if not necessarily determining, policy agenda will be set or altered there, to which others may have to respond, whether by accommodation or resistance. More pragmatically, from the researcher's point of view, it is also considerably easier to track policy as it is constructed from the top down, where the sources are relatively open and easy to access, rather than from the bottom up, where one must take into account the potentially different 'translations' of 376 separate CDRPs, and other relevant local bodies such as Local Strategic Partnerships (LSPs), which vary in terms of political alignment, in terms of their placement on an urban–rural divide, in terms of the nature of their local crime problems and so forth. They are likely to vary also, therefore, in terms of local crime control policies and practices. It is not that this variation is unimportant – far from it, although the number of research studies concentrating upon aspects of this variation remains few and far-between (though see, for example, Skinns [2005] or Fletcher [2006]). Rather, the point is that the focus in this book upon the role of central government is informed by a desire to uncover the essential attributes of the New Labour project in this area. Such a project is rendered problematic by the questionable insistence that it is a pragmatic project and not an ideological one, that its ends are informed by an ambiguous 'third way', and that it can somehow marry up the two purposes of being 'tough on crime and tough on the causes of crime', to quote an infamous and well-used phrase of Tony Blair's apparent design (see Chapter 2).

The structure of this book

My attempt to map out the New Labour project in the domain of local crime control is set out as follows. This chapter has outlined the problem that the book is intended to address, namely the characterisation of the New Labour project of local crime control, and a determination of the extent to which its discourse of crime and disorder reduction adheres to or diverts from the paths set by the earlier discourses of crime prevention and community safety. As we have just discussed, this political project is constrained by the structural conditions in which it is positioned, and particularly those set by a neo-liberal hegemony and its particular vision of freedom, although the project itself helps to frame such conditions. It is also constrained by the power-dependence that any central political authority faces when seeking to pursue a particular course of action through a policy process over which it has limited control, especially as the conditions of governing are undergoing something of a transformation, characterised by many as a shift from government to governance.

In Chapter 2, we turn our attention to the New Labour project. We examine the phoenix-like renewal of Labour as New Labour, emerging out of the ashes of a radicalised and disorganised Old Labour Party, whose 1983 election manifesto had made them, in many people's eyes, unelectable. As a political project, New Labour comprised a strategy of reorganisation and centralisation under a more moderate, capital-friendly political elite, intended to appeal to the material and moral interests of a putative 'middle England'. This project is examined, focusing particularly upon the emergence of a law and order programme that dropped its association with penal welfarism, and that embraced a much-trumpeted 'toughness', both on crime and on its causes, that, in concert with a media-savvy communications strategy, enabled New Labour to outflank the Conservatives on what the latter had come to regard as essentially their natural 'home' ground. The chapter then moves on to offer an interpretation of New Labour's 'third way' as a political strategy that has been presented as a pragmatic response to the pressures of globalisation. In the case of crime control this has involved positioning urban Britain as a collection of safe, sanitised and thus 'competitive' spaces ready for inward-investment, not least in the governance of this safety; and, through a moral authoritarian communitarian agenda, moulding the souls of responsible free neo-liberal subjects. The final sections of the chapter then examine the tools that New Labour has deployed to shape its governmental project of steering from the centre, using the strictures of evidence-based policy, joined-up policy, and new public management, which coalesce together in the general theme of modernisation.

Chapter 3 is the first of a series of four chapters looking at the unfolding of local crime control under New Labour. It begins with a brief review of the Conservative legacy, which demonstrated a bias towards situational crime prevention, but a 'tolerance' towards community safety that was an inevitable corollary of a policy approach that stopped short, for political reasons, of 'enforcing' a partnership approach upon local agencies, particularly local authorities. New Labour appeared to go more boldly, mandating local partnership working through CDRPs, and simultaneously encouraging a localism that seemed to fit with what local agencies wanted, and with what they claimed they were capable of delivering. Yet this apparent localism, which was perhaps itself an inevitable corollary of an initial reluctance to provide additional central funding for CDRPs, sat uneasily with an increasingly prescriptive approach that came more to the fore after 1999, following the launch of the Crime Reduction Programme. The chapter documents the way increased central funding from 1999 was accompanied by the control mechanisms associated with evidence-based policy and particularly new public management, as tools designed to attain central ends by curtailing the powers of local 'provider interests'.

Chapter 4 takes up the story of local crime and disorder reduction from the beginning of New Labour's second term of office in 2001 through to 2006, again focusing upon the evolving role of the CDRPs. This story becomes increasingly complicated as the business of CDRPs is entwined in the wider processes of police reform and local government reform, which means, in turn, that the narrow Home Office emphasis upon crime and disorder reduction is joined by a more expansive focus upon issues such as democratic accountability and reassurance, centring upon neighbourhoods as the spatial expression of 'community'. As a result of this, CDRPs have found themselves sitting awkwardly between a tightly controlled performance management framework oriented towards crime reduction, and the drive towards a *new localism* that affords the possibility of drawing local crime control more in the direction of community safety. The review of CDRPs, which was announced in 2004 and which resulted in the 2006 Police and Justice Act, implemented in the summer of 2007, can be read as an attempt to resolve this awkward position, although whether it does so remains to be seen.

Two indicators of a possible 'softening' of the crime reduction agenda, and an accommodation of an alternative community safety future, are the increasing emphasis given to low-level disorder-related concerns, represented by the new policy domain of anti-social behaviour, and the potentially related focus upon social causation, represented by policy developments falling out of the work of the Social Exclusion Unit (SEU). These form the focus, respectively of Chapter 5 and Chapter 6. We start Chapter 5 by looking at how anti-social behaviour has been made governable through its conceptualisation in policy, and through its measurement in the British Crime Survey (BCS), where it has been 'fingered' as the issue responsible for the much-problematised 'reassurance gap'. We examine how the edifice of anti-social behaviour has been built through the thematic linking of the fear of crime with 'nuisance neighbours', with the incivilities that have been targeted by zero-tolerance policing, with the 'pre-delinquent' behaviour of young people, and more recently with alcohol-related disorder. We look at the balanced approach to anti-social behaviour that was recommended by the SEU, and we look at how, in practice, New Labour has been happier to construct tools that are predominantly enforcement-oriented and too frequently exclusionary in their application. This enforcement-oriented approach allows New Labour to play to the galleries, demonstrating its sovereign authority through populist punitiveness. But it is also a means by which it hopes to pursue a moral agenda that seeks to constitute a neo-liberal vision of responsible freedom. Such an approach falls short of a progressive model of community safety, and has a number of negative consequences that are briefly considered. However, there is, nevertheless, space for a more progressive approach, as has been demonstrated by a number of localities that have not been so quick to resort to the anti-social behaviour order (ASBO), and so, as in other areas, the New Labour agenda here has been limited by its own power-dependence.

In Chapter 6, the focus switches from the role of CDRPs in crime and disorder reduction, to the role of social exclusion in informing a more progressive 'social' approach to local crime control, such as one might find in the normative model of community safety. The chapter looks at the different ways in which social exclusion has been conceptualised, and it is suggested that while New Labour flirts with all of these it tends to sail closest to a moral underclass discourse (Levitas 2005), which fits neatly with the moral authoritarian communitarianism to which it also subscribes (see Chapter 2). It then goes on to examine New Labour's strategies to tackle social exclusion through work, through childcare and parenting, and particularly through neighbourhood renewal. Such neighbourhood renewal, it is argued, has tended to give more weight to the physical side of the 'urban renaissance', and certain barriers have stood in the way of a more progressive social regeneration. Beyond the moral focus which has obscured the structural causes of social exclusion, these include the failure of joined-up government to get beyond a new public management-induced silo-mentality in public service organisational cultures, and a rather impoverished understanding and implementation of community participation, whether with regard to bodies such as LSPs, or with regard to crime-specific initiatives. More recently, policy to tackle social exclusion and neighbourhood renewal has been reconceived as the attempt to build social capital, and the chapter ends with a lengthy discussion when I get on my high horse about the dangers and limitations of attempting to do this through crime control.

Finally, we are left in Chapter 7 with a conclusion that returns us to our original question, posed at the beginning of this chapter, about the true character of New Labour's local crime control project. Clearly it has moved well beyond the Conservatives' narrow focus upon crime prevention, and their particular ideological preference for situational crime prevention, although there is a strong element of crime and disorder reduction that takes this situationalism on board, that is seduced by *crime science*, and that combines situationalism with an enforcement orientation that is geared to managing the risks of so-called volume crimes, which are political as well as criminogenic. Yet in the focus upon the neighbourhoods agenda, upon anti-social behaviour, and upon social exclusion and social capital there are also strong hints of community safety, but such hints as we can find are suggestive of problems with the theory and practice of community safety, and with its capture by and for a neo-liberal agenda of governing through freedom to which, ultimately, the New Labour project accedes. But let us first begin by examining, in the next chapter, the contours of that project.

Chapter 2

The New Labour project

Introduction

In this chapter, prior to exploring in subsequent chapters the way that crime prevention policy has unfolded since 1997, we shine the analytic spotlight on to the political project of New Labour. This is something that mainstream criminology too frequently fails to do, and Stan Cohen's (1988) identification of a 'correctional bias' in criminology still largely holds true. For various reasons, contemporary criminologists come under pressure to demonstrate a 'policy relevance' to their work (Walters 2003) which generally entails an assessment of crime control practices as technocratic solutions to putative crime and social problems, and subscription to misleadingly rationalistic assumptions about the policy process that actually serve to mystify rather than to enlighten our understanding of crime control. It is not the idea of policy relevance per se that is problematic, so much as its technocratic representation, which serves to foreclose more critical agendas of policy relevance. But then such foreclosure and mystification may be exactly what governments want as they seek to convey an image of policy-making as a wholly pragmatic affair. To be fair, such an image is not totally without foundation, as policy is frequently adjusted to counter new threats and risks, and to manage new crises, such as that concerning the release of foreign national prisoners that ultimately cost Labour's third Home Secretary, Charles Clarke, his job. Consequently, it is no surprise that, in his study of Labour's policy-making at the Home Office, Randall (2004) identifies pragmatism as one of the 'three faces of New Labour', but the other two faces he identifies, namely principle and populism, are equally and probably more important, and deserve more attention than many criminologists are prepared to offer, although there are some notable exceptions. Most of this chapter is devoted to a study of these other two faces, and it is contended that an understanding of these ingredients of New Labour's political project will aid us in the task of explaining the direction that policy has taken since 1997, and will help us to shed light on some of the tensions, ambiguities and contradictions that beset that policy. It is important to remember in this regard, lest it be thought that our guns are trained too tightly on New Labour's political project, that all such projects – even those of absolute monarchs, despots, dictators and Tony Blair – are inherently unstable.

Under Tony Blair's leadership, the Labour Party, or at least the political elite within it, has been renewed, and this theme of renewal, of a shift from Old Labour to New Labour, was an important means of distinguishing the asserted uniqueness of the new elite's political project. Many have quite rightly questioned exactly how new or unique New Labour is, and as previously noted many have characterised New Labour as little more than a mark II version of Thatcherism. Yet despite or possibly because of this, the theme of renewal continues to be inscribed upon the New Labour project, facilitating the kind of permanent campaigning that has become a hallmark of late-modern politics (McLaughlin *et al.* 2001), even if the label of New Labour carries less salience than it once did. Currently, the subject of renewal is applied less to the political party, and more to the country, or at least to those parts of it that stand in need of, for example, *neighbourhood* renewal or *civil* renewal – both important parts of the story that unfolds as the book progresses. But we are getting ahead of ourselves here, and it is necessary first of all to return our focus to the emergence and character of the New Labour project.

The structure of this chapter broadly follows the distinction made by Chadwick and Heffernan (2003) between office and policy, which constitute the two central goals of all major political parties. These two goals, concerned with seeking political power and using it, are not necessarily complementary: 'Managing the relevant tensions and compatibilities between office and policy are part and parcel of any major political party's existence' (ibid.: 7). We start by looking at New Labour's attempts to return the party back to office, and to keep it there, before moving on, in the latter part of the chapter to examine the main influences upon its policy agenda, focusing especially upon the much-vaunted third way.

Finding the road back to office

Before the spectacular success of the 1997 general election, albeit more spectacular in terms of seats won than in terms of the proportion of the vote obtained, Labour had failed to secure a general election victory since 1974, a year I remember well for getting two days off school, and for indulging a dubious taste in *Hot Hits* albums. From 1979 onwards, as Margaret Thatcher took an ever-tightening grip on power, Old Labour showed itself to be particularly inept in the art of seeking office, producing what many regard as its most radical manifesto in 1983, which MP Gerald Kaufman, with his characteristically dry wit, later referred to as 'the longest suicide note in history'. The radicalism that the Party had shown in 1983 was perceived by many as being badly out of step with the socio-political conditions created by the fiscal, economic and legitimacy crises of the mid-1970s, that the Conservatives had so effectively exploited, in so doing unleashing the forces of globalisation that the architects of New Labour were later to regard, questionably, as irreversible (Hirst 2000). Driver and Martell (2002) locate the origins of New Labour to this 1983 election defeat, and to Michael Foot's replacement by Neil Kinnock, whose left-wing credentials softened the longer he remained in office as party leader. Under Neil Kinnock a reform process began which involved the reorganisation of the Party so that decision-making became more centralised and concentrated in the hands of a moderate leadership, and less vulnerable to capture from the more radical fringes, and particularly from sections of the trade union movement. Tony Blair completed this process of centralisation and carried it into the office of Prime Minister through the mixture of a presidential style and the sort of conviction politics that had been pioneered by Margaret Thatcher, who numbered Tony Blair amongst her list of not-so-secret admirers. Hennessy (2000) describes Blair's style as that of a *command premiership*, which for him leads to a concentration of too much power in the hands of one individual, and such power, as we shall see, has frequently been used to steer the course of crime control policy, which remained a pet interest of his even after he assumed the leadership of the Party.

While Neil Kinnock may well have started the centralisation and control process which gave the political elite more control over the direction of the Party, another important part of Labour's office-seeking agenda entailed the modification of its policy agenda, and after the 1987 general election defeat a major policy review was announced. For

Hay (1999) this policy review resulted in the effective abandonment of the social democratic principles that had steered the Labour Party for the best part of the twentieth century, but that 'modernisers' regarded as being increasingly outmoded. Importantly, by the end of the 1980s these modernisers included the likes of Gordon Brown and Tony Blair amongst their number, and they were instrumental in helping to steer Neil Kinnock away from the left-wing credentials that had initially brought him to the leadership of the Party. The 1992 general election defeat, when Labour spectacularly snatched defeat from the jaws of victory (Heffernan and Marqusee 1992), and when the relatively charismatic Neil Kinnock was up against the relatively charisma-less John Major, suggested that this modernisation project was unfinished business. This was despite the fact that, by the time of the 1992 election, Labour had in Hay's (1999) view effectively sold out to the neo-liberal hegemonic project of Thatcherism, based as it was on the memorable assertion of Margaret Thatcher that there was no alternative.

The next phase of the reform and modernisation project began with the replacement of Neil Kinnock by John Smith, and, in the fashion of the 1987 policy review, the establishment of the Commission on Social Justice (1994), although the Commission was run by the think tank at the Institute for Public Policy Research (IPPR), which as Levitas (2005) reminds us is largely male-dominated, part of the metropolitan elite, unaccountable, and yet remarkably well connected to the key architects of Labour's renewal as New Labour. The Commission did not produce its final report until late in 1994 when more attention was being devoted to debates about Labour's constitution, and the replacement, as leader, of John Smith by Tony Blair, following the former's untimely death. This means that the report did not receive the attention that it deserved (ibid.), because if the 1987 policy review had propelled Labour into a sort of limbo in which it had dropped its social democratic principles but not yet fixed an alternative vision securely in their place, the 1994 report of the Commission on Social Justice, significantly entitled *Social Justice: Strategies for National Renewal*, alighted upon such an alternative, namely a furrow that Labour could plough and claim as its own, the third way. The details of the Commission's report are considered below, but for now it is worth pointing out that the third way was by this time already crystallising in the minds of Labour's political elite, and bearing in mind Levitas's point about the IPPR, the Commission's report may best be seen as providing a legitimacy that enabled the third way to be taken up as the mantle of New Labour.

On a not unrelated point, with Tony Blair now at the helm, Labour's constitution was rewritten with the ditching of the symbolic Clause IV, which had committed Old Labour to a strategy of public ownership that did not fit the abandonment of social democratic principles and the new third way, and thus New Labour was born, although there were two more pieces of the jigsaw yet to be put in place which, notwithstanding the declining electoral popularity of the Conservatives in the wake of concerns of economic mismanagement, rampant sleaze and an ill-fated injunction from John Major to get 'back to basics', served to enhance New Labour's office-seeking credentials.

Firstly, as Driver and Martell (2002) observe, New Labour's political elite learnt a great deal from the electoral successes of Bill Clinton's New Democrats, who like Labour had previously spent some years in the political wilderness. In particular, they had seen the importance of tightly managed and controlled political communications to both seeking and holding on to political power, and they set about replicating this model through the media centre at Labour's headquarters at Millbank, and through the key figures of Peter Mandelson, Philip Gould and particularly Alistair Campbell. In this way, the Party was increasingly kept 'on message', political leaks were plugged, and 'spin' and presentation became a part of a new democratic politics in which direct communications with the electorate played a significant part in setting a policy agenda that, in a self-fulfilling way, New Labour could then be seen to 'respond' to (Franklin 2000) – this was certainly the case with law and order (see below). Although the spin was by no means the only thing, the priority given to presentation, which for Franklin (2000) is attributable to the managerialist and centralising tendencies of modern political parties, but also of considerable importance when there is not a great deal of political distance between the main political parties, did make it difficult at times to discern the substance and distinctiveness of the New Labour project, and did raise suspicions that it was just Thatcherism by another name.

The second piece of the jigsaw that helped to cement New Labour's credentials for office may be found in its electoral strategy, which recognised that social and demographic changes by the end of the twentieth century had fundamentally altered the structure of Britain's electoral constituency, replacing the binary divide between the traditional working class and others with a more differentiated polity, described by some such as Hutton (1995) as the 40:30:30 society (see Levitas 2005). The differentiation is supposedly founded more on employment status than income, but whatever its precise nature its significance lies in the fact that those in the middle become the most important group electorally, and thus the outcome of general elections turns generally upon the relative success of the two main political parties in winning the support of what has come to be known, in somewhat pejorative terms, as middle England. This loose social grouping, made up of the likes of young couples, modestly paid mid-lifers, and retired people on modest pensions (Bennington and Donnison 1999), may be relatively well off compared both to those below them and to the material standards of previous generations, but one of their defining features is their insecurity and anxiety (Morgan 2000), with their existence lending credibility to the idea of the emergence of a risk society, but also perhaps to the 'success' of the neo-liberal project of freedom. The risks these people face are mostly to their material interests, in terms of excessively high mortgage payments, vulnerable pension schemes and threats of redundancy in jobs that are increasingly short term and at risk of contracting out and downsizing (Bennington and Donnison 1999). This, as Bennington and Donnison (1999: 57) depressingly note, gives them '... less reason than their predecessors had for solidarity with those worse off for themselves', and this inevitably reduces the electoral appeal of a redistributive strategy for social justice. Instead New Labour's office-seeking strategy was to address the concerns of middle England (or fan their flames?), particularly but not exclusively with regard to questions of social order (see below). It was also to sell a *one nation* vision of inclusion into this middle stratum (Driver and Martell 2002), particularly through a discourse of stakeholding, although such language was dropped because of its association with a more progressive view of stakeholding propounded by and popularised in the work of Will Hutton (1995). Of course, the flip side to this inclusive vision was the exclusion of 'non-stakeholders', against whom a language of control has been deployed (Morgan 2000), and this has particular relevance for New Labour's approach towards law and order, to which we now turn.

Following the law and order path

New Labour's office-seeking strategy can be summarised largely in terms of modernising the Party by centralising power into the hands of a moderate political elite, overhauling political communications, orienting such communications in the direction of a strategically important middle England, and dropping policies that had, in the leadership's eyes, made the Party previously unelectable. In this section, we focus particularly on the changes that were made to Labour's law and order policies, seeing these changes very much as part of New Labour's office-seeking strategy, particularly because Old Labour's approach to law and order had, in the eyes of New Labour's political elite, made the Party previously unelectable. As in the previous section, we focus on the period from 1979 through to 1997.

In the 1979 general election, Labour's apparently poor record on law and order played a key part in bringing about the downfall of the Callaghan government. The Conservative Party's adept manipulation of the law and order issue, meanwhile, played an equally important part in the rise to power of the new Prime Minister Margaret Thatcher. As Downes and Morgan (2002) show in their review, prior to the 1970s the post-war politics of law and order had been low-key, marked by some degree of a Butskellite consensus which ensured it was never made a high profile political issue at election times. Stenson (2001) suggests that for most of this period crime control was regarded as a part of the routine business of government, based on a mixture of penality and welfare that prioritised rehabilitation, but that was backed up by repression beneath this soft rehabilitative underbelly. While there may have been differences between the two main political parties, criminal justice was regarded more as a routine administrative domain from which politicians were by and large excluded.

In the course of the 1970s, however, this consensus, like the welfare consensus, was rudely broken by a resurgent New Right, responding to the fiscal and legitimacy crises of that decade by pointing out, Cassandra-like, that the welfare liberal path was also a path to the breakdown of law and order, and to the rise of the spectre of 'ungovernable Britain'. In their 1979 general election campaign, consequently, the Conservatives identified 'restoring the rule of law' as one of the five major tasks they set themselves were they to be voted into government, which they duly were. Just how ungovernable Britain had become is a point of debate: the work of Cohen (1972) and Hall et al. (1978) suggests that media and official responses to putative problems such as youth subculture violence and 'mugging' epidemics were both over-reactions, and it may be that studies into other 1970s problems, like football hooliganism, vandalism and unnecessarily wide flared trousers, would have reached similar conclusions. Yet whatever the true extent of these problems, the important point is that the Conservatives were adept at linking them to parallel issues, specifically industrial unrest and militancy, so that the ungovernable whole could be portrayed as much larger than the sum of its constituent parts, particularly in the immediate wake of the notorious 1978/1979 'winter of discontent', and particularly when this could be linked in turn to the Labour government's apparent failure to invest properly in the (police) forces of law and order. As later events were to show (see below), the example of the Conservatives' success with their manipulation of the law and order issue was not lost on the architects of New Labour.

For their part, Old Labour remained shackled to an orthodox 'social democratic criminology' (Young 1988). Hence, for example, their 1979 manifesto promised that '... we shall attack the social deprivation which allows crime to flourish. Our policies on fighting deprivation and social injustice, on arresting the decay of our inner cities, on youth employment and helping the family, will all contribute to a happier and more law-abiding society' (Labour Party 1979). In the 1970s, such a welfare liberal approach patently lacked credibility as a means of tackling 'ungovernable Britain', and it is interesting that although many of these same themes appear in New Labour's approach to controlling crime, they do so in ways that do not allow them to be confused with an approach that is 'soft' on crime. In the 1970s, this welfare liberal approach had come under sustained attack from James Q. Wilson (1975), who argued that such an approach not only did not control crime, but in fact actively encouraged it, particularly when combined with a weak criminal justice response. The target of Wilson's attack may have been the social democratic criminological orthodoxy that underpinned the USA's 1960s *War on Poverty* programme, but the right-wing views that he espoused were certainly starting to feed themselves through to these shores. Within the UK Home Office, there may have been no sudden outburst of Wilson's 'right realism', but Home Office researchers who had been given a certain amount of freedom to act as policy entrepreneurs were, as it turned out, deeply sceptical of the 'dispositional criminology' that informed welfare liberal responses to crime that had failed to control the rise in crime, or account for this rise in the post-war years despite obvious improvements in social conditions and living standards (Cornish and Clarke 1986). And the approach to crime control that they worked on, based on the notion of crime as opportunity (Clarke and Mayhew 1980) that later informed the emergence of situational crime prevention, had some elective affinity with, even if it was not actively supportive of, this right realism.

If Labour's criminology had become a liability by 1979, then so had its principal friends. A key part of the Conservative 'ungovernability' discourse was the association that it managed to make between the Labour Party and lawless causes, such as trade union strikes and other political protests such as Campaign for Nuclear Disarmament (CND) marches (Morgan 2000), although the latter was to become more prominent into the 1980s. Thus, not only had Labour failed to control crime, but it also hung out with delinquent friends, a well-known deviancy risk factor. And this problem, ideologically manufactured though it may have been, continued into the 1980s as elements of Labour in opposition supported causes such as that of the striking miners in 1984 and 1985, which Margaret Thatcher famously portrayed as part of 'the enemy within', thereby damning parts of the Labour Party by association. Other such 'enemies' who attracted the sympathies of certain parts of the Labour Party included those inner city residents, often members of minority ethnic groups, who had rioted within various urban areas throughout the UK, particularly in 1981 and 1985, and especially in Brixton, Handsworth, Moss Side and Toxteth. As the Conservatives set about their self-appointed task of rolling back the frontiers of the welfare state, they simultaneously rolled forward the forces of a criminal justice state, building new prisons and investing heavily in paramilitarised policing to soak up the social fall-out that was an inevitable consequence of such a policy agenda.

While the Labour Party offered political support to the victims of such harsh social policies, the Conservatives rode the crest of a wave of authoritarian populism that allowed them to re-cast the victims as perpetrators, and as law and order crept up the list of pollsters' priority concerns, so Labour's support for unpopular causes, and its soft welfare liberalism, remained an electoral liability. Some of the new urban socialist local authorities, such as those in Greater Manchester and Greater London, established police monitoring units that joined forces with critical criminologists and some Labour MPs to lobby for greater controls on the exercise of police powers, and for more democratic accountability. For the Conservatives, it was easy to portray all of this as distinctly anti-police, if not seditious, and in Parliament an early attempt to limit police powers, interestingly introduced by a young Jack Straw (see Scraton 1985), was easily blocked. It is perhaps testimony to the success of 'the Thatcher project' that despite enduring some of the steepest annual rises in recorded crime, particularly in the first half of the decade of the 1980s, the Conservatives never lost the political high ground on the issue of law and order, and its projected self-image as the natural party of law and order remained intact, and seemed largely justified.

There are signs that under the stewardship of Neil Kinnock the reform process intended to address Labour's apparent unelectability began finally to touch the issue of law and order. The hard-left image of some Labour-controlled urban authorities began to soften partly because of the abolition of the highly oppositional metropolitan authorities, but partly also because the remaining urban authorities started to take up the new left realist cause, and particularly the cause of community safety (see McLaughlin 1994). Left realism, whose criminological architects quite deliberately intended its use as a means of reinvigorating Labour's position on law and order (Taylor 1999), did not imply the abandonment of concern for issues such as police powers and accountability, which had animated the Party for much of the early 1980s. But in its desire to take crime seriously it offered conceptual and methodological priority to criminal victimisation, and in so doing it backed law enforcement strategies to tackle urban crime and the fear of crime, as well as multi-agency approaches to crime prevention and community safety, that recognised the simultaneous need to address criminal opportunities and criminal motivations, and to activate networks of informal social control. In left realist terms such an approach recognised the complexities of the square of crime, but for many Labour-controlled local authorities it offered the prospects of addressing the lived experiences and concerns of their urban electorates (McLaughlin 1994), and it appears that this political position started to feed through to the Labour Party at large. Hence, in the 1987 and 1992 manifestos (Labour Party 1987; 1992) the earlier line on police powers and accountability is softened, and the emphasis switches to the more familiar refrains of more bobbies on the beat and support for crime prevention and community safety, and much of the welfare liberal language found in earlier manifestos is quietly dropped. In other words, these manifestos show Labour taking on parts of the left realist mantle that, as critics of left realism are quick to point out, often leads to the adoption and support of crime control policies that are barely distinguishable from those emanating from that bastion of administrative criminology (a pejorative term coined by Jock Young, the principal architect of left realism), the UK Home Office.

To be fair, there are important lines of difference: the Home Office's backing in the 1980s for a mainly situational model of crime prevention is quite different from a left realist-informed model of community safety, which in addition to its local focus requires that action be taken at the structural level to address those social inequalities that feed criminal motivations. Yet at the presentational level this difference is not always so manifest, partly because the terms crime prevention and community safety are often used interchangeably, although as we have seen in Chapter 1, they are quite different things.

If the adoption of a realist crime control agenda saw Labour moving closer to the Conservatives on the question of law and order, the picture was further complicated by the fact that towards the end of the 1980s, the Conservatives themselves started to move more in the direction of the centre ground. From 1987 onwards, for example, Downes and Morgan (2002) refer to a period of 'greater realism and restraint', whilst for Savage and Nash (1994) it was 'an age of reason'. Crime rates remained historically high, and the Conservatives may have been mindful that the continuation of too much punitive law and order rhetoric looked disingenuous given that it had been in office for nearly a decade, and that such rhetoric might shine a spotlight on its own policy failings in this area. But towards the end of the decade there was also a liberalising moment, albeit ultimately rather brief, when the limits of criminal justice appeared to be recognised in the ascendance of a just deserts sentencing philosophy and a responsibilising discourse in crime prevention (Faulkner 2003). For the Conservatives this may well have been neo-liberal in emphasis, yet as Stenson (2001) rightly points out, when manifested in community-based approaches to risk management this responsibilising discourse can be empowering in a way that questions the extent to which such approaches really do herald 'the death of the social'.

For all Labour's efforts at enhancing its office-seeking credentials by making its law and order policies more compatible with the tastes of an electorate subjected to well over a decade of Conservative rule, and showing a sustained concern about crime, it still was not enough to help the Party secure victory in 1992. In all probability, law and order would not have been a decisive electoral issue in 1992, even had Labour played a blinder on this theme, but as events transpired, perhaps because of the narrowing of the ground between the two main political parties, crime was not given a high profile in the manifestos of that year, and during the election campaign Labour chose not to make crime a campaigning issue. This turned out to be a major tactical error because the Conservatives used Labour's silence to infer that Labour was still 'soft' on crime (Downes and Morgan 2002), and such a political error probably did Neil Kinnock's chances of survival after the election no favours at all.

Before Tony Blair became leader of the Labour Party in 1994, and was thus enabled to launch his New Labour project, he took the position of Shadow Home Secretary in John Smith's Shadow Cabinet, a position for which Tony Blair had volunteered, thereby signalling a personal interest in matters of law and order that has not since waned. Indeed, his role in the Street Crime Initiative in 2002, and in launching the *Respect* action plan in 2006, both show him still driving the law and order agenda very much from the front. His position as Shadow Home Secretary under John Smith's leadership gave him an opportunity to stamp his reform agenda on a policy area where, as we have seen, Labour had quite clearly lost the initiative since 1979. Giddens' point that 'New Labour took over from the US Democrats the idea that political opponents should not be able to "own" any issues' (2002: 23) is particularly instructive in informing our understanding of Tony Blair's commitment to seize the initiative back.

While Tony Blair's time as Shadow Home Secretary was brief, it is best remembered for the coining of the memorable phrase 'tough on crime, tough on the causes of crime'. It is tempting to dismiss this as a relatively meaningless catchphrase or soundbite, but it would be a mistake to do so. Barnett (2000) recognises that New Labour's marketing of its policy product is much more than empty words. Hence '[t]hey understand that the way a policy is projected is an essential part of the policy, much in the way that the design of a consumer durable is today part of the product itself' (2000: 89). The 'tough on crime, tough on the causes of crime' design works so well on a number of levels. It appeals to middle Englanders, whose anxieties are not just about their material well-being, but also about a quality of life that is adversely affected by the environmental footprint left by problems of crime and disorder, as have been capably uncovered by Girling *et al.* (2000) in their research in the quintessentially middle England town of Macclesfield. It also effectively shrinks the space that might have existed between right and left so that, according to its logic, the third way – which is well epitomised by the term – becomes the only way. Hence, as Blair notes in an article penned for the *New Statesman and Society* magazine, in which the phrase first appeared in print, '... we are moving the debate beyond the choice between personal and social responsibility, the notion that there are only two sides to the "law and order" debate – those who want to punish the criminal and those who point to the poor social conditions in which crime breeds. The obvious common sense of the matter – which would be recognised by any member of the public is that the choice is false and indeed misleading' (1993: 27). Taking this choice away from the law and order debate effectively and skilfully leaves New Labour in a position where it commands the high ground, offering something for everyone, pulling in right and left, addressing the anxieties of the included but also the aspirations of those unfortunately excluded in those criminologically well-known urban breeding grounds of crime, who as left realists show are only too well aware of the reality of the crime problem.

Elsewhere in this 1993 article relatively little is said about the concrete features of New Labour's likely crime control policy, but importantly in terms of office-seeking, Tony Blair does include amongst five objectives for his Party a preparedness to support the incumbent Conservative government 'if it does things that are right' (1993: 28). This was a political masterstroke. Where the Conservatives had portrayed Labour's silence about law and order in the 1992 election as evidence of 'softness' on crime, Blair's objective of conditionally supporting Conservative policy effectively neutralised such a prospective charge in future, as well as denying the Conservatives the easy target of a 'bleeding heart liberal' response to their policies, which had been the norm over much of the preceding two decades. In affording the prospect of conditional support, moreover, it set the Labour opposition in judgement of government policy, and taken together these things did a great deal to wrestle the law and order initiative from the Conservatives. The Conservatives may have tried to seize the initiative back by putting Michael Howard in charge of the Home Office and by pursuing a policy of populist punitiveness (Bottoms 1995) based around the very dubious premise that 'prison works', but Labour's preparedness to support tough measures, such as the 1994 Criminal Justice and Public Order Act, and proposals for the mandatory sentencing of certain repeat offenders, effectively drew the Conservative sting.

As Shadow Home Secretary Tony Blair may have shown the kind of political astuteness that eventually earned him the leadership of the Labour Party, but it also demonstrated the lengths that he was prepared to go, and the direction in which New Labour was prepared to travel, in order to obtain political power. In his pledge to be tough on crime, and in his preparedness to support tough Conservative policies, Blair has an instrumental role in reversing the liberalising moment that had occurred at the turn of the decade, with the passing of the 1991 Criminal Justice Act, which had been premised upon the idea of minimum intervention, even though such an aspiration probably lay closer to the heart of the Act's principal architect, the senior civil servant David Faulkner, than to the hearts of his political masters. Rutherford (1996: 127) suggests that in backtracking from the more progressive elements of the 1991 Act Home Secretary Kenneth Clarke was '… too well aware that his opposite number on the Labour Party benches, Tony Blair, was in the process of stealing his party's law and order mantle'. In this way, it could be argued that, notwithstanding the social structural factors to which both main political parties were in some ways responding (albeit in ways of their own choosing), the shift to the right in law and order politics, and towards a culture of control (Garland 2001), was precipitated in the UK not by the Conservatives, but by Labour. The Conservatives may have been holding the smoking gun, but arguably it was New Labour that had pulled the trigger.

New Labour's preparedness to countenance tough measures of crime control did not rely simply upon their support for what the Conservative government proposed. When Tony Blair became Party leader in 1994, Jack Straw took over as Shadow Home Secretary, and within the course of the next year he had been packed off to New York City to witness the much-vaunted zero-tolerance policing miracle, though many have subsequently doubted or debated the veracity of that particular miracle. Jack Straw, however, returned suitably impressed, and full of the desire to bring down the strong arm of the law on the likes of 'winos, addicts and squeegee merchants', and others who were allegedly undermining the quality of life in towns and cities up and down the country. Again, perhaps what impressed New Labour most about zero-tolerance was the message it communicated, which could not have been designed more effectively to satisfy the needs of those who wanted to demonstrate the Party's tough law and order credentials, and thus the term was appropriated for the 1997 election manifesto (Freeden 1999; Jones and Newburn 2004), and well used both before, during and after the campaign.

In addition to their enthusiasm for zero-tolerance policing, and in many ways related to it, New Labour were also able to pick up on the issue of disorder and anti-social behaviour which had been brought to attention by social landlord groups dealing with the problems of managing increasingly residualised social housing areas (Burney 1999). Although the Conservatives had responded to their concerns by passing legislation that facilitated easier evictions in the shape of the 1996 Housing Act, there evidently remained political mileage in the problem of anti-social behaviour. In raising the lid of this particular Pandora's Box, which is discussed in greater detail in Chapter 5, Labour were able to tap into popular concerns about disorder and the fear of crime, and to be seen to take crime seriously, to quote the left realist injunction. Like zero-tolerance towards minor incivilities, tackling the anti-social behaviour of nuisance neighbours spoke to Wilson and Kelling's (1982) openly populist theory of broken windows, and their rationale for 'nipping crime in the bud'. New Labour's proposals here were set out in the policy document *A Quiet Life* (Labour Party 1995), which based the force of its argument on a small handful of nuisance neighbour case studies, one of which was drawn from Jack Straw's parliamentary constituency of Blackburn. Armed with what was to become the notorious ASBO, a nifty soundbite, a discourse of zero-tolerance, and a preparedness to out-tough an opposition in political decline, New Labour entered the 1997 general election with, possibly for the first time, more than a little confidence on the issue of law and order. Arguably, just as the Conservatives had been able to create and exploit a theme of ungovernability at the end of the 1970s, so New Labour were able to do likewise towards the end of the millennium, as the powerful imagery of out-of-control 'white trash' youths on working-class housing estates (Campbell 1993), persistent young offenders, 'bail bandits', child murderers inspired by 'video nasties', nuisance neighbours and sleazy Conservative politicians all coalesced into a growing sense of lawlessness that something like zero-tolerance was perfectly equipped to simultaneously cultivate and challenge.

As noted above, one of the structural changes made to the New Labour machine was a tighter and better-managed system of political communications. In addition to its media centre, this included an imperative for parliamentary candidates to remain 'on message'. An example of this, cited by Downes and Morgan (2002: 299), was that the leadership forbade '... any discussion by shadow ministers of changes to the drugs laws, even to the point of reprimanding those who sought to reopen discussion in decriminalising cannabis'. This exercise in political control, which continued after 1997, demands a kind of loyalty to 'the firm' that is more reminiscent of the corporate sector than some ideals of democratic politics, but in this particular case it raised the question of whether, with the message being the thing, New Labour's approach in the build-up to the 1997 election was all about office-seeking rather than policy. To those on both the right and the left, serious questions remained about whether word and deed would really be matched were Labour to take office. Would New Labour practice what they preached in terms of toughness, or was this all a case of electioneering? While subsequent chapters in this book go on to explore policy developments after 1997, we can at least begin to answer this question by looking at the main influences on New Labour's political project beyond those discussed above, that are predominantly about matters of office-seeking.

New Labour's policy programme: the third way explored

The previous sections have set out New Labour's strategy for seeking office, both generally and with specific regard to law and order. Much of this involved ditching the policies of Old Labour that it was thought in one way or another had made the Party virtually unelectable, and some, as we have seen in the case of law and order, involved taking up populist policies that made the Party more electable and suitable for office in the changed context that existed at the turn of the twentieth century. Partly because New Labour appeared to put office-seeking ahead of policies, and partly because their media-savvy political communications were geared more to presentation than substance, questions remained about what it was, if it was not Old Labour's social democratic philosophical underpinnings, that was to guide New Labour's policy programme. It was not that New Labour did not have a policy programme, and it was not even that New Labour did not have a philosophy – the third way – that purported to guide that policy programme. Rather, the problem was that this philosophy, if that was indeed what the third way amounted to, was essentially ambiguous. It was ambiguous because it was new, but more especially because it was defined by something that it was not, rather than by something that it was (Driver and Martell 2002). Thus the third way was not the old right, and nor was it the old left, but given that left–right politics had dominated the political landscape of Britain over at least the last half of the twentieth century, this did not exactly amount to a clarification of what the third way actually was. Consequently, in this part of the chapter we devote a good deal of our attention to deconstructing the third way, taking it to be a primary influence – but not the only influence – on New Labour's policy programme, and particularly on its programme for law and order, which remains our principal focus. In doing this, we should not make the mistake of thinking that the third way has been a static entity since its early articulation by New Labour's political elite in the 1990s, or of thinking that there is complete unanimity over what it constitutes, for its essential ambiguity cannot simply be defined away. Nor should we assume a clear correspondence between the normative content of the third way, its inscription on New

Labour's policy programme, and the unfolding of that programme in action, because the policy process never corresponds to such a neat, top-down model of the relationship between intention and action. Here, however, our focus is more on the intention than the action, and this warrants our attention to the details of the third way, even if it is a construction that we should not afford too much solidity.

Perhaps, as its name suggests, because the third way seeks to steer a course between the big 'isms' of conservatism and socialism, not to mention liberalism, it is bound to attract criticism for being philosophically incomplete, insubstantial and contradictory, and such criticism may indeed be well founded. Yet such criticism also misses the significance of the third way as a discursive project, which is how Janet Newman (2001) sees it. Her cultural analysis, which '... emphasises the way in which social arrangements are constructed as a result of the production of meanings and the repression, subordination or incorporation of alternative meanings' (2001: 6), helps us to understand that the discourse of the third way had a particular '... practical function [which] was to define the impossibility of alternatives rather than to identify a specific programme of reform' (2001: 45). This is well illustrated in Tony Blair's (1993) dismissal of the old 'two sides of the law and order debate' which simultaneously conflated them into the third way. The genius of the third way lies in its capacity to hook us in to its common sense, in much the same way that Margaret Thatcher succeeded in convincing most of us in the 1980s that 'there is no alternative', but then given the population's penchant for dodgy mullets and 'big hair' hairstyles in that decade, we were obviously a gullible lot back then. In the case of the third way, other 'ways' are dismissed as failures, whether that be the nanny state or the atomising, fragmenting market, the 'hard' approach to punishing criminals or the 'soft' approach to addressing crime's causes. Yet in the moment of their dismissal these oppositional values are somehow drawn together, and in the process of doing so their opposition is resolved, so that the rights that go with the state can be combined with the responsibilities that go with the market, or the 'tough on crime' punitive logic can sit alongside the 'tough on the causes of crime' interest in addressing criminal aetiology. In this way the third way presents itself as being somehow more complete than and superior to its alternatives, which is why it works so well as an office-seeking strategy, but leaves unanswered questions when used as a guide for policy. How can one combine rights and responsibilities in any particular instance, and is it possible to be simultaneously tough on crime and tough on its causes?

The dismissal of other 'ways' and the resolution of their oppositional values holds the third way up as a pragmatic project rather than an ideological one. The pragmatism is discursive in the sense that the third way visualises a path between ideological extremes, but it is also very real, because in the final analysis it makes New Labour's politics subservient to the economy, rather than vice versa, as it was under Old Labour's Keynesian project (Byrne 2005). This is a defining feature of the third way. In its keenness to avoid being ideological, it inevitably accepts the Conservative legacy of a neo-liberal hegemonic project of globalisation as its starting premise, even if, unlike the Conservatives, it does not simply have such blind faith in the free market. This position is well illustrated in the influential report of the Commission on Social Justice, published in 1994. This report, using classic third way tactics, identified different visions of social welfare: there were, it said, Levellers, who sought social justice by redistribution; Deregulators, who relied upon the market and entrepreneurialism; and Investors, who sought to use supply side measures such as education and training to maximise opportunities to compete in the marketplace.

New Labour's vision, needless to say, was to be that of an Investors' Britain (Blackman and Palmer 1999), maximising Britain's fitness for the competitive challenges of globalisation, thereby responding to the agenda set by its political predecessors, rather than looking to set its own more progressive one. To this extent, New Labour's third way concurs with the third way outlined by Giddens (2002), who is quick to point out, lest it be thought that it is some kind of electoral gimmick, that the third way is actually an international movement, and a means by which social democratic parties have reformed their policy programmes in order to hold office on spaces now occupied by the impregnable forces of global capitalism. Not all commentators, however, are quite so convinced by the determining force of globalisation (Hirst 2000), which, after all, has largely been the creation of the macro-economic policies of nation states, and which third way parties such as New Labour presume to be some Frankenstein's monster, that once made cannot be unmade. If the third way is an accommodation of globalisation, then as Driver and Martell (2002) point out, it is not necessarily the case that different countries have plotted exactly the same course, and in the UK the course has been set by a Thatcherite inheritance which means, despite the protestations of pragmatism over how best to organise and deliver public services within a mixed economy framework, that there is a tendency to fall back on a belief in the competitive market as a naturally superior economic mechanism (Newman 2001).

In terms of crime control the third way's accommodation to the forces of globalisation is indicative of policy responses that have the purpose of shoring up Britain's economic competitiveness: crime control is an investment in such competitiveness. Just as the neo-liberal thinking World Bank requires developing countries to demonstrate their creditworthiness through a capacity for 'good governance', so it would appear that global capitalism 'requires' nation states to demonstrate that the spaces over which they hold sovereignty are safe and secure. Ian Taylor (1996, 1999) made valuable contributions about the importance of crime control to urban fortunes, and the same point applies, writ large, to nation states. Thus, beyond evidence of a 'credible' criminal justice system that catches and punishes its criminals, capital may attach particular importance to the sanitisation of public space, using the kinds of 'sanitary ware' – CCTV and zero-tolerance policing, for example – that have been taken up with some enthusiasm by New Labour in power. And while crime control may play its part in sanitising public space to make it suitable for inward investment, it also provides opportunities for investment of its own, as the massive expansion of the private security industry bears testimony to. New Labour has not blazed its own trail here, because the Conservatives' Safer Cities Programme, launched in 1988, first tied local crime control to the coat-tails of urban economic regeneration (Gilling 1997), but it has certainly continued the trend, providing a good example of the way in which the third way has accommodated this neo-liberal political agenda. In many ways New Labour's project here may have been chiselled partly out of the 'urban boosterist' experiences of erstwhile urban socialist local authority areas such as Manchester or Sheffield in the 1990s.

While the third way's 'bottom line' may be to accommodate Britain to the hegemonic project of neo-liberal globalisation, it would be wrong to suggest that it is devoid of a principled vision of how this might be done: it is not simply a case of New Labour pimping Britain to the global economy. The vision that informs its policy programme is largely a moral one that takes its cue from the moral authoritarian (Hughes 1996) communitarianism expressed by the American Amitai Etzioni, which ultimately sets out a prescriptive normative programme for how individuals and communities should conduct themselves in a way that is conducive to the neo-liberal economic order. To qualify this, Etzioni's work is, as he says, explicitly about the question of moral order, and for this reason he does not actually address economic questions. The implication of this is that moral issues are somehow divorced from other spheres of social life (Byrne 2005), but this is nonsense, and in practice this means taking unequal capitalist social relations for granted (Levitas 2005), as well as other sources of inequality. Implicitly, therefore, Etzioni's communitarianism is about shoring up the existing economic order, even if he does not say as much.

As Hughes (1998) points out, communitarianism gathered influence in the 1980s as a critique of the individualistic excesses of market liberalism, and it chimed well with the New Labour project, not least because of its Janus-faced third way qualities: the morality that underpins appeals to community attracts conservatives, while the collectivist implications appeal to socialists. By combining the two sides, communitarianism magically presents itself, like the third way, as non-ideological common sense that rises above politics (Little 2002).

As well as being critical of the ideology of market liberalism – if not the economic base that sustains it – Etzioni also writes critically about the dependency-inducing qualities of rights-based welfare liberalism, thereby following a line that has already been well trodden by the right realist likes of James Q. Wilson and Charles Murray. In criticising market liberalism and welfare liberalism, Prideaux's observation, that '... Etzioni selects polarised extremes in an attempt to substantiate a middle course that is already predetermined by his moral sensibilities' (2005: 42), is accurate, and might just as well have been applied to Tony Blair's third way. Like many who have been caught up in the seductions of community, Etzioni harks back to the apparently orderly society of 1950s America, when work and the work ethic were both widespread. Exposing his conservative leanings, Etzioni sees 1950s America as a moral society, and a moral yardstick against which contemporary society falls woefully short. Human association, which endows us with our fundamentally social identities, has fallen apart as communities have crumbled, and identity has therefore lost its moorings, floating off in the direction of abstract and unhelpful systemic influences such as market liberal ideology, which has spawned a rampant individualism, and brought in its wake a host of moral problems, amongst which crime, disorder and family breakdown are prominent. The solution to these problems is to recreate the communities that have crumbled away, because these communities are primarily vehicles for attaining social order (Levitas 2005), with community interests taking precedence over the particularistic interests of individuals. In many ways, in proposing the use of communities to take on moral problems such as crime and disorder, and a culture of dependency, in Etzioni's vision communities take on the tasks previously performed by disciplinary institutions such as the prison or the factory, which in the nineteenth century sought to produce a compliant workforce for industrial capitalism. In place of these disciplinary institutions, compliance in late-modernity can be achieved by governing through communities (Rose 1999). Communities become sites where individuals can become self-actualised as social beings, putting their responsibilities before their rights, just as the community comes before the individual.

Such moral authoritarian principles have become inscribed upon Blair's (1998) characterisation of the third way, two of whose four core values he identifies as community and responsibility. One key question is how these values, this moral authoritarian communitarianism, are to be translated from theory into practice. What kind of policy programme would transpose an equivalent normative model of 1950s America on to the very different social context of late-modern Britain? Clearly, given Etzioni's diagnosis, it cannot be expected to happen spontaneously, but rather requires some form of state action to both build and support community action, without inducing dependency. It is apparent from Etzioni's work, and the work of others commenting upon it, that this action is to be concentrated upon particular features of community life. In particular, the targets of Etzioni's attention are the family, the school, work, and collective action within the community, particularly through community and voluntary associations which, in contemporary discourse, are conceived of as 'the third sector', the social space for the third way. Within the family, the priority is to cultivate good parenting and parental responsibility, and within schools, the priority is moral education and discipline, all things that have at one time or another fallen on to James Q. Wilson's radar screen. In this way of thinking, work is moralising by its very nature, inculcating habits of industry and a sense of discipline and responsibility to others, the latter also being a feature of participation within the third sector. These targets can be worked on in part by what Little (2002) describes as a 'politics of enforcement', which clearly distinguished Etzioni's communitarianism and New Labour's third way from any form of 'soft' welfare liberalism that might have been associated with Old Labour, and which made the 'mistake' of putting rights before responsibilities. It is, rather, 'a crusade to reinstate lost values' (Little 2002: 65) where, as we shall see in subsequent chapters, policy initiatives can make parental responsibility legally enforceable through court orders, and where former recipients of welfare benefits can be placed under compulsion to find or take whatever work opportunities are made available to them. Only in the field of participation within the third sector can this politics of enforcement not be prosecuted, and here there is more reliance upon moral pressure and state subsidy to encourage the growth of the third sector.

We will examine some of these areas in more detail in subsequent chapters, particularly because their role in producing order, by creating 'stakeholders' or by turning the excluded into the included, signifies their importance in local strategies of crime control: the politics of enforcement is also, inevitably, a politics of crime control. The communitarian assumption, evident in Etzioni's work, is that the creation of a moral order around ideal typical community attributes such as family, schooling, work and voluntary association will insulate such communities from crime, by endowing them with a capacity for moral conformity, but also with a capacity for community policing, neighbourhood watch and public shaming, all of which Etzioni has offered his support for as crime control measures (Hughes 1998). But of course, if communities cannot hold together their own moral orders, there is always the prospect of falling back on the moral authority of a strong state through its law enforcement and penal machinery.

As a number of commentators have noted, New Labour's communitarianism has endowed its policy programme with a *one nation* feel, where the aspiration is that people will pull together as a single socially cohesive mass of included stakeholders, voting for New Labour and committing themselves to a New Britain. Such an aspiration compares favourably against Conservative policies that promised little more than a trickle down effect to those at the bottom (which never materialised), and a fragile safety net of welfare for those who were most deprived and marginalised, and this may be why the other third way core values mentioned by Blair (1998), namely equal worth and opportunity for all, can be seen, albeit more indirectly, as communitarian in emphasis. These values appear to be less moral authoritarian and more progressive (albeit mildly so) in nature, aspiring to bring those excluded by discrimination or disadvantage in to the bosom of the community, so that they may have an equal opportunity to demonstrate their moral worth. This is the sense in which concepts such as 'stakeholder' and 'inclusion' are utilised in third way speak, and certainly any idea of a more progressive politics, associated with Old Labour values such as equality of outcome, is completely absent.

There are a number of problems with the moral authoritarian communitarian vision that has been inscribed upon New Labour's third way. Firstly, as Prideaux (2005) points out, it smacks of a consensus functionalism that assumes an unwarranted harmony to community life, as if somehow it can be divorced from the wider social conflicts and inequalities that exist, as if morality, like love, can conquer all. In particular, secondly, communities by themselves cannot overcome or compensate for the destructiveness of market relations that remain untouched by Etzioni's exclusively moral focus, even though he may be critical of individualistic market liberal ideology. In its acquiescence to a neo-liberal hegemony, New Labour's communitarianism has a hollow ring to it because the free market is destructive of the very attributes – mutuality, voluntarism, trust and friendship – that communities require to thrive (Little 2002). The market brings competition and insecurity which is unlikely to provide the firm foundations for a communitarian moral order, without the continuance of a politics of enforcement that will always rely more on state action than spontaneous community action, particularly in those areas – typically those also suffering highest rates of criminal victimisation – that feel the fullest force of market inequalities.

Thirdly, the idea of imposing community cohesion, on a diverse society such as that inhabiting late-modern Britain, through a single moral authority – *the community* – is both anachronistic and dangerous. Identity may well come from human association, but it is not all chiselled off the same cultural block, but rather comes from multiple connections and relations (Little 2002) that are always in a state of change (Clarke 1999). To assume otherwise, as moral authoritarian communitarianism does, is to risk unleashing an exclusionary dynamic that 'others' those that do not fit or belong (see Young 1999). And even amongst 'the included' there is a failure to respect diversity, and not just ethnic diversity, that is likely to lead to very unequal treatment, such as that dished out to single mothers (Levitas 2005). Etzioni's nostalgic view of 1950s America is precisely that, observed through the proverbial rose-tinted spectacles, and, as students of criminology would do well to remember, observed quite differently by the American subculture theorists, and by a young Edwin Lemert, who presumably would have had little to write about had the America of the 1950s really been quite as Etzioni imagines it. Perhaps New Labour's third way commits the same error, falling for an impossibly homogeneous view of a New Britain, composed of 'the people' with whom Tony Blair liked to think he communed, and to whom he frequently referred in his political rhetoric.

Writing with characteristic prescience, when New Labour's governmental project had barely been unwrapped, Hughes (1998) foresaw three possible ideal typical futures for crime prevention, as previously discussed in Chapter 1. One of these, the 'high trust, authoritarian communitarian' model, comes very close to plotting the actual course of the third way, in intent if not always in delivery. The model seeks to build strong communities, established and backed-up by an authoritarian state, and it reads very much like the politics of enforcement through which New Labour has sought to strengthen communities. It is no coincidence that this model is most strongly associated with the so-called economically successful 'Tiger economies' of the 1980s and 1990s in South and East Asia, and interestingly this shows that while communitarianism might be the end to which the third way aspires, the third way in turn is the means to the end of competitiveness in a global economy, and this is why it does not challenge, but in fact actively supports, the neo-liberal hegemony. As we shall see in Chapter 6, a similar argument could be advanced against New Labour's conversion to the cause of building social capital, which fits the end of stronger communities, but which is so enthusiastically pursued because of the putative links, set out in Putnam's (2000) work on Italy, between strong social capital and strong economic performance. This model, of strong communities and authoritarian governments, might fit best in the mind of its authors such as Etzioni. Hughes (1998), however, is wary that such a model may not fit societies such as contemporary Britain, which are less traditional, less hierarchically organised, and have a stronger tradition of liberal rights. It may also be unstable when grafted on to a neo-liberal market society, which as noted above continually undermines the values on which strong communities depend, thereby requiring a yet more authoritarian state to enforce the moral boundaries against increasingly excluded 'others'. Much of this tension is played out in New Labour's responses to anti-social behaviour, which are considered in more detail later.

As Hughes (1998) and Little (2002) would doubtless be quick to point out, while the third way's communitarianism is deeply problematic, the problem lies less with communitarianism per se, and more with its moral authoritarian variant. There is an alternative radical pluralist version of communitarianism that recognises the fluidity of identity and of individual connectedness to multiple communities, and that provides the basis not for inevitable exclusion, but for constructive, respectful dialogue that is democratic and that seeks to resolve the inevitable conflicts of a diverse and fluid society. But this would require the sort of socially just levelling of the playing field that New Labour is evidently not prepared to countenance.

From ideas to action: moving along the third way

Thus far, the focus of our attention on New Labour's policy programme has been on the third way, which sets out an apparently pragmatic accommodation to a neo-liberal hegemony, and a moral emphasis upon community as the source of social order, mediated and indeed established through the responsibilising contributions of work, voluntary association, the family, schooling and community-based crime control. In the final part of this chapter before the summary, we switch our attention to those rationalities that have characterised the practical content of New Labour's policy programme, which have become more apparent since taking office, and particularly since 1999, when New Labour had served its time in self-imposed adherence to Conservative spending plans, thereby demonstrating its prudence, before launching itself into a more expansive period of 'delivery-oriented' public service reform, fuelled by a distinctly favourable economic climate and the proceeds of a not inconsiderable windfall tax on the former public utilities. We do not have the space here to review specific policy developments which lie outside the scope of this book, and our emphasis, rather, is on the 'big ideas' that have tended to recur across developments in different policy domains, and particularly in the areas related to crime control in which we are especially interested.

New Labour's policy programme has been strongly orientated to the reform of public services, particularly drawing upon the general, and rhetorically much-used, theme of modernisation. In so far as modernisation means renewal, it plays very strongly to the theme of 'newness' that New Labour's permanent revolution has been all about. Yet inevitably modernisation as a concept lacks precision and means different things to different people, deliberately so. Rather than seek some quasi-authoritative definition of the term, therefore, in this section I will restrict my attention to three features of New Labour's governmental project that characterise and help to comprise this theme of modernisation, that run through the policy developments that we shall be addressing later on in the book, and that therefore merit our attention here in helping to make sense of such developments. These three features are firstly, New Labour's pragmatic commitment to 'what works', or to evidence-based policy; secondly, their 'big idea' (Clark 2002) of joined-up policy; and thirdly, their faith in the potential of new public management to deliver more economic, efficient, effective and value for money public services. With the usual proviso that looking at each in turn is a heuristic device that meets our analytic needs but is a somewhat artificial exercise, we will proceed nevertheless to do exactly that.

Evidence-based policy

Tony Blair (1998: 31) has set out the tenets of evidence-based policy thus:

> As I say continually, what matters is what works to give effect to our values. Some commentators are disconcerted by this insistence on fixed values and goals but pragmatism about means. There are even claims that it is unprincipled. But I believe that a critical dimension of the Third Way is that policies flow from values, not vice versa.

Seen in this light, evidence-based policy represents a decisive move away from Old Labour's dogmatic and ideological commitment to the idea that 'the public sector is best' when it comes to the matter of organising and delivering public goods. It recognises the Conservative legacy in the shape of privatisation and marketisation, which has brought the private sector into areas of public service provision, or which has made the public sector more private sector-like in its bid to compete for service delivery contracts or to operate within quasi-markets such as in health care. And it also recognises, in a way that the highly statist, modernist project often did not, that public policy outcomes are the accomplishment of mixed economies that take in not only the efforts of state agencies, but also those from private, voluntary and informal providers. While this is true of areas such as social welfare, where needs are invariably met (though too frequently remain unmet) through a combination of these sectors, often through a heavy reliance on the informal sector and the emotional labour of caring women, it is equally true of areas like crime control, where the major push of crime prevention policy under the Conservatives in the direction of active citizenship, for example, was a clear acknowledgement of the instrumental role that individuals, families and communities make in preventing crime, beyond the criminal justice system.

Evidence-based policy is not just about the question of *who* delivers public goods such as crime control, it is also about *how* such goods are delivered, the implication being that the best way is the one that produces the best outcomes: what matters is what works. In practice, questions of who and how are often difficult to disentangle, because how a good is delivered is often dependent upon who is delivering it. But this openness to different approaches suggests that in theory evidence-based practice is anti-traditional, and open to innovation and flexibility. Thus it is not a case of delivering public goods in a particular way because 'we have always done it this way' or because it fits a certain ideological predilection, but rather it is a case of delivering them in a way that maximises positive outcomes.

In theory, evidence-based practice fits well with the problem-orientation of crime prevention, because it means matching crime prevention responses to the particularistic circumstances of specific crime problems. Whereas the Conservatives were suspected of promoting situational approaches to crime prevention that fitted their responsibilising ideology, and their lack of interest in social causation (see Chapter 3 for a fuller discussion), New Labour's much-vaunted evidence-based philosophy suggested an approach that would be unfettered by such bias, giving more space, rather, to objective 'scientific' judgements about what works. An early indication that this indeed was to be the road travelled was Chancellor Gordon Brown's comprehensive spending review methodology, which implied the fundamental scrutiny of central government department spending to ensure it maximised positive policy outcomes. In the case of crime control the upshot of this was a quest for examples of effective practice (Goldblatt and Lewis 1998), and a commitment to apply the 'evidence base' to contemporary practice, which is the idea that the 1999 Crime Reduction Programme was largely premised upon. All this was particularly good news for evaluation researchers, whose task it was to provide unambiguous answers to the question of what works, although in the event, as we shall see, this turned out for various reasons to be not such an easy question to answer.

On the face of it, evidence-based policy is an immensely attractive discourse that promises a focus upon the 'business end' of public policy delivery, and the negation of unhelpful distractions such as tradition and provider interests, notably those emanating from obstructive trade unions or public service professions. However, in practice, as countless efforts at public service reform have shown, such distractions are not so easy or so wise to negate, and the aspiration to negate them rests upon too technocratic a view of the policy process, and an implicit and often undermining mistrust of professional discretion (Tilley 2001). On a related point, evidence-based policy may also rest upon a flawed natural science-inspired understanding of policy interventions which, in reducing them to the question of what works, and to an implicit expectation of their replicability, dangerously oversimplifies and decontextualises such interventions. Put simply, the discourse of what works raises expectations more than is warranted by what remains a complex and difficult to understand social world, as Tilley's (ibid.) realist critique of natural scientific experimentalism makes clear. Also, in giving priority to questions of what works, there is a danger that priority is given to an ends-orientation that neglects important questions of value, if these are not clearly articulated within articulations of what works. In the case of crime control, particularly given the exercise of power that may be involved, it is important, for example, that questions of effectiveness are balanced by questions of accountability, and it is also important that crime control is not pursued at the expense of other values such as tolerance and fairness. To put it more starkly, Mike Davis's (1990) dystopian *City of Quartz*, even were it to be an example of effective crime control in its creation of fortified spaces, is not necessarily the kind of place where we would all want to live. Many of us, similarly, would shirk from Shearing and Stenning's (1984) less threatening, yet nevertheless discomforting, portrayal of Disney World. Finally, there remains a suspicion that the valorisation of evidence-based policy conceals a potential downsizing of the public sector, with its professed pragmatism being used to justify a mixture of load-shedding, privatisation, marketisation and government at a distance, because, it may be argued, public sector agencies may be less able directly to provide and deliver what works. Thus, just as the third way capitulates to the neo-liberal hegemony of globalisation, so evidence-based policy capitulates to governance, as if the shift from government to governance is an unstoppable social force.

All of these points suggest that we should treat evidence-based policy with some caution. It is aspirational, and its professed pragmatism remains unconvincing, just as the third way's claim to being non-ideological is similarly so. Given the difficulty if not the impossibility of a purely pragmatic approach to governing, one may legitimately ask whether evidence-based policy is honoured more in the breach than the observance, whether its pursuit has come at the neglect of other less outcome-oriented ends, and whether the suspicion alluded to above is justified.

Joined-up policy

We examine joined-up policy in more detail later in the book, but it is important here to acknowledge its centrality to New Labour's modernisation project. Clark (2002) refers to it as New Labour's 'big idea', although it would be erroneous to assume that it was in any way a *new* idea, because it is based upon notions such as partnership that were by no means anathema to the previous Conservative governments, in domains such as community care, urban regeneration, and, significantly, crime prevention. What is different about joined-up policy under New Labour is partly the recurrent use of the discourse as a motif of modernisation, but also the priority given to it. This priority is evidenced in the cross-departmental machinery that has been established within central government, typified by bodies such as the SEU. In the case of crime control, it is also evidenced by the introduction of a regional link between the centre and the periphery, in the shape of the Government Offices for the English Regions and Welsh Assembly, and particularly the Crime Reduction Directorates that have been established within them, and that have come to play an increasingly important part in the governmental architecture. And, also in the case of local crime control, it is also evidenced in the preparedness to move beyond the Conservatives' approach of merely promoting partnership working, to mandating it, through such bodies as local CDRPs, Youth Offending Teams (YOTs) and LSPs, although the mandatory force can only be applied to statutory bodies.

There are two core aspects to New Labour's joined-up approach. The first aspect, joined-up government, is about establishing better linkages between statutory bodies, whether that be within particular tiers of government, or across them: the purpose here is better horizontal or vertical coordination. The second aspect is really about the shift from government to governance: in theory it is about establishing networks between statutory bodies and those from the private, voluntary and community sectors, so that the contribution of each sector to the business of governing is recognised, but also coordinated to ensure maximum effectiveness. Like evidence-based policy, therefore, joined-up government has a certain pragmatic outcome orientation: it is about delivering effective policy, but as with the former, we should be mindful that this apparent pragmatism is never ideologically neutral. As Fitzpatrick (2005: 163) quite rightly points out, '... discursive techniques of governance and managerialism create the very social world to which they offer themselves as the solution'.

There is a well-established rationale for joined-up government. Generally this is based upon a critique of existing approaches to problems such as crime, which stand accused of operating with too narrow a focus: they are too 'departmentalised', or work with a deficient 'silo mentality', and they show that for too long the administrative tail has been wagging the problem dog. This is usually regarded as the fault of bureau-professional approaches to public policy problems, that draw upon too narrow or specialist a knowledge-base, and too inflexible an administrative process. Advocates of joined-up policy recognise that, contrary to the discourses of competence that are purveyed by departmentalised bureau-professionals, some problems are 'wicked issues' (Stewart and Clarke 1997) that do not fit easily into neat administrative categories and boundaries, but rather provide 'cross-cutting themes' for governmental bodies. This is perfectly illustrated in New Labour's use of the concept of social exclusion, but it is also present in their approach to crime, and to anti-social behaviour. In the case of crime, then, joined-up policy aspires to connect central government departments whose field of operations impact upon, or are impacted upon by, crime, such as transport, health, employment, education, physical and social regeneration, and of course criminal justice. And it aspires to connect the networks of local 'players', such as business interests, a wide range of local government services, the police, voluntary agencies such as Victim Support, and community bodies and representatives, whose resources and interests can be tapped into to provide more joined-up, and more holistic, approaches to the problem of crime.

It is important to recognise that joined-up policy is aspirational, and like evidence-based policy it is an attractive aspiration that gives it suitable third way appeal. Yet just as evidence-based policy is somewhat ambiguous about precisely what this evidence is that will illuminate the way to effective policy outcomes, so joined-up policy remains vague about what a joined-up approach to policy really looks like. For some, there is a sense that we are talking here about a fundamentally new mode of governing, which shifts us from hierarchies and markets towards networked governance, which operates not on the legal authority of the state, nor on the contractual relations of the market, but rather on the much more ephemeral quality of trust (Gilling 2005). This implies that governmental power shifts from a vertical to a more horizontal form, and that the modality of such power shifts from a 'command and control' style to one based more on negotiation and bargaining. Yet while those involved in 'partnership working' may recognise the importance of negotiation and bargaining to their work, and while trust looms large as an issue for them, the elephant in the room is still central government, and the pressing question we need to ask is just how far this apparent shift from government to governance really does represent a new mode of governing. The other aspect of joined-up policy, namely joined-up government, if anything *strengthens* the 'command and control' role of the centre, giving it a tighter grip over local policy responses. In this way, the priorities of the centre can work to fracture the negotiated equilibrium of local partnerships, pressurising local statutory agencies, in particular, to dance to the centre's tune. This explains the co-existence of centrifugal and centripetal forces (Clarke and Newman 1997), or the decentring/recentring dialectic (Crawford 1997), identified by others in their research into partnership working.

Joined-up policy at the local level does appear to demonstrate a sharing of the responsibility for problems such as crime across the sectors of the mixed economy, and it does appear to represent the pragmatic acceptance of the limitations of government agencies, and certainly of central government, in being able to address 'wicked issues', yet there is also a sense that ideology may be at work here. Normatively, joined-up policy as governance pays homage to a neo-liberal hegemony which recognises the limitations of government action – although neo-liberalism's conservative underbelly (O'Malley 2004) means that this does not always extend to questions of law and order, except where there may be market opportunities, as indeed there are in the business of private security. Yet it may be ideological also in the sense that it conveys the impression of central government relinquishing control to networks of trust relations, when in reality attempts are being made to reconfigure such control in an attempt to govern at a distance, through bodies upon whom central government is dependent for the success of its political project. Since many practitioners testify to the immense difficulties of partnership working, this is, it should be stressed, no easy feat.

As can be seen from this limited discussion, joined-up policy raises some very big questions about the nature of government action and about the relationship between government and other sectors of the mixed economy, including 'the community'. For New Labour, it is presented as a pragmatic means through which the third way can be realised in practice and policy outcomes, but for the purposes of this book it is important that we acknowledge that, while it is very easy to become seduced by the self-evident 'common sense' of partnership working, we do not lose sight of these bigger questions about the significance of the partnership approach and the form it may take, and we do not fall into the trap, that so many people do fall into (Gilling 2005), of seeing partnership working in purely pragmatic terms, and seeing the difficulties that arise as wholly practical, rather than to a large degree political.

New public management

As with joined-up policy, New Labour's ardent enthusiasm for the rationalities and technologies of new public management should not be taken to imply that such managerialism is in any way unique to the New Labour project. Rather, it is a global phenomenon that varies internationally in shape, but that is associated particularly closely with the previous Conservative governments, who between them developed and refined it after its initially rather narrow focus upon financial management, and cost-savings. It was given renewed emphasis through the publication of the immensely influential work of Osborne and Gaebler (1992) on *Reinventing Government*, which received a personal endorsement from then President Bill Clinton, and which therefore, given the general influence of Clinton's New Democrats on the emergent New Labour project, made quite an impression on this side of the Atlantic.

It should come as no surprise to the reader that, like evidence-based policy and joined-up policy, new public management sells itself on its pragmatic appeal. Its existence is justified as a means of improving the performance of government in terms of the economy, efficiency, effectiveness and value for money of its operations, although there are subtle but nevertheless important differences between these different criteria. Because it is pragmatic, it can be presented as non-ideological, although its origins lie very strongly in an ideological assault on state, bureau-professional power. This assault is dressed up in the language of public choice theory (Niskanen 1973), which castigates the self-interest of providers, who, it appears, are always looking to maximise their own utility, to build their own empires and to line their own pockets, rather than to deliver true public service. Why else, after all, would one become a child protection social worker, a police officer or even a university lecturer, for that matter? Against the self-seeking bureau-professional model of public administration is set the market discipline of the private sector, where performance is measured in terms of profitability, and where only the fittest survive. New public management therefore becomes a matter, largely, of bringing this market discipline into the business of government, in various different ways.

The implicit 'private is best' assumption supports a strategy of using the private sector wherever possible, such as the Private Finance Initiative, which forces a rather sceptical eye to be turned on the imputed objectivity, neutrality and pragmatism of the claim for evidence-based practice. But if the private sector cannot be used, then the task becomes that of making the public sector more private sector-like, and particularly more competitive. As with the Conservatives' policy of compulsory (some might say compulsive) competitive tendering (CCT), public sector organisations, or parts of them, might be forced to compete with the private sector for contracts to deliver public services, or as with the internal market introduced after the Conservatives' National Health Service reforms, 'purchasers' and 'providers' may be separated from one another, and public sector providers may be forced to compete with one another for the purchasers' contracts. But New Labour has generally shunned such approaches in favour of a less obviously market-friendly third way approach that relies more upon the quasi-competitive discipline that can be instilled through the use of performance standards and targets. These standards and targets are mainly externally imposed upon public sector agencies – the whole point is that the bureau-professionals that staff them cannot be trusted to set sufficiently challenging targets for themselves, although over time, through practices such as self-assessment and appraisal, and through enticements such as performance-related pay or the granting of certain 'freedoms and flexibilities' to 'performing' agencies and authorities, the aspiration is that individuals and the agencies that they work for can become self-governing, enterprising bodies, and very much a part of the neo-liberal hegemonic landscape that surrounds them.

New Labour's adoption of new public management has resulted in the institutionalisation of an audit culture (Power 1997) of performance management – the relentless setting of standards and targets, and the equally relentless measurement of progress relative to those standards and targets, and relative to the 'performance' of others in meeting those same standards and targets. It has been well described as 'the institutionalisation of mistrust' (Crawford 2001), because it involves a constant 'checking up', although this is not necessarily a bad thing and can, in the right circumstances, if the performance measurement is appropriate, enhance public accountability. It is also mistrustful in the sense that performance standards are externally imposed, although as individuals and agencies are encouraged to set their own targets, once they have demonstrated their merit as enterprising souls, this is perhaps better conceived as conditional trust.

Yet just how pragmatic is this new public management, which in the case of local crime control is expressed through the public service agreements (PSAs) that the Home Office negotiates with the Treasury and then imposes as targets upon local agencies; the Best Value Performance Indicators that are derived from and concretise the targets in the PSAs; the Best Value audits and inspections to which local authorities and the police must submit themselves; the i-Quanta statistical framework that the Home Office compiles and uses to assess the performance of individual CDRPs, the partnership self-assessments that CDRPs are obliged to conduct, and so forth (see Chapters 3 and 4)? There is a burgeoning critical literature on new public management that raises a number of issues that cast doubt upon or find fault in many of the claims of new public management to act as a pragmatic guide for better public policy.

Firstly, in specifying standards and targets, performance management regimes inevitably prioritise what is measurable over that which is not, and in so doing they seek to shape organisational business around what is measured, and around the temporal and spatial frames that are deployed by the measurement regime. In an area such as local crime control, this becomes immensely significant. As noted in Chapter 1, one of the key issues for us concerns the fundamental nature of the local crime control enterprise, and specifically whether it moves in the direction of community safety, which is a label used by many local practitioners as a normative description of what they do, or in the narrower direction of crime prevention, with its more short-termist, risk management focus. When the performance management regime is conceived largely in terms of crime reduction targets, then it would appear to mobilise bias in the direction of this narrower vision, and this is a very good example of the way that a governmental technology, performance management, constitutes the social world (in this case the notion of 'crime reduction') that it offers itself as a solution to. Its success in shaping the policy domain in a particular, favoured way may depend upon the capacity of those with alternative discourses to impose their constructions, and to resist the power of this managerial discourse, which is by no means absolute. But this focus on 'the measurable' undoubtedly distorts organisational activities away from activities that are not so easily or obviously measurable, some of which might be relatively unimportant, but some of which may be absolutely fundamental to organisational action. As Hough (2004) has pointed out with regard to policing, the performance management regime generally neglects the legitimacy-building activities that may occupy a considerable proportion of the energies of the local police which provide a necessary condition for effective police crime control operations and which, if neglected, because they are not easily 'countable', would significantly and negatively impact on police effectiveness. The problem is by no means peculiar to policing.

Secondly, performance management has been found to impose a 'core business' mentality that militates against joined-up policy (Crawford 1997). We should not be surprised that discursive formations have their contradictions (Clarke 1999), and in the case of the third way here is one, where the pursuit of new public management undermines the pursuit of joined-up policy, imposing upon public agencies the very 'silo mentality' that joined-up policy is supposed to address. The vertical command and control framework imposed by performance management thus cuts through the fragile horizontal networks of trust that partnership working is said to require, pulling statutory agencies out of these networks in a way that could be interpreted by others either as a lack of commitment to partnership working, or as arrogance, both of which impact negatively on the formation of trust.

Thirdly, and as another example of contradiction, performance management, supposedly founded upon the anti-bureaucratic principles of dynamic action-oriented management, can end up reproducing bureaucracy to an even greater degree. As one police officer once observed to me, with a heavy dose of cynicism but possibly an equal measure of truth, 'we're no good at controlling crime, but we're damn good at counting it'. If the pejorative use of the term 'bureaucracy' is taken as a shorthand for the problem of goal displacement, where means become ends, then performance management, with its industry of endlessly collecting, processing, analysing, presenting and comparing or 'benchmarking' data, is a case in point. It is frequently pointed out that crime rates are vulnerable to potentially quite wild temporal variations beyond any specific seasonal effect, and while this can provide a major issue for those looking to evaluate the effectiveness of specific individual crime control interventions, it is rarely recognised as an issue in more general performance management regimes, where temporal variations are read as variations in 'performance'. When these variations mark a downward trend, as they may and arguably did in the earlier years of New Labour's administration as a result of a marked economic upturn, they can lead to a self-congratulatory approach to the assessment of performance that exaggerates the tendency of performance management towards bureaucratic goal displacement, reconfigured as the manufacture of good news. If one adds to this the kind of techno-fetishism to which local crime control is now vulnerable, in the age of the all-singing, all-dancing geographical information system (GIS) and the like, it is easy to see how likely is such goal displacement, or de-coupling, as Power (1997) describes it.

Again, then, as the third way moves from ideas into action, we are left with important questions about its policy programme, and about its professed pragmatism. New public management, which in Osborne and Gaebler's (1992) terms is all about 'steering not rowing', does indeed steer policy on a particular course. But whereas for Osborne and Gaebler this might have been all about improving performance, employing the ideology of management as something that 'makes things better', and that pushes the textbooks of self-styled management gurus onto the best-seller lists, in reality this steering plots a more uncertain, and more political course. Performance management can shape the content of that which it professes simply to measure; it can undermine other policy objectives like joined-up policy and evidence-based policy (one could question, for example, the wisdom of measuring the performance of localities in terms of the number of ASBOs they have issued, if, as many would argue, ASBOs are ineffective policy tools); and it can repeat the very bureaucratic 'sins' that managerialism presented itself as a cure for. This is not an exhaustive list of its flaws, and this is not to suggest that it is always entirely without merit, but there is enough here to caution against blind faith, and to guard us against accepting new public management on its own ideological terms.

Chapter summary

The purpose of this chapter has been to equip the reader with a knowledge and understanding of the New Labour project, to foreground our subsequent exploration of the way this project has unfolded in the field of local crime control. It has examined the New Labour project in terms of the two goals of office and policy, which, as we said at the outset, are familiar to all mainstream political parties with a will to power. In the case of office, the success of New Labour has been to transform an apparently 'unelectable' Old Labour Party into electorally successful New Labour, which has with relative ease, and despite the shameful shadow cast by the Iraq War, won three straight general elections, although with the demise of Tony Blair's leadership, its star may now be fading. Alongside reforms to the structure, organisation, constitution and electoral tactics of the Party, which began under Neil Kinnock but which were taken forward with greater energy and enthusiasm by Tony Blair, changes to the Party's law and order policies played a major part in enhancing their office-seeking credentials, by neutralising the advantage that the Conservatives had enjoyed on the law and order issue at least since 1979, but also by shifting the law and order 'debate', such as it was, onto populist punitive grounds from which it has yet to retreat, if ever it can. Yet despite this populist punitiveness, New Labour has provided space for the growth of a potentially more progressive architecture of local crime control, to which we shall turn our attention in a moment, although, perhaps as a forewarning, one should not expect this 'preventive turn' (Hughes 2006) to be unaffected by the 'punitive turn' that preceded it – but more about ASBOs in Chapter 5.

Perhaps more important and influential than law and order, New Labour's office-seeking credentials may have been consolidated particularly by its happy or resigned acquiescence to the hegemony of neo-liberal globalisation, which means that its political strategy and policy programme is framed by this, rather than a more progressive politics that challenges this hegemony, and that looks to lead rather than to follow a public opinion formed by nearly 20 years of Conservative rule, which has left its cultural as well as its political mark. Without falling into the trap of economic determinism, we should not expect this accommodation of neo-liberal hegemony to be without significance on the unfolding canvas of local crime control, although nor should we be surprised by local resistance and opposition to it.

This architecture for local crime control bears many of the hallmarks of the third way, which serves as a philosophical as well as a practical guide for New Labour's policy programme. Key features of the third way were explored, notably its moral authoritarian communitarian underpinnings, which shows New Labour operating with the same mix of neo-conservatism and neo-liberalism as did Thatcherism, providing a simultaneous and contradictory desire both to responsibilise, but also to set the moral terms to such responsibilisation, and if necessary to enforce it – hence the combination of a strong state and a strong moral community. But in addition to its communitarian underpinnings the third ways sells itself as a non-ideological and highly pragmatic political project, and this has manifested itself in a commitment to modernisation in which three themes have stood out for further scrutiny in the latter parts of the chapter, namely evidence-based policy, joined-up policy and new public management. Our examination of these has been necessarily brief, but it has been sufficient to show that their apparent pragmatism is more than a little misleading. These rationalities and technologies of government have the capacity to mould and shape the domain of local crime control in significant ways, in pursuit of a reconfigured governmental programme that may be at odds with the priorities of others, and that may hold particular consequences for the way that local communities are governed through crime. It is this capacity of the third way in practice that we now set out to explore over the next few chapters.

Chapter 3

Imposing the crime reduction agenda

Introduction

In the last chapter, the distinctive characteristics of the New Labour project were outlined. New Labour clearly marks a departure from Old Labour, and its third way discourse places it somewhere between the latter, with its allegedly out-of-touch social democratic aspirations for egalitarian, redistributive state intervention, and the New Right, with its apparently excessive free market liberalism. Precisely where the third way sits, however, is open to contention, and probably varies from one policy domain to another. In this chapter we shift the focus from politics to policy – in so far as one can analytically separate the two. This serves the descriptive purpose of mapping out the changing terrain of local crime control since 1997, based upon the belief that good description – which is far from easy given the number and complexity of policy changes that have taken place – provides a firm bedrock for good analysis. It also provides us with an opportunity to examine the extent to which local crime control under New Labour had adhered to or departed from the path set by the previous Conservative administrations. In so doing, we will find ourselves in a better position to discern the distinctiveness of the third way in this area, as rhetoric is translated into policy. A note of caution is worth sounding, however, since the focus here is upon developments at the top of the implementation chain, rather than at the bottom, where policy is translated into action. We are looking in this chapter, then, at policy as it is expressed through legislation, guidance and a host of initiatives, rather than as it necessarily appears in practice, though there is obviously some relation between the two.

The Conservative inheritance

One major problem with evolutionary accounts of social phenomena is that the phenomena themselves do not remain the same over time, and the implication that they do risks applying not only a progressive logic, but also a coherence and order that are really not justified in reality. Crime and disorder reduction under New Labour, in other words, is a different beast to whatever existed under the Conservatives, which in Chapter 1 we represented as crime prevention. The change in nomenclature, from crime prevention to crime reduction should help us to remember this. Effectively, it is a domain that is both fluid and open-textured, that is in a constant state of invention and reinvention, although analytically it is possible to draw out certain lines of policy continuity and discontinuity that serve our broader purposes here.

There is broad agreement that crime prevention as a distinct policy domain 'took off' under the Conservatives, even though certain institutional structures and practices can be traced back much earlier (Gilling 1997). Crime prevention provided the Conservatives with an opportunity to make a virtue out of necessity. The necessity lay in the manifest failure of existing criminal justice approaches to stem the tide of rising crime, or to halt the alarming increases in the prison population. The first was an electoral, and thus a political liability, while the second was a fiscal one, and together they formed the 'twin pincers' that Windlesham (1987) neatly depicts as holding crime control policy in their grip. Certainly other factors of a more structural nature, such as globalisation, the advance of the neo-liberal project and the various socio-political and cultural transformations of late-modernity could be pressed into use in explaining the 'necessity' of a shift to crime prevention, which was also evidenced in other advanced liberal states, but we should not lose sight – as some do – of the more practical and down-to-earth factors that stimulate policy change. Radzinowicz (1991) neatly refers to this as 'crime pressure', which pushes governments from a normative concern with criminal *justice*, to a more instrumental concern with crime *control*, that in turn motivates them to attain greater influence over the local practices of such control, including crime prevention, rather than leaving them to the judicial domain.

61

The virtue that the Conservatives sought to make out of crime prevention policy was an ideological one, although that is not to say that they did not also have faith in the prospect of its practical effectiveness, which had been demonstrated earlier (see Clarke and Mayhew 1980). Crime prevention could be harnessed to the neo-liberal project by stressing the centrality of individual responsibility: just as citizens should not be dependent upon the state for their welfare, so they should not be dependent upon the state for their safety. This ideological message could be seen particularly strongly in the Conservatives' heavy promotion of neighbourhood watch, with Douglas Hurd being a particularly ardent enthusiast of such 'active citizenship'. It could also be seen in the proliferation of government-sponsored campaigns that brought crime prevention publicity and advice right down to the household level, with practical suggestions explaining how individuals and families should protect their property and selves from criminal depredation. Regardless of the effectiveness of such measures in terms of actually preventing crime – and there has been considerable doubt expressed about the effectiveness of both neighbourhood watch and crime prevention publicity campaigns – they certainly contributed to an ideological shift in the direction of responsibilisation (Garland 1996).

While one aspect of responsibilisation is its impact upon private citizens, another is its impact upon agencies. Private businesses were also targets of crime prevention publicity and advice, as well as being 'incentivised' by threats of charges for public police services, or the withdrawal of such services, and the success of such a strategy, although it may be entwined with other factors, may be evidenced in the massive expansion of the private security industry at this time (Johnston 1992). But the focus was also on public agencies, as a result of the clear acknowledgement of the limitations of the criminal justice system as a tool of crime control (because it touched only the tip of the crime iceberg), and as a result of the recognition that resources for crime control lay elsewhere, such as in land-use planning, architectural design and product design decisions. Successful crime prevention depended upon getting others 'on board', by recognising their responsibilities and overcoming their dependency upon the criminal justice system.

The chosen tool for responsibilising agencies beyond the formal criminal justice system was the multi-agency or partnership approach, which chimed very well with the Scarman-inspired discourse of community policing at the beginning of the 1980s (Gilling 1997). The first formal attempt to promote the partnership approach was Home

Office *Circular 8/84* (Home Office 1984), and it was followed up with a number of attempts to establish a model infrastructure for such partnerships, including the Five Towns Initiative, the Safer Cities Programme, a further Home Office circular in 1990 requiring a formal response from the police and local authorities, and the publication of a national guidance booklet (for a fuller account see Gilling 1997).

As many have observed, the New Right project comprises a somewhat contradictory mix of neo-liberalism and neo-conservatism. The former valorises the free market and individual responsibility and is effectively anti-statist, whereas the latter is supportive of the idea of a strong state, to maintain social order in what could be regarded as the flip side to the disintegrative effects of a neo-liberal market order, but also to shape responsible free subjects. In other words, there is a limit to the ideological project of responsibilisation, because of the need to impose social discipline on those who refuse or are unable to act as responsible, law-abiding citizens. A large proportion of these could be regarded as the casualties of an economy run on neo-liberal lines, characterised under the Conservatives by welfare retrenchment, mass unemployment, low wages and widening social inequalities. This limit is also political: in responsibilising citizens, neo-liberal governments must at some point confront their own mortality, recognising that their survival depends upon their ability to manage a state whose legitimacy is founded upon its ability to deliver safety and security to its citizens. Pushing the responsibilisation line too far looks too much like off-loading responsibility and shifting the blame. The 'discovery' of the fear of crime as a problem in the 1980s could be regarded as an indicator of a threat to this legitimacy, because the presence of the fear of crime betrays the lack of a sense of such safety and security, regardless of how rationally-founded such a sense might be.

The significance of the need to temper a neo-liberal strategy of responsibilisation, whether of citizens or of other agencies, with a neo-conservative strong 'order maintenance' state lies in the fact that the latter continually serves to undo the former. Thus, while citizens might come to take on more of a responsibility for their own protection, their dependency upon state action in the field of law and order is not entirely shaken off, as government simultaneously pursues a populist punitiveness (Bottoms 1995) that seeks to convince that the state is still the guarantor of safety and security. Similarly, while other agencies might recognise the contribution that they make in their own fields to crime prevention, there is still an inclination to leave criminal justice agencies, and in the case of crime prevention notably the police, in charge. Such an inclination is not only a consequence of the 'get tough' rhetoric of populist punitiveness, but also of criminal justice agencies' own claims to professional expertise. Overall, therefore, such agencies as the police are simultaneously in charge and not in charge, responsible but not responsible. This means that the partnership approach poses fundamental problems for the neo-liberal responsibilisation project, and hence this element of Conservative policy proved, at the very least, troublesome.

There are also other difficulties with the partnership approach which need to be taken into consideration when assessing Conservative policy. Ideologically, the Conservatives found it difficult to support the premises of penal welfarism. As discussed in Chapter 2, the political success of Thatcherism lay in part in its authoritarian populism, which it was able to direct against a range of folk devils, including offenders and delinquent youth in particular, to justify essentially punitive responses. This required a criminology of the 'other' (Garland 2001) that located criminal responsibility with the offenders themselves, and not with their social circumstances, which characterised the 'soft' approach of penal welfarism. Such a criminology at least had an elective affinity with the criminology that supported situational crime prevention, if only because situationalism was relatively disinterested in offenders' biographies (which tended also to be 'othered' from the 'criminologies of everyday life' [ibid.]), focusing instead upon criminal events and the way that opportunities for such events might be effectively blocked or designed out. Not surprisingly, then, Conservative policy in the 1980s showed a strong bias in favour of situational crime prevention, and this was the kind of crime prevention that government wanted local partnerships to pursue, as was made explicit in Home Office *Circular 8/84*.

The problem for the government, however, was that its position of power-dependence left it poorly placed to ensure that local partnerships did indeed pursue the situational agenda suggested to them, even when it was able to offer financial incentives for local partnership working (Tilley 1993). At the local level, many of the public agencies involved in crime prevention had a stronger affinity to social crime prevention, which sought to tackle criminal motivations, and was supported by criminological paradigms more in tune with what for the Conservatives was a then-discredited penal welfarism. This left local agencies with little incentive to form partnerships, as there were no additional resources available to them, and little common ground on which to decide the way ahead, given the political differences that existed between the social and situational approaches (Gilling 1994).

This diagnosis of the difficulties faced by local partnerships is broadly consistent with the findings of the Morgan committee (Home Office 1991), which had been set up by the Home Office specifically to explore the reasons behind the disappointingly slow adoption of the partnership approach as a new, mainstream approach to crime control in the UK. Although the Morgan Report had a number of more practical things to say about the effective management of local partnerships, its more significant findings were as follows. Firstly, in an acknowledgement of the situational versus social crime prevention politics alluded to above, Morgan suggested that the business of the partnerships was better conceived of in terms of the more inclusive notion of community safety. Secondly, it was proposed that local authorities needed to be given a lead responsibility, rather than simply being encouraged to participate with the police. And thirdly, it was recommended that a ring-fenced budget be allocated for local community safety, so that partnerships had resources to support meaningful local action. In addition to the 'situational versus social' politics, then, Morgan had uncovered the other major political stumbling block to the development of local crime control, namely the Conservatives' reluctance to give additional governmental responsibilities or resources to local authorities, for whom central government reserved spectacular hostility, not unconnected to their alternative political alignment, particularly with the urban socialist left.

Predictably, the blockages that Morgan had identified were not going to be unblocked, although of the three main findings cited above, the recommendation about a name change to community safety probably attracted the least hostility. This is because, despite the Conservatives' strong neo-liberal and neo-conservative underpinnings, by the end of the 1980s they had entered something of an 'age of reason' (Savage and Nash 1994). Such reason was imposed upon them partly by a continued failure to tackle the rising crime rate, which made their existing programme vulnerable to political criticism, but also by the growing influence of key Home Office officials, notably David Faulkner (Rutherford 1996), who advised the pursuit of a more moderate criminal justice policy. Although crime prevention was not Faulkner's 'brief', because responsibility for it sat in the Home Office's Police Department, Faulkner's sphere of influence extended across to it. Faulkner's enthusiasm lay less in situational crime prevention and more in the sort of inclusive crime prevention found in France, and for him an effective crime prevention policy was a necessary condition for the effective operation of penal policy based on the principle of just deserts, calibrated at a level of minimum intervention. This was so because effective crime prevention would serve to prevent the system from being flooded with offenders, whose numbers had to be controlled for minimum intervention just deserts to remain politically viable.

As studies of the contents of the Safer Cities Programme show, the local practice of partnerships tended to look more like community safety than the much narrower model of situational crime prevention, and it would seem likely that there was official tolerance of this by the government, even if it was not loudly cheered by them (Tilley 1993; Sutton 1996). This suggests that the community safety being practised locally was not that much of a political threat to the neo-liberal project – a point to which we shall return later.

By the mid-1990s, as we have seen, New Labour had started to crank up its political strategy for outflanking the Conservatives on the law and order issue. This led, in effect, to a loss of patience with local partnerships (Taylor 1993), and little additional effort was expended on seeking to extend the partnership approach beyond nominated 'Safer Cities' and those other areas – particularly urban left local authorities – that had most enthusiastically adopted it. Instead, greater emphasis was placed upon encouraging the local up-take of CCTV schemes, unjustifiably regarded by many as a 'silver bullet' solution. CCTV did, however, fit more comfortably with the neo-conservative, punitive discourse of Michael Howard, the last Conservative Home Secretary, because both the surveillance and the punitiveness could be focused upon the same target, namely the 'underclass'.

In summary, then, the Conservatives had attempted to launch crime prevention into the crime control mainstream, under the key theme of responsibilisation. While this played a part in encouraging the expansion of the private security industry, and of privatised prudentialism (O'Malley 1992), it was a very unstable project when it came to the matter of responsibilising agencies through local partnerships. Attempts to control the direction of such partnerships were always likely to flounder on the power-dependence of central government; on the hostility to local government which meant the whole initiative was insufficiently supported; and on the political limits to responsibilisation, which ensured the crime control spotlight was never really taken off criminal justice agencies such as the police. From 1993, the emphasis upon the partnership approach diminished, and policy moved sadly away from the age of reason. Moreover, if a primary goal was to extend central government influence over local practice, then the passing of the 1994 Police and Magistrates' Courts

Act provided the Conservatives with a better opportunity than that provided by putative partnerships. This is because the imposition of a new performance management framework allowed the Home Secretary centrally to set national objectives for the police service, and this, combined with a new-found confidence that police law enforcement could, after all, make a significant contribution against crime (especially against the small proportion of persistent offenders that was thought to be responsible for a disproportionate amount of crime), signalled the stagnation, if not the demise, of a central plank of crime prevention policy.

Crime reduction in New Labour's first term

The Labour Party had promoted crime prevention in each of its manifestos from 1983 onwards, and in both 1992 and 1997 it had committed itself to a partnership approach. Significantly, so too had both the Association of Chief Police Officers (ACPO), as the most influential representative police body (ACPO Sub-Committee on Crime Prevention 1996), and the combined local authority associations (Local Government Association 1997). Interestingly, ACPO's support for the partnership approach was premised upon an understanding that the police service occupied 'the most prominent place' in the partnership framework. By contrast, the local authority associations' support was premised upon the idea that the leadership role should be given to them and not the police, on the basis that 'councils are best qualified to take the lead because they are democratically accountable to their local communities and are responsible for most of the services which have a key part to play in community safety' (Local Government Association 1997: 4). There was, therefore, some different of opinion about where the lead responsibility should lie.

On taking office, it was not entirely clear where New Labour stood on this issue. In his *New Statesman* article, Tony Blair (1993: 28) had written: 'There should be a comprehensive crime prevention strategy, *led nationally* but *implemented locally* ...' (emphasis added). This suggests that his concern lay less with who led local policy and practice, and more with the capacity of central government to direct the process. Such a position confirms Rutherford's (1996) point about the way 'crime pressure' pushes central government to intervene in local practice, and raises questions over the true extent of localism in such arrangements. It also belies the dirigisme that many commentators have noted in New Labour's subsequent governing style.

The 1997 manifesto (Labour Party 1997), in which crime prevention gets a rather low profile, offered this in the way of clarification: 'We will place a new responsibility on local authorities to develop statutory partnerships to help prevent crime. Local councils will then be required to set targets for the reduction of crime and disorder in their area.' This does not make clear whether this new local authority responsibility would be a *lead* responsibility, or otherwise, although it certainly does not discount this, and the ambiguity could be interpreted as a politically astute apparent concession to the local government lobby, which in its manifesto *Crime: The Local Solution* (Local Government Association 1997), was, as we have seen, pushing hard for a local authority leadership role.

Prior to the 1998 Crime and Disorder Act, in September 1997 the New Labour government issued a consultation document entitled *Getting to Grips with Crime: A New Framework for Local Action* (Home Office 1997). Amongst other things, this document set out the intended local infrastructure for crime prevention. The government made it clear that they were 'not persuaded by' the view that local authorities should occupy the lead role, despite the extensive role that many local authorities apparently played in crime prevention (Local Government Management Board 1996), having effectively implemented the Morgan recommendations that the Conservative central government had elected to ignore. New Labour were concerned, they said, that a lead role for local authorities would give them undue influence over the resource deployments of other agencies, notably the police. Equal stakes in leadership, they suggested, would provide some balance of local powers. By the same logic, of course, New Labour might have wanted to abolish the Home Secretary's powers, obtained under the 1994 Police and Magistrates' Courts Act, to set national objectives for local police forces, but that was a different matter for a dirigiste central government!

The 1998 Crime and Disorder Act, when finally drafted, placed a statutory duty upon what it described as 'responsible authorities' to establish a CDRP that was expected to produce a three-yearly crime and disorder reduction strategy, with clear objectives and targets, to tackle locally-identified problems. The strategy was to be evidence-based, arrived at following the production and analysis of a local crime audit, and following local consultation on the results of that analysis. Although the strategy was to be of three years' duration, it was also expected to be reviewed on an annual basis, so that it could be modified in line with changing local conditions. This required some form of ongoing monitoring and evaluation.

The legislation diverged from Morgan (Home Office 1991) on two of the latter's key recommendations. Morgan had suggested a reconceptualisation of crime prevention as community safety, whereas the chosen language of the legislation and the accompanying guidance was crime and disorder reduction. Morgan had also recommended the ring-fenced funding of local practice, but the government made clear that no new funds were to be made available to the CDRPs. Rather, while CDRPs could make use of existing funding streams such as that of the single regeneration budget (SRB), the expectation was, in an echo of *Circular 8/84*, that crime and disorder reduction would set in motion a virtuous circle of cost-savings that would ensure that the work of CDRPs, in formulating and implementing crime reduction strategies, would effectively pay for itself. This, of course, also made a virtue of political 'necessity', as an important part of New Labour's electoral platform had been its promise to adhere to Conservative spending plans in its first two years of office, thereby demonstrating its prudence and trustworthiness in fiscal affairs. What *had* been taken from Morgan, meanwhile, had been the affirmation of partnership as the way ahead; the desire to see this partnership extended out from statutory agencies and into the business and voluntary sectors; and the proposal that local crime prevention work should be premised upon a factual analysis of local crime and disorder problems – hence the audit.

Perhaps in order to focus the minds, and enforce the compliance, of the two responsible authorities, particularly when additional funding was not to be forthcoming, Section 17 of the 1998 Act placed upon them a new obligation to consider the crime and disorder implications of all of their activities, and to do all they reasonably can to prevent crime and disorder. This Section therefore spoke of the problems that the police service had had, and importantly had acknowledged, in seeking to prioritise crime prevention over other features of operational policing (ACPO Sub-Committee on Crime Prevention 1996). It also perhaps pre-empted the objections of those local authorities, albeit now a minority, that had not engaged with crime prevention, and that saw the lack of additional funding as a big disincentive to participation in the new partnerships.

Section 17 can be interpreted as a potentially radical way of mainstreaming crime prevention into the business of local governance (Moss 2006). This more radical interpretation, which to some extent is shared in the Audit Commission's (1999) first major report on community safety, sees Section 17 as a way of shifting decisively away from the short-termist project orientation that had dogged local practice under the Conservatives, as the Morgan Report (Home Office 1991) had previously noted, and of pushing a crime prevention consciousness out into parts of local governance, such as planning and health, from which it had hitherto been mainly absent.

Subsequent to the legislation, local authorities and the police were bombarded with a significant quantity of advice and guidance that sought to set out to them how they might go about realising their new-found statutory responsibilities. Here we focus specifically upon the statutory guidance (Home Office 1998), much of which can be interpreted as an attempt to ensure that local CDRPs operated within the parameters of evidence-based practice. This is a theme which has been repeated across a number of different policy domains, and which has become a characteristic element of New Labour's modernisation agenda and governing style, as explored in Chapter 2. The evidence-based approach was apparent, for example, from the significant input made by two criminologists who had been heavily involved in Home Office policy developments in this area, namely Mike Hough and Nick Tilley (Hough and Tilley 1998), as well as in the acknowledgement that '[t]he material contained in this guidance reflects much of the accumulated understanding of what makes crime reduction partnerships work which has built up over the last decade' (Home Office 1998: 2). The influence of previous research studies on good practice in partnership working, such as that by Liddle and Gelsthorpe (1994a, 1994b and 1994c) was also clearly apparent.

The research that was used for the guidance fits an orthodox view that crime prevention partnerships often flounder because they have not adopted the correct recipe for success for 'what makes a good partnership' (see Gilling 2005). Thus the statutory guidance makes reference to such things as:

- the need to informally 'network' as a preliminary step before a formal meeting of the CDRP;
- the need to ensure that agency representatives are of sufficient seniority to make commitments on behalf of that agency;
- the need to ensure agency representatives communicate CDRP decisions and their implications back to their 'parent' agencies;
- the need to break data collection practices down into small spatial units to overcome the potential problems wrought by a lack of coterminosity in agency boundaries;
- the need for effective leadership and management;

- the need for a 'business orientation' and an agreed process for decision making; and
- the need to prioritise objectives rather than to seek to 'do everything'.

It would be difficult to disagree with much of this 'good sense'. However, notwithstanding the guidance, this does not mean that partnerships only flounder because of a failure to follow such guidance, as there may be important structural constraints that affect their capacity to 'perform' in such ways.

As in other areas, the guidance illustrated a reluctance from the centre to be too prescriptive. This was set out very clearly in Jack Straw's foreword (Home Office 1998: 1):

Crucially, the Act will not prescribe in any detail what the agenda for the local partnership should be, nor what structures will be needed to deliver that agenda. The people who live and work in an area are best placed to identify the problems facing them and the options available for tackling those problems, and we kept that maxim very much in mind when drafting the legislation.

This was consistent with the theme of *local solutions for local problems* that underpinned the Act, and in the case of local structures it was justified in the guidance by the need to maintain a focus on the end of crime reduction, rather than the means to that end – the partnership itself. Again, this is an indicator of the pragmatism of New Labour's evidence-based approach, where what counts is what works.

Implicit within this emphasis on pragmatism, however, was the hint that in the past partnerships have been distracted by questions of structure. Another quote from the guidance (Home Office 1998: 29) bears this out:

It is sometimes tempting to spend so much time putting in place steering groups, support mechanisms and channels for communication that the need to deliver hard outcomes is lost. Bureaucracies must not be allowed to get in the way of the ultimate purpose of this work, which is to reduce crime and disorder and make communities safer.

The anti-bureaucratic sentiment in this statement is a rhetorical device that is often used to legitimate the discourses of new public management, which valorise a more pragmatic 'business' and 'results' orientation. However, the implication that it is 'bureaucracy' that might be getting in the way is at best misleading. A concern about structures is important for a variety of reasons. There is, for example, an inter-agency politics that cannot be ignored (Crawford 1997). Hence the competition between the police and local authorities over which agency should take on a lead responsibility, which was referred to above, cannot be expected to disappear simply as a result of a legislative wave of the hand that employs the wisdom of Solomon in dividing the responsibility between each. Whilst police and local authority relations, especially in the major urban conurbations, were immeasurably better in 1998 than they had been in the mid-1980s, the conflicts that existed then were an integral part of differences in the very understanding of local community safety, and they have not vanished altogether. The local authority case for a lead role in the late-1990s depended in part upon a claim to democratic accountability, an issue that can hardly be dismissed as the unwelcome intervention of 'bureaucracy'. Similarly, concerns about structure draw attention to a politics of inclusion and exclusion. Which agencies were 'allowed' to participate in CDRPs? And upon which rung on the ladder of participation (Arnstein 1969) were they expected to stand? These representational politics are a lot more than just the rearing of the ugly head of bureaucracy, which itself often gets unwarranted bad press (Du Gay 2000).

There were other structural issues raised by the 1998 Act that could not be so easily dismissed, and that perhaps rendered this pragmatic ends-orientation dangerously simplistic.

Firstly, the legislation effectively created three classes of agencies, as far as membership of the CDRP is concerned. These were the *responsible authorities* (specifically the divisional police commander and the borough, unitary or district council chief executive); the *cooperating bodies* (agencies legally obliged to cooperate with the responsible authorities, including the police authority, the probation committee, the fire authority and the health authority); and finally *agencies invited to participate* (including both statutory and non-statutory bodies, and a reserve power for the Home Secretary to direct CDRPs to invite certain agencies). The problem was that whilst the three separate classes were not intended necessarily to stratify local agency relations, and thus power dynamics within CDRPs, it is difficult to see how they could have done otherwise. If CDRPs were supposed to represent a genuine shift to the local *governance* of crime, then there was a fundamental problem in seeking to legislate for their existence, that this particular problem highlights. This is because legislation requires an accompanying accountability that simply cannot be extended beyond the limits of the state's formal powers into the non-statutory sector, thus inevitably creating at least two possible classes of CDRP membership. Moreover, CDRPs were endowed with responsibility for a high profile party political issue, namely crime, and inevitably this gave central government a results-orientation for which it was always likely to want to hold local agencies to account. This results in driving a wedge between those that were primarily responsible for crime (the responsible authorities), and others that may have been only tangentially responsible, and may not therefore have been fully involved in the process. Such a phenomenon was clearly evidenced in the results of Phillips *et al.*'s (2002) research. The rhetoric that was in favour of partnership working was thus undone by a reality that rendered mandated partnership working in a politically highly-charged domain such as crime control unworkable in any genuine sense.

Secondly, while CDRPs were responsible for creating crime and disorder reduction strategies, the agencies that were expected to be involved in this process all had their own strategies and plans to follow, and these were not necessarily in synchronicity with each other, or with the crime and disorder reduction strategy. The statutory guidance acknowledged this issue, but suggested that '[w]ith a little common sense, the different demands can be reconciled' (1998: 6). The problem is that it may take more than common sense. The proliferation of sometimes heavily prescriptive plans, which is another feature of the new public management agenda, effectively prioritised for agencies what they took to be their 'core business', thereby endowing them with their own particular 'silo mentality'. Given that public agencies often find themselves operating in conditions where demand for their services outstrips supply, they inevitably prioritise their core business and de-emphasise ancillary responsibilities. Particularly for those that are not designated as responsible authorities, this operates as a disincentive against full participation in CDRPs, and thus a fragmenting logic is built in to the process (see also Clarke and Newman 1997; Newman 2001).

Yet even among the responsible authorities there were difficulties, particularly as a result of the national objective-setting process which was put in place for policing following the implementation of this part of the 1994 Police and Magistrates' Courts Act. What in 1998 had become key national objectives for the police service focused the police's attention on objectives that were more likely to be regarded as core business than crime reduction strategy objectives, and that were unlikely to be the same as them in terms of content. One solution might have been to subsume CDRP objectives within key national objectives, and in theory there was space to do this in the local objectives part of the annual local policing plan. In practice, however, the police might have found it easier to prioritise objectives that had been set nationally, rather than risking the creation of local hostages to fortune, which had to be set for three years rather than the single year of the policing plan, and which may have varied markedly amongst each of the CDRPs within a police force area. Alternatively, for those who subscribed to the more all-embracing idea of community safety, there was attraction in the idea that the community safety strategy (which is what many CDRPs preferred to call it) should be superordinate, encompassing all other plans and strategies within it (Cramphorn 1998), not least because it should be, 'the community' that determines local priorities. This is a nice idea that, notwithstanding the emergence of the community plan (see below), is based more on faith than fact, and an over-homogenised reading of 'the community'. Although the co-existence of different and ill-fitting plans is undoubtedly a problem, it is not necessarily a problem that requires solution, and in the short term it was possible for agencies simply to 'muddle through', in the hope that no crisis would be precipitated by the co-existence of potentially conflicting plans.

A third structural issue applied specifically to the case of non-unitary authorities. The problem here was that crime reduction strategies were required to be set at district council level, but the strategies were supposed to draw in the resources of agencies that had a county-wide level of operation. Consequently, such county-wide agencies would have had to adjust their level of service provision according to the different requirements of each district area. Some county-wide agencies may have been equipped to do this, such as the police service, where over recent years there has been a clear shift towards decentralised service provision based upon basic command unit (BCU) boundaries. However, not all county-wide agencies may have been so well placed, and service provision might not be so easily tailored to individual district circumstances. Furthermore, there could be good reasons for not tailoring service provision too closely to the demands of each district: it could result, for example, in the withdrawal of services from already under-resourced rural areas, into urban areas where crime and disorder-related problems can be more easily demonstrated.

Fourthly, and finally, potential structural problems arise from the co-existence of CDRPs with other bodies that share similar concerns or responsibilities, such as crime prevention panels. The guidance disclosed that 'the government thinks it would make sense for their work to be brought under the umbrella of the new crime and disorder strategy' (1998: 19), although it did not rule out the possibility that some might prefer to remain autonomous. If they were to do so, there was no guaranteed way of preventing some duplication of effort. More important, perhaps, was the overlap between CDRPs and YOTs, that were also brought into existence by the 1998 Act, although most YOTs did not begin operating until April 2000. Since youth crime was likely to figure prominently in local crime problems, the guidance suggested, CDRPs were likely to want to prioritise measures to tackle youth crime, but in so doing they entered YOT territory, populated with its own YOT strategy. The guidance suggested that '[d]ecisions as to the nature of any objectives and targets set within each strategy, and their ownership, must be taken locally' (Home Office 1998: 41), and it went on to propose that the YOT's focus may be more on youth criminality, and less on the 'wider needs of young people'. As logical as this may sound, the distinction was of course more difficult to hold in practice, and there remained the distinct possibility that YOTs and CDRPs may not see eye-to-eye on the problem of youth crime and how to address it – something that has become increasingly apparent as anti-social behaviour strategies have moved more to the fore (see Chapter 5). It is not clear how or whether such potential differences could have been resolved, but it is of considerable importance when questions of intervention and non-intervention loom large in the aetiology of youth crime.

Overall, the point here is that CDRPs were born with some pretty fundamental structural instabilities, some of which subsequent policy changes have sought to rectify, as we document in later chapters. The presence of such instabilities, however, made it difficult for CDRPs to attain the normative ideal of spontaneous joined-up government, and ultimately a mandated approach to partnership working was never going to be enough to overcome them.

If one side of central government's 'non-prescriptive stance' related to the structure of CDRPs, the other side related to the contents of the crime reduction strategies. Again, the importance of the local determination of crime reduction strategies, based upon the findings of the crime audit, was stressed. Thus the guidance (Home Office 1998: 20–21) noted that 'the content of strategies must be driven by what matters to local people, and not constrained by prerequisites or artificial definitions imposed by central government. ... Within reason, nothing is ruled out and nothing is ruled in.'

However, despite this, the guidance went on to list a number of issues that might well figure in CDRP strategies. These included:

- racial crime;
- witness intimidation;
- fear of crime;
- repeat victimisation;
- domestic violence;
- youth crime;
- drug-related crime; and
- homophobic crime.

The inclusion of many of these issues, which were often marginalised in national objectives, or relate to groups within the population that find themselves marginalised, may have been highly desirable, but they do hint at the possibility that, despite its protestations to the contrary, the Home Office was looking to impose strategic priorities upon CDRPs. The inclusion of witness intimidation was a good example of this, because it arose from a 1998 Interdepartmental Working Group report on Vulnerable or Intimidated Witnesses, which carried the recommendation that CDRPs might consider measures to tackle the problem of witness intimidation, if identified as a local issue of concern. The proviso suggested that this was not compulsory, but the problem is that the suggestion emanated from a dirigiste government that left room for doubt about the optionality of the recommendation.

To summarise this section, it is apparent that New Labour intended to breathe new life into crime prevention partnerships, following the stagnation of policy at the national level in the last few years of the Conservative administration, even if local practice seemed quite buoyant. Its solution to the problem faced by the Conservatives was to make such partnerships a mandatory requirement, but in so doing it encountered a number of difficulties. The compulsion of legislative mandate sits uneasily with the implied voluntarism of partnership working, and the trick could only be pulled off at the cost of endowing CDRPs with certain structural instabilities, such as the stratification that left responsible authorities feeling a good deal more responsible for the business of CDRPs than others. The legislation and its accompanying guidance also demonstrated a strong bias in favour of a pragmatic, evidence-based approach that was extended to the mechanics of partnership working itself, and neglected the more critical research literature on partnership working assembled over the previous decade (Crawford 1998; Hughes 1998). Consequently, there was a tendency in the guidance to dismiss or misrepresent the local politics of partnership working as just so much bureaucratic 'noise'. Such politics were unlikely to quieten in the context of a strategy-setting process that on the face of it looked localised, but in the guidance looked more like gentle persuasion from the top down. Initial suspicion, in this regard, might have been provoked by central insistence on the terminology of crime and disorder reduction, rather than that of community safety.

The Crime and Disorder Act received royal assent in the summer of 1998, and local responsible authorities – constituting some 376 CDRPs in total across England and Wales – were given very little time to get the show on the road. They were required to produce their first crime reduction strategies by the beginning of April 1999, which had to be informed by an extensive audit, drawing upon disparate sources of not necessarily compatible information from a range of agencies that had not necessarily yet mustered an information-sharing protocol between them. They were expected to analyse this information, although it was not clear how well-honed local analytic skills were; they were supposed to consult with 'the community' on the results of this analysis, even though 'the community' had not necessarily been clearly identified, consultative machinery had not necessarily been put in place, and little thought had been given to what should happen if there was a divergence of opinion within 'the community', or between 'the community' and the partnerships.

With the benefit of hindsight, central government might have over-estimated the preparedness and ability of local responsible authorities to get the job done. Perhaps in part this was because local government had over-sold the extent of its crime prevention involvement and expertise before 1998 (LGMB [Local Government Management Board] 1996). Nevertheless, there was plenty of advice issued for practitioners, beyond the statutory guidance discussed above. There was, first of all, a Her Majesty's Inspectorate of Constabulary (HMIC) (1998) report entitled *Beating Crime*, based upon a thematic inspection headed by John Stevens which had been set up in February 1997, perhaps by those with a keen eye on the way the political wind was blowing before the 1997 general election. The report sought to establish a practical framework for the police where crime reduction was a core function, rather than peripheral, as it had hitherto been in most forces. This core function, the report argued, should be delivered through a partnership-based, problem-solving approach – exactly that put in place by the 1998 Act, by happy coincidence. But while HMIC found plenty of good examples along such lines in their force inspections, their overall message was that there was a lack of systemic management of this process. Thus, for example, progress was not always clearly monitored against targets; crime reduction effort was sometimes unfocused rather than problem-oriented; and partnerships did not always pull individual contributions together into an effective coordinated approach. The report went on to provide a checklist for practitioners to ensure there was better management and support for local crime reduction work.

The second source of advice was the wonderfully named Home Office Police Research Group publication *Getting the Grease to the Squeak* (Hough and Tilley 1998), which was directed mainly at the police, and which had been requested as a sister publication to the HMIC report. As such, it offered a little more detail on the way that the police might go about their crime reduction work – more operational that strategic in focus. Thus, for example, the SARA model (scan, analyse, respond and assess) was promoted as the means of ensuring a problem-oriented approach. Further advice was given with regard to how technology such as GIS systems might facilitate scanning and analysis; how responding to crime problems should span both prevention and detection, and how responses should be routinely monitored.

The third source of advice was the Audit Commission report *Safety in Numbers* (1999), although perhaps this is best seen as a 'taking stock' exercise, rather than a source of practical advice, which is just as well given the timing of its publication (only a couple of months before crime reduction strategies had to be set in place). As such, the report picked up a number of long-standing problems with crime prevention partnerships, some of which harked back to the Morgan Report, if not earlier. These included the lack of priority given by the key agencies to crime prevention; the short-term project orientation of much work; the lack of a clear problem-orientation; and the limited knowledge of 'what works' and what is cost-effective. While this was pretty standard fare, two particularly interesting features of the report – if only for their later significance – stand out. The first of these relates to a general failure of partnerships to analyse or reflect local concerns, or to really get to grips with understanding the localised causes of crime and disorder. The second relates to a prescient concern that local authorities should not be tempted to 'rebrand' much of what they were currently doing as crime prevention work, in lieu of really committing themselves to the new CDRP structures created by the legislation.

Like the statutory guidance, the HMIC report and *Getting the Grease to the Squeak* (Hough and Tilley 1998) were understandably positive and promotional, whereas the Audit Commission was more cautious. It was this more cautious tone, moreover, that reflected the Home Office's own position as it embarked upon a more ambitious programme of reform after the two-year period of self-imposed spending restraint came to an end in 1999, following the first of New Labour's comprehensive spending reviews.

Beyond 1999: the focus upon delivery

Although the major New Labour push around the themes of modernisation and delivery took place after the 2001 election, in crime reduction, things started a good deal earlier. The policy changes beyond 1999 proved to be both an opportunity and a threat to CDRPs. They were an opportunity because we saw in the Crime Reduction Programme (see below) and other related funding streams the injection of an unprecedented amount of money into the future development of crime reduction, albeit slanted towards certain priority themes, and higher crime areas. But it was a threat for a number of reasons. Firstly, having been told that there was no extra money to fund the business of CDRPs, and having cut their cloths accordingly in the first round of strategies produced in April 1999, these same bodies now found out that there *was* money to spend, but not necessarily on the objectives that they had identified in their strategies. In other words, the goalposts had been shifted, and not just by a few inches. Secondly, although money was now available, it came with strings attached, in so far as it was to be accompanied by an overhauled performance management regime. This was likely to lead to considerably more central influence or direction over CDRPs, as well as profoundly altering their day-to-day business, as we shall see in Chapter 4.

For New Labour, as has been established, there was always the suspicion that the idea of 'local solutions for local problems' carried more rhetorical support than genuine commitment. But in the 'prospectus' that announced the Crime Reduction Strategy (Home Office 1999a), even the rhetorical support was dropping away. One might speculate as to what brought about the change. The availability of increased funding, for example, provided New

Labour with an opportunity to establish a much more rigorous governmental infrastructure for crime reduction, which chimed with its dirigiste predilection. This was a government, after all, that had always wanted to govern from the centre, and that was more than a little mistrustful of the governmental capacity of local authorities and other public sector bodies.

On a more practical level, as Jack Straw's foreword to the Crime Reduction Programme's 'prospectus' elucidated, while crime rates had fallen for a number of years in succession, crime in England and Wales was still much higher than in the rest of Europe, and prospective demographic pressures (specifically the proportionate demographic increase in young males, the most crime-prone group by far) meant that sustaining this fall was going to be a major challenge in the years ahead. In such circumstances, given the importance of crime to New Labour's electoral fortunes (it may have stolen the Conservatives' clothes of 'tough' law and order, but there were still questions to be asked about their fit), it was perhaps thought to be essential that policy was driven firmly from the top, rather than relying upon those further along the implementation chain.

Importantly for our purposes, by 1999 news was starting to come back from the crime reduction front which indicated that all was not well in the world of CDRPs. From the discussion above, this can be explained in terms of their structural instabilities, but this is not necessarily how central government was likely to see it. In this regard, the Audit Commission (1999) set the tone, for although many of its findings were not based on a particularly close empirical analysis of CDRP work, since many had barely formed during the period of its investigations, the issues that it raised were being validated in what little information was percolating through to the centre. Thus, for example, the Home Office conducted an analysis of the first round of crime reduction audits and strategies (Phillips *et al.* 2000), and it found that target-setting in particular was a rather haphazard affair, with some even refusing to set targets at all. Also, although the results were not published until later (Phillips *et al.* 2002) a Home Office study of three partnerships had confirmed not only these problems with target-setting, but also the problem anticipated by the Audit Commission, namely the use of 'umbrella strategies' that repackaged a whole range of existing initiatives under the CDRP brand. At the very least, there must have been a suspicion that in return for the lack of central funding, some CDRPs were indulging in an exercise of 'paper compliance', with strategies being used presentationally, rather than indicating any fundamental reform of the local governance of crime. Such a suspicion would have fanned the flames of New Labour's mistrust of local service provider interests.

The 'prospectus' for the Crime Reduction Strategy identified a number of distinct changes that were likely to impact upon the business of CDRPs. The most significant of these were the planned investments of the Crime Reduction Programme; the incorporation of CDRPs into the Best Value performance regime; and the establishment of Crime Reduction Directorates in each of the regional government offices in England, and the Welsh Assembly. We will look at each of these in turn.

The Crime Reduction Programme

After two years of self-imposed spending restraint, by 1999 New Labour found themselves in a favourable fiscal position where they could countenance a substantial increase in public expenditure; although they were never going to countenance profligacy over prudence, or any kind of return to the 'tax and spend' style of Old Labour. Rather, with the Treasury very much at the helm, the new comprehensive spending review process was used to identify areas for public investment over a three-year period, rather than the more chaotic one-year cycle that had hitherto been the case. For the comprehensive spending review, central government departments were required to engage in a thorough analysis of their objectives and priorities, and an exploration of the most efficient and cost-effective means through which these could be achieved. In the case of the Home Office, one of these objectives was crime reduction, and the review published by Goldblatt and Lewis (1998) provided a number of examples of 'what works' to achieve this objective.

This promise of 'what works' was enough to convince the Treasury to invest what in the crime prevention domain was an unprecedented £250 million in the ambitious Crime Reduction Programme, although in the context of other central government initiatives, it was a relative drop in the ocean. The funding was for three years in the first instance, but with the possibility – which was not in the end realised – of an extension to ten (Maguire 2004). The basic idea was that the funding would be used to support the local implementation of 'what works' projects in crime reduction, across a number of distinct themed areas (see Tilley 2004). These projects were to be thoroughly evaluated (10% of the budget was for evaluation, thus meeting the threshold set for 'gold standard' evaluations set by Sherman *et al.*

[1998]), and the results of the evaluations were to be used to promote evidence-based practice that could be rolled out across the country. Major beneficiaries of the funding were to be CDRPs, although there were elements of the programme that were channelled towards other agencies, such as YOTs or the probation service. Importantly, the funding was made available only on a competitive basis: applicants had to demonstrate that they had disproportionate problems in the themed areas for which they could apply; they had to demonstrate an understanding of 'what works' and how it could be applied in their areas; and they had to show that their projects would be properly evaluated.

As noted above, the Crime Reduction Programme brought turbulence into the domain of local practice. All CDRPs had put in place their crime reduction strategies to cover the period from April 1999 to March 2002, only to discover, within months, that central government funding was now likely to be available for localities that could demonstrate a localised problem in specified areas, particularly burglary. In theory, it might have been assumed that since CDRPs had already identified their local problems in their audits and strategies, this funding would merely facilitate local action that was already underway. In practice, however, given the variable quality of audits and strategies, the instability of so many new partnerships, and the low knowledge base from which many partnerships had started, such an assumption was not necessarily warranted. There was no guarantee that the problems that the Crime Reduction Programme prioritised, and that local partnerships were supposed to demonstrate in their applications for the funding, had been discovered in the earlier local audits and strategies. This was especially true because the level of resolution for the Programme was set very much at sub-partnership level, so that such problems as existed could be obscured by scaling-up, which some partnerships were inclined to do deliberately because they did not want to identify geographical hotspots within their areas that might lead to local stereotyping and fraught local politics. In addition, even if such problems had been identified as the focus of local action in crime reduction strategies, there was no guarantee that the problems were being addressed according to the tenets of 'what works', and thus, if Programme funding was obtained, significant change was likely to be required in local practice.

If the Home Office were to be imagined as a parent, it would be as an inconsistent one. The 1998 Crime and Disorder Act effectively sought to convince the CDRP kids of the health merits of eating up their vegetables (the virtuous cycle of unfunded crime prevention), only for the Crime Reduction Programme to stick a whopping great cake on the table. Vegetables look very unappealing when there's cake, and not surprisingly many wanted a slice of it. However, the competitive funding meant that the cake was not shared out evenly, but was given to those who could demonstrate the greatest hunger – mostly the urban areas with the highest crime rates and high crime estates. Those who did not get cake were upset, and some resented the advantage gained by others, who could now start to implement part of a crime reduction strategy, even if it was not the one originally envisaged. Those who did get cake, meanwhile, were perhaps less inclined to return to their vegetables, because the parental message appeared only half-hearted. In other words, losing enthusiasm for any further continuation of the analogy, in subtle but important ways the Crime Reduction Programme started to undermine the infrastructure put in place by the 1998 Act.

More was to come. As Hope (2004), Hough (2004), Maguire (2004), Tilley (2004) and others have all capably documented and described, the Crime Reduction Programme, or certainly significant parts of it such as the Burglary Reduction Initiative, turned out to be something of a disappointment, for two main reasons. Firstly, there was considerable 'implementation failure' (a 'top-down' understanding of what went wrong), so that what was promised often failed to materialise, either by way of crime reduction action, or by way of evaluation. Secondly, the scientific aspirations of the Programme, which provided a real window of opportunity for the launch of effective local practice (Maguire 2004), and which as Hope's (2004) concerns reveal, could have made a real difference in disadvantaged areas blighted by crime, were effectively corrupted by the political underpinnings of New Labour's modernisation project. Both of these important issues need to be considered in more detail.

Implementation failure

'Implementation failure' conceals a multitude of sins, and conveniently de-personalised a process so that it becomes less easy to attribute blame to individuals. However, since, according to the classical distinction, implementation is the responsibility of those at the bottom rather than the top of the policy hierarchy, there is at least a movement of intent in popular understandings of the concept towards blaming those at the bottom, in this case, for our purposes, the CDRPs. If, alternatively, we are to conceive of policy as action (Barrett and Fudge 1981), then policy-making and implementation are entwined, constitutive processes, and difficult to separate out for analytic purposes.

Tilley (2004) seeks to explain the difficulties of the Crime Reduction Programme in terms of the gap between what interventions were supposed to do, and what, in practice, they otherwise or also did. The existence of such a gap was due in part to limitations in local capacity (Maguire 2004), including skills such as project management (Hough 2004), that others (Hedderman and Williams 2001) have also noted. However, much of local 'capacity' problems have less to do with ability, as might be implied by the term, and more to do with cultural leanings that did not fit the model of crime reduction that the Programme sought to develop. Thus, for example, Maguire (2004) identifies a culture of bidding for competitive funding that had evolved over years of the availability of funding streams such as City Challenge, the SRB, and various European sources. The culture turned bidding into a game or perhaps even an art form, where the bids told a story of what would happen, but once the funding was secured, the reality was always somewhat different. There is no reason why practitioners versed in these games should treat the Crime Reduction Programme any differently – it was just another source of scarce funds for local governance.

Similarly, Hough (2004: 248) cogently argues that the idea of crime reduction as the police's priority core business, that underpinned much of those elements of the Crime Reduction Programme that related to policing, failed to take into account the realities of the police order maintenance role: '[t]he central preoccupations of effective police middle managers are those that relate to the maintenance of organisational legitimacy in a complex and unpredictable environment.' Put simply, the police often had far more important things to do than getting around to targeted crime reduction, even though this is something their professional claims-making makes them reluctant to admit.

The Crime Reduction Programme also opened up the old wounds of partnership politics. Thus, as Maguire (2004) documents, local concerns about the police domination of partnerships, and their strong enforcement orientation, could easily get in the way of local progress. Such progress, moreover, was not effectively monitored by a largely London-based Home Office that itself did not have the infrastructure to police the activities of those CDRPs in receipt of Crime Reduction Programme funding, let alone all 376. Once the Programme was up and running, this issue was addressed in so far as a monitoring responsibility was given to the new regional Crime Reduction Directors (see below), overseen by a very short-lived Crime Reduction Taskforce, that evidently promised more than it delivered. But the capacity of the Directors and the teams they acquired was also limited, and between them, the Home Office, as well as the National Association for the Care and Resettlement of Offenders (NACRO) and Crime Concern (who had both been given the task of 'supporting' the development of the Programme), the result was a confusing, overlapping arrangement of bodies, and less than effective monitoring (see Homel *et al.* 2005). And if monitoring was problematic, so too was evaluation, with Hough (2004) reporting, among other things, problems with data quality and availability; problems finding comparison areas without similar interventions in them; and problems distinguishing cause and effect.

The corruption of the Crime Reduction Programme

There are different accounts of the way in which the Programme was corrupted. Much of the corruption, it would appear, was due to political intervention, or to the political pressures being exerted upon those running the scheme. Thus, for example, if the Programme had started out with rational scientific principles oriented towards establishing high-quality evidence about what works, then the sudden introduction of an additional £150 million to be spent on CCTV projects, that had very equivocal evidence of success to date, but that were popular with the public (Maguire 2004), seemed to undermine this premise (Tilley 2004).

There was also a reluctance to leave the Programme to the researchers, particularly because in return for Treasury funds the Home Office was committed to its own performance management regime, set out in a number of PSAs that specified targeted reductions in particular crimes over a five-year period. The sudden rise in crime figures in late 1999 (Tilley 2004) raised Home Office anxiety that the targets might not be reached, and this increased pressure for the Programme to be used not so much for experimental practice and research, but rather for the more mainstream aim of meeting PSA targets. In this way, then, 'policy' pushed out 'research', and the imperative shifted to the need to spend the Programme's funds on 'tried and tested' interventions that would reduce those crime problems specified in PSA targets.

More fundamental causes of the Programme's corruption are identified by Hough (2004). His view is that the highly rationalistic problem-oriented premises of the Programme were never likely to be realised by what was effectively a mobilisation of bias at the problem identification stage. With available data focusing heavily upon crime events rather than offenders, the result was that crime problems could be poorly identified or misidentified, while '… some preventive solutions tend to be privileged and others ignored or downplayed' (2004: 248). He points here to the effective situational bias of the problem-oriented approach, which has been well documented by others (Gilling 1994).

The most critical perspective on the corruption of the Programme is provided by Hope (2004). He attributes the problem not specifically to politicians, but more to the 'network of governance' that has built up between politicians, Home Office officials, and crime scientists, those 'experts-cum-policy-entrepreneurs' who are associated particularly with the Jill Dando Institute at the University of London. Like Hough he picks up on a bias in favour of situational crime prevention, but he suggests that this is used by crime scientists effectively to sell their policy utility to officials and politicians, who are swayed by their credibility, which chimes so well with New Labour's predilection for evidence-based practice. This may be because situational crime prevention tends to be based on 'hard data', and in the course of the last couple of decades a considerable volume of work has built up around successful case studies (Clarke 1997; Tilley 2005). It is probably also because situational crime prevention steers well clear of any Old Labour preoccupation with questions of aetiology. The problem for Hope (2004) is that in the pursuit of policy utility, crime science may end up compromising its scientific aspirations, evading accountability to scientific standards and being somewhat selective in its use and interpretation of evidence. In this way, the allegation is that crime science, through the blurred boundaries of its network of governance, contributes to the populist agenda in which excessive claims are made both for the prospects and effectiveness of certain crime reduction interventions.

Crime reduction and Best Value

Best Value and the Crime Reduction Programme are connected, by default if not original design, in so far as both are set within a performance management framework headed by the Treasury's PSAs. Thus, while the PSAs provide the Home Office with their performance targets, these in turn are cascaded down to local agencies through BVPIs that are key elements of the Best Value performance regime. A little elucidation is probably in order.

In opposition to the Conservatives, Labour had been opposed to the policy of CCT that was used to reduce public expenditure, by forcing certain local government services to compete for service delivery contracts with the private sector. Local authorities were required to award service delivery contracts to those providing the lowest cost tender. Such a policy facilitated privatisation, and proved to be particularly damaging to public sector trade unions. This, of course, was no accident, as an integral part of Conservative policy was to weaken trade union power, given the belief that unions served only 'provider interests', and distorted the operation of the market. New Labour's opposition to CCT, however, did not mean a lack of sympathy with this viewpoint, and as Entwistle and Laffin (2005) observe, this left them with the need to find some other means by which provider interests could be controlled. The concern was that such interests might get out of hand under a New Labour government, particularly when manifested in the shape of some of the urban socialist local authorities that had once attracted from the media the 'loony left' label. As Entwistle and Laffin suggest (2005: 207), '... the leadership had started to see some of its councils as an electoral liability'.

While in opposition, Labour sought to develop an alternative to CCT, as part of the office-seeking agenda that had been started after the 1987 general election defeat, and that shifted Labour into what was to become the New Labour path. Interestingly, two future Home Secretaries, David Blunkett and Jack Straw, were a part of a policy review group that sought to steer Labour policy more in the direction of a consumerist, quality-oriented vision of local government services. Like so much of New Labour's pre-election policy developments, the solution was discovered in a soundbite, namely 'Best Value'. The idea was that local authorities would be made responsible for delivering services that were best value for their citizens, not by requiring them to put services out to tender, which anyway was principally about cost, but rather by subjecting them to some kind of inspection, and by inviting them, if they felt the need, to market test some of their services. This was a classic bit of third way trickery, positioning the idea of Best Value in an indefinable space somewhere between privatisation and state provision, so that '... it meant different things to different people' (Entwistle and Laffin 2005: 214). Just like tough on crime and tough on the causes of crime, in fact.

New Labour's masterstroke was to sell the idea of Best Value to local government before the 1997 election: rather like crime prevention, it was a 'hurrah concept' that was difficult to oppose:

who would not want best value services for their local electorates? After the election, more flesh was put on the bones of Best Value, introducing details about which local authorities might have been rather less pleased, but by then, of course, it was too late, and the juggernaut was impossible to halt.

Best Value is an integral part of New Labour's modernisation agenda that seeks to improve the delivery of public services. It was piloted in a few areas before being introduced more widely in 1999, requiring local authority services to engage in an overall process of continuous improvement. This improvement was to be obtained, in theory, through the production of annual Best Value performance plans, which show how local services will meet nationally set BVPI measures and targets. In addition, under the original formulation of the scheme, each local authority service area, such as community safety, was to be comprehensively reviewed once every five years, following a methodology that subscribes to the '4 Cs' of challenge, comparison, consult and competition. Finally, the performance of each local authority was subjected to periodic Best Value inspections from the Audit Commission, which on the basis of such inspections was able to place local authority services into various categories, namely, in descending order, *beacon*, *striving*, *coasting* and *failing*. The categorisation of an authority as failing brings with it a power of outside intervention.

So, what exactly did the Best Value performance regime mean for CDRPs? Its most significant feature probably lies in the BVPIs, which effectively provide the crime reduction targets that many CDRPs evidently failed to set properly for themselves in the 1999 strategies. But more than this, they also bring the Home Office's PSAs down to the local level, and in so doing they impose upon CDRPs not only the targets, but also the objectives that they should orient their crime reduction strategies towards. Failure to do so, it should be remembered, risks a negative assessment and worse. In this way, then, the Best Value regime marks a significant shift away from the manifest principle of local solutions for local problems, which more and more takes on the status of empty rhetoric. Entwistle and Laffin (2005) argue that Best Value is best thought of as an initiative that fits a political purpose of pulling provider interests into line. In its own terms, it is not necessarily the best means of ensuring best value, because it is heavily centralised and over-bureaucratic, which is more than a little ironic given that it is overseen by the Audit Commission, whose stated mission is the evangelical sounding one of being *against bureaucracy*. Certainly those who have been lead officers in the Best Value process remain to be convinced of the merits of all parts of it (Higgins *et al.* 2004), although they do think (but then wouldn't they?) that the whole process has probably resulted in service improvements. Others less involved might suggest that it encourages a more cynical paper compliance that, as Higgins *et al.* (2004) observe, neglects the 'softer' side of people management, and perhaps in so doing promotes a jaundiced view of public service that stifles creativity and commitment. We will say more about this when we discuss the role of community safety officers (CSOs) in a later chapter.

The Crime Reduction Directorates

As noted above, some way into the slow implementation of the Crime Reduction Programme, a responsibility for the oversight of projects within their region was passed to the Crime Reduction Directors. These Directors were put in place in 2000, and their establishment can be seen as a belated response by the Home Office to the lack of an established regional presence, the problematic nature of which had been exposed by the implementation problems of the Programme, and by the apparent distance between 376 CDRPs and the Home Office in London. The Directors were assisted in their tasks by Crime Reduction Teams, comprising a small number of civil servants who did not necessarily have any crime reduction or criminal justice backgrounds. Some time later, they were also joined by small research support teams.

The main aim of each Crime Reduction Director has been to improve the effectiveness of CDRPs within the region, through a combination of performance monitoring and support. In terms of monitoring, this includes the scrutiny of the contents of CDRP audits and strategies; assessing CDRP performance against their targets and against published crime statistics; and managing the allocation of central government funding, initially through the Crime Reduction Programme, but after the 2001 election, through a number of other funding streams (see Chapter 4). In terms of support, the Crime Reduction Director has been responsible for identifying training and development needs within the region, and setting about meeting them. Overall, the position of the Crime Reduction Directors and regional Crime Reduction Teams fits very well into the performance management framework that came to be established, as we have seen, as the Home Office's strategy started to unfold after 1999.

Chapter summary

This chapter has covered a long period from the development of crime prevention policy under the Conservatives in the 1980s, through to the end of New Labour's first term of office, in 2001. The Conservatives brought crime prevention into the mainstream, but the active citizenship element of its programme was probably more successful than the partnership element. The latter floundered on the rocks of Conservative antipathy towards local government, although as the LGMB survey (1996) showed, a large number of local authorities nevertheless seized the initiative in pushing the partnership process forward, quite possibly alarming the police service in the process, by threatening their monopolistic hold on the domain.

New Labour sought to build upon the apparent enthusiasm of local authorities and the police service for crime prevention and community safety by mandating the formation of local CDRPs. Such a mandate, it was hoped, would make a reality of joined-up policy at the local level, although the awkward accommodation of 'hands off' localism and central prescription in the statutory guidance perhaps belied an uncertainty about exactly how such a joined-up approach could be engineered from the centre.

In the event it did not take long for the centre to become disillusioned with the performance of CDRPs, although the causes of such disillusionment had as much to do with the structural instabilities that had been built into the design of CDRPs, as it did with any limitations in local capacity. In effect, although New Labour did not extend the same political antipathy towards local authorities that the Conservatives had shown, their mistrust of 'provider interests' produced much the same effect. Consequently, the emphasis upon localism as the route to joined-up policy was gradually replaced by an emphasis upon evidence-based practice and new public management techniques of command and control. Joined-up policy, it seemed, was less of a priority that performance in terms of crime reduction, measured according to criteria imposed through PSAs and the Best Value performance regime. In this way, New Labour's dirigism came more to the fore, evidenced particularly clearly in the experience of the Crime Reduction Programme. The great irony was that this Programme provided the missing ingredient – namely funding – that may well have oiled the wheels of joined-up policy, as it had done in other policy areas such as community care, had it been made available in the first place, when CDRPs were first established. But when the funding finally arrived it came with strings attached, intended to further the cause of crime reduction rather than joined-up policy as such.

The problem, however, was that the failure of the Crime Reduction Programme meant that knowledge of how best to attain crime reduction, through evidence-based practice, remained limited and patchy. As the character of New Labour's policy of crime reduction began to take shape as a very instrumental approach to reducing headline rates of volume crimes, this problem was concealed by the fact that, broadly speaking, headline crime rates were anyway showing a reduction in crime, linked in all probability to the sustained economic upturn over which New Labour presided in their first term of office. The PSAs and the Best Value performance regime may have pushed CDRPs towards prioritising the reduction of specific crime problems such as burglary and vehicle-related crime, but they did not provide clear guidance on how this should be done, though the three-year problem-oriented strategy cycle did institutionalise bias in favour of situational approaches

Overall, as New Labour approached the end of its first term of office, and as CDRPs therefore started to look towards their next three-yearly audit and strategy, there remained a good deal of uncertainty about what CDRPs had been doing, and what they were to do in the future. Worryingly, the BCS, which had been reorganised into an annual survey that could be used for performance management purposes alongside police crime statistics, showed a persistent 'reassurance gap' in which the public continued to think that crime was rising, and continued to show signs of anxiety about victimisation and disorder, despite the apparent fall in the headline crime rate. In the next chapter, we will look at the direction crime reduction policy took in New Labour's second term of office and beyond, as the Home Office sought unrealistically (given that such insecurity is a corollary of neo-liberal freedom) to plug this gap.

Chapter 4

From crime reduction to community safety?

Introduction

In its first term of office, New Labour's policy of local crime control had been premised upon a particular set of rational expectations. The 1998 Crime and Disorder Act established an infrastructure for the local governance of crime. The 1999 Crime Reduction Strategy then fed this infrastructure with funding that was designed to tease out the constituent elements of an evidence-based crime reduction policy that could then be rolled out across the country, into the second term. The problem, however, was that such expectations were broken up on the rocks of a confounding social reality. The infrastructure built for the local governance of crime was, for many reasons, far from solid or robust. There had been no funding to support it; little time to develop it; and beyond the responsible authorities the commitment of other partners fell a long way short of what had been hoped for. Funding from the Crime Reduction Programme ended up being diverted from a research and development agenda into measures that met the Home Office's PSA targets (Homel *et al.* 2005); whilst locally the funding sometimes disturbed the balance of, or undermined, existing local crime reduction strategies, and connected to an implementation structure that in many places simply was not there – hence the frequent lack of project management and project monitoring (Hedderman and Williams 2001). As evidence of these difficulties began to emerge, it became apparent that Home Office expectations had been unrealistic. Faced with this reality, or at least those parts of it that it was prepared to accept, the natural inclination of a government that was heavily committed to the controlling imperatives of new public management, and particularly an institutionalised mistrust of provider interests, was to cast a sceptical eye at the local capacity to deliver. An ideological commitment to new public management ensured that the solution was likely to be seen in terms of much stronger central 'steering', along with capacity-building to facilitate the local 'rowing' (Osborne and Gaebler 1992).

New Labour's apparent first term prudence, combined with very favourable economic circumstances, had provided the opportunity for an ambitious and expansionist public policy, but this was not going to be unrestrained. Rather, while Tony Blair made the future of the public services the dominant theme of the 2001 election (Driver and Martell 2002), it was a future that was to be built upon the principle of modernisation, the tools for which we have already reviewed in Chapter 2. Although in many ways this was another of New Labour's loose soundbites, it generally meant that public services had to be kicked into shape to deliver the ambitious objectives set for them, both broadly in the sustained promise to be tough on crime and tough on its causes; and more narrowly, in the more specific goals that had been set through the Home Office's PSAs, and in manifesto commitments. In this sense, then, CDRPs were cursed to have been born in 'interesting times'. They had just been established, but now they were to be subjected to the spotlight of a modernisation project, that as events transpired (see below) turned out to be more than a little convoluted.

Up until the beginning of New Labour's second term, the story of local crime control had really been the story of a struggle to shift crime prevention from the margins to the mainstream. Under the Conservatives, crime prevention had been put firmly on the agenda, and this certainly posed challenges to a police service that had traditionally marginalised crime prevention, both as an occupational specialism (Harvey *et al.* 1989), and more generally as a function (although its elasticity allowed it to be repackaged to some extent as detection). The Conservatives' refusal to implement the Morgan Report's (Home Office 1991) recommendations to impose a statutory responsibility for crime prevention (as community safety) upon local authorities ensured that, despite all the exhortation and pump-priming, through initiatives such as the Safer Cities Programme, crime prevention remained relatively marginal. It remained marginal throughout the remaining years of Conservative administrations, as we have seen in Chapter 3, in no small part because of the populist pressure imposed by a resurgent Labour Party, under first Tony Blair, and then Jack Straw, who both served as Shadow Home Secretary during this period.

Within local government, crime prevention as community safety was also relatively marginal. There may well have been a growing interest in community safety among urban local authorities, and among the local authority associations, culminating in their own manifesto in 1997 to have the Morgan recommendations implemented by the in-coming government, but in the overall scheme of local government affairs, community safety was small beer, and relatively insignificant. This was only to be expected, given that there was no strongly established professional base from which to advance or defend its interests. This also remains a problem in the present.

The important point about crime prevention's marginality is that it was perceived locally as an adjunct. Consequently, the partnership structures were regarded as a 'bolt-on' to the mainstream services. For some service managers, for example, they were the occasional morning or afternoon's diversion, sitting around a collaborative table with peers from other agencies, working through agendas that were often aspirational, rather than dealing with the 'nuts and bolts' of core business service delivery, performance management and so forth. For practitioners, they were often a welcome relief from the day job – although for some – such as the growing numbers of local authority CSOs or police service 'secondees', this *was* their day job. But despite the importance that many attributed to this new area of local governance, it did not figure prominently on the agendas of most.

Evidence would appear to suggest that, despite putting partnerships onto a statutory footing in 1998, this marginality remained throughout New Labour's first term of office. This was due in part to the lack of core funding; to the fact that government policy such as the Crime Reduction Programme rode roughshod over three-year strategies (thus rendering them marginal in areas that successfully scrambled for Programme funding); and to the structural instabilities that encouraged others to defer to the responsible authorities, and to play hard-to-get over key issues such as information exchange. Importantly, however, the marginality of CDRPs in New Labour's first term was also a consequence of poor design and bad policy-making. The marginality had not been intended. Rather, although this might have been an over-ambitious aspiration, the infrastructure established by the 1998 Crime and Disorder Act, which importantly included not only the CDRPs, but also the general crime prevention duty found in Section 17, which applied to both responsible authorities, was intended to put crime and disorder reduction at the centre of a new structure for local crime control.

The most obvious aspect of this centrality was the Home Office's deliberate emphasis upon crime reduction, evidenced particularly in PSA targets and BVPIs, as opposed to community safety. This marked an instrumental re-invention of the partnership approach that effectively pushed it firmly in the direction of the police service mainstream, given that the police service too was being put under a performance management regime that was shifting away from detection and much more closely towards crime reduction. In other words, crime reduction was the glue that should have stuck the police service and CDRPs together. But towards the end of New Labour's first term, and moving into its second, other developments, that were not necessarily complementary to the Home Office's firm emphasis upon crime reduction, were serving to demonstrate the centrality of local crime control to local governance. These, which will be discussed in more detail below and in subsequent chapters, include changing perceptions on the role and functions of local government, as well as changes in the understanding of 'the crime problem', which led, as we saw at the end of the last chapter, to the problematization of the fear of crime and of the 'reassurance gap'.

What this all means, for the purposes of this chapter, is that policy in this domain, geared in general terms towards moving crime reduction more into the mainstream, became more closely entwined with policy developments elsewhere. In particular, as the story of local crime control under New Labour unfolds, Home Office crime reduction policy became caught up in the reform and modernisation programmes affecting institutions of local governance such as local authorities and the police service. The effect of such entanglement, which is still being felt, has been to muddy the waters of crime reduction, as will become apparent in what follows.

Police reform

For many observers, at the beginning of the twenty-first century the police service represented the last unreformed public service. The neo-liberal and neo-conservative project undertaken by the Thatcher governments in the 1980s required a strong police service to maintain order in the face of challenges from the likes of the trades union movement and errant inner city populations, and for this reason the police remained largely (but not totally) untouched from the kind of radical reforms and rationalisations that had been imposed upon other public services. In the 1990s, the continued rise in crime pushed the spotlight more firmly in the direction of police performance, but the intended reforms of Kenneth Clarke's period of office as Home Secretary failed to materialise, and from the mid-1990s, as New Labour sought to seize the law and order initiative from the Conservatives, both main political parties found it politically unwise to take on the cause of police reform, preferring instead to compete on unashamedly populist promises to provide more and more 'bobbies on the beat'.

However, under the politically astute theme of modernisation, which avoids many of the 'cutback' connotations of earlier public sector reform efforts, New Labour was able to place the police service firmly within their sights. Before the 2001 election, perhaps as an indicator of things to come, the police service had already been brought within the continuous improvement performance management regime of Best Value, but within a relatively short space of time, and under a new Home Secretary, David Blunkett, plans for further change were revealed in a White Paper, appropriately entitled *Policing a New Century* (Home Office 2001a).

The White Paper set out the manifest reasons for the police reform agenda. These included the observations that there had been an alarming fall in police detection rates; that BCU performance tended to vary wildly across police force areas; and that there was a need to maintain public confidence in the police, particularly in terms of their accessibility. In addition, while crime rates were falling they still remained too high in some areas, and crucially public perceptions remained that crime was rising, not falling – the 'reassurance gap'. Such perceptions were correlated with a persistently high fear of crime, that in turn was linked to concern about anti-social behaviour – all 'facts' generated from the BCS, which had become a much more important and instrumental governmental technology under New Labour. Indeed, perhaps pre-empting the White Paper, some of the BVPIs imposed upon the police service for use in 2000/1 were to be based on the 2001 BCS questions about perceptions of the level of crime, the fear of crime, feelings of public safety, and public confidence in the criminal justice system.

Overall, a key theme that this White Paper, and the subsequent 2002 Police Reform Act, alighted upon was reassurance (Hallam 2002), to address the problems mentioned above. This theme of reassurance had also been prominent in an ACPO (2001) policy paper entitled

Policing in the 21st Century, which had been critical of the pressure that the Home Office had exerted over the police to demonstrate their crime reduction performance against volume crimes such as burglary and vehicle-related crime. Too narrow a focus upon such crime reduction, the paper said, was unwise because it neglected the important role the police had in dealing with minor crimes and incivilities, and public reassurance. Reassurance had also been an important theme in the HMIC (2001) paper entitled *Open All Hours*, which had argued that such reassurance could be achieved through the three key criteria of visibility, accessibility and familiarity (Innes 2005).

The police service's neglect of reassurance could be traced back to the performance management agenda that was imposed upon them from the mid-1990s onwards, even if more radical reforms had failed to materialise at that time. Thus, the Conservatives had placed a very firm emphasis upon the centrality of the police's crime-fighting role, baldly stating in a White Paper of their own that 'the main job of the police is to catch criminals' (Home Office 1993: para. 2.3). The Audit Commission (1993) effectively backed this message up, saying that the police needed to adopt a model of crime management that was oriented particularly towards catching that small proportion of persistent offenders that was responsible for a disproportionate amount of all crime. The priority, therefore, had to be detection (Morgan and Newburn 1997; Crawford 1998).

The problem for the police service is that this narrow focus on detection did not address public concerns, which was particularly worrying given declining public support for the police (Waters 1996). Nor did it fit with the police service's own consumerist bid for relegitimation, which had been launched by the Operational Policing Review in 1990 (Joint Consultative Committee 1990). And nor did it appear to fit well with an emergent crime prevention policy that had been premised upon the fact that the police alone could not be expected to control crime, and thus needed to work in partnership with others. Consequently, one way of interpreting the emergence of the reassurance policing agenda at the beginning of the twenty-first century is as an explicit recognition that policing policy had been going down the wrong path.

In reality, attempts had been made at the beginning of New Labour's first term of office to steer the police service performance agenda away from detection and towards crime reduction, thus putting them on the right path. Thus, for example, the Audit Commission (1999) had urged for a stronger focus on crime reduction as a way of addressing community concerns, while HMIC's (1998) *Beating Crime* promoted a culture of sustainable crime reduction within the police service, which it felt should be supported more strongly in key national objectives. The emphasis upon crime reduction does not necessarily neglect detection. Rather, it gives prevention and detection equal prominence in an integrated model of crime management. But while Home Office policy in New Labour's first term pushed the crime reduction agenda forward, it did so in a narrower way than either the Audit Commission or HMIC had envisaged. Thus, as ACPO (2001) pointed out, the problem was the exclusive focus upon the reduction of volume-serious crimes such as burglary, rather than the reduction of minor crimes and disorder, that were key to any public sense of reassurance. This probably also meant that, in the pursuit of these volume crimes, too much emphasis had been given to detection over prevention.

Consequently, the key point to take from this complicated story is that in the 2002 Police Reform Act, and in the emphasis this gave to reassurance, the Home Office appeared to have started to grasp the importance of a more expansive notion of crime reduction, beyond the narrow focus upon headline volume crimes. Accommodating the idea of reassurance meant being prepared to tackle low-level, quality of life concerns, that would address the fear of crime, insecurity and declining public confidence. In the 2002 Act, provision was made to do this through the encouragement and support of 'the extended police family', particularly through the position of the police community support officer (PCSO), which provided a relatively cheap resource for increasing a patrolling policing presence across the country. Additionally, PCSOs and others, including regular uniformed officers, were provided with the potential to have additional powers to tackle low-level disorder through a range of sanctions, including new penalty notices for disorder (PNDs). We shall return to the reassurance agenda later.

While one part of the 2002 Police Reform Act appeared to show an appreciation of reassurance and a broader understanding of crime reduction, the other part – concerned more with steering than rowing – was more orthodox, and oriented towards imposing a strict performance management regime (which, as we have seen from the above discussion, can end up undermining the reassurance agenda). Thus the Act empowered the Home Secretary to set down a National Policing Plan, and to intervene, if needs be, in the management of poorly performing BCUs or forces, which were to be identified in a performance management framework that included monitoring from a new Police Standards Unit (PSU), revamped inspections by HMIC, and the compulsory adoption of the National Intelligence Model (NIM) as good practice in intelligence-led policing.

If, as I have argued at the beginning of this chapter, crime reduction was regarded as integral to the local governance of crime, an obvious question to ask is where CDRPs fitted in to this reform agenda. Importantly, they were not neglected. The 2002 Act firstly proposed a merger between CDRPs and local drug action teams (DATs), which made sense given the prominence of drug-related crime in many if not all localities. Secondly, it required a revision to the constitution of CDRPs, which saw the attribution of responsible authority status extended from the police commander and the local authority to the police authority, the fire authority, and the primary care trust (PCT). While this extension partly reflected changes in expectations placed upon these bodies between 1998 and 2002 (e.g. the potential combination of CDRPs and DATs necessitated a more central role for PCTs as the DATs' major strategic funding body), it also represents an acknowledgement that the boundaries for responsible authorities had been drawn too tightly in 1998, thus providing insufficient incentive for such bodies to participate in a strategic approach to local crime and disorder reduction. Implicitly, it was recognition of some of the structural instabilities that had been created back in 1998.

The legislative changes made to the CDRPs represented only relatively minor structural reforms, and did not solve the riddle as to how they could be brought into the mainstream. Confirmation that this was where they were thought to belong can be found, however, in Home Office *Circular 14/2002*, which launched the Safer Communities Initiative (SCI) (see below), as the main successor funding stream to the Crime Reduction Programme. That circular opines that:

> Partnerships' strategies will be driven by the mainstream activity of public agencies coordinated in a way to achieve the maximum impact. Partnerships can also supplement mainstream service delivery with programme funded activity which can, when targeted in a highly focused way, make a difference to outcomes. (Home Office 2002a: 3)

Yet research-informed critiques of the first round of strategies from 1999 to 2002 suggest that those strategies did not necessarily live up to this model. The idea from this circular that CDRP strategies would be driven by mainstream activities gave the strategies, and the CDRPs that constructed them, much greater prominence than they actually had in practice at the local level. We have already considered some of the reasons why this was the case, given the CDRPs' inherited structural instabilities. Thus, while the circular offers a statement of principle, it does not go any further than that, and it may be plausible to suggest that much of the policy development in this area, and from the beginning of New Labour's second term and beyond, was about finding a 'way in' for CDRPs. Although CDRPs were there for crime reduction, it was by no means clear what this actually meant for them in practice. However, it was clear that, whatever it was they were supposed to be doing, evidence suggested that they were not necessarily doing it that well.

There have been increasingly loud mutterings of discontent about the capacity and performance of CDRPs. A pathfinder report (Home Office 1999b) into the early experiences of 12 CDRPs, for example, had shown cultural differences between police and local authority representatives; significant problems with data exchange despite the permissive legislation; and problems in engaging partner agencies that were exacerbated by a lack of coterminosity, which meant that some upper-tier agencies incorporated several CDRPs within their boundaries, making collaboration prohibitively resource-intensive for them. The Crime Reduction Programme then showed up a very limited CDRP capacity for essential functions such as project management and project monitoring, and the Home Office's own case study research of three CDRPs (Phillips *et al.* 2002) provided very limited grounds for optimism.

The difficulties experienced by CDRPs might have been thought of as teething troubles that would be sorted out over time, by the kinds of incremental structural changes brought in by the 2002 Police Reform Act. However, the publication of the Audit Commission's (2002) report on the partnerships brought these difficulties more firmly out into the limelight, and suggested that there were fundamental difficulties that needed to be addressed if CDRPs were to play a more prominent part in the local governance of crime, along the lines suggested by the 2002 circular.

The Audit Commission report was based upon its experiences of inspecting and auditing local authority practice, and upon the results of a survey conducted by the Local Government Association (LGA) in 2001. Clearly such experiences were not overwhelmingly positive, as the report baldly notes at the outset that 'local partnerships have not made an obvious impact on community safety' (Audit Commission 2002). The rest of the report seeks to explain why this is the case, focusing particularly upon problems with government policy, and with local capacity (Gilling 2003).

On one level, the report can be interpreted as belonging to the stable of orthodox managerial critiques that one would expect from bodies such as the Audit Commission. Thus, for example, the report notes deficiencies with the skills-base of local authority practitioners; it complains about difficulties with poorly developed performance management frameworks; and it criticises the absence of information exchange between partner agencies. This confirms what other previous studies have found, and thus provides a useful validity check, without actually saying anything particularly new. However, on another level the report comes across as a radical critique of the direction of government policy, coming from a rather unlikely source. As such, it speaks to the issue of bringing the CDRPs in from the margins to the mainstream.

The grounds for this critique are established around the Audit Commission's insistence that the domain be described as community safety rather than crime reduction. It discerns a tension, for example, between the top-down crime reduction that emanates from the Home Office, and the bottom-up community safety that is expressed (but not necessarily well acted out) through *community safety* partnerships (the term CDRP is not used in the report). And it also notes that the Audit Commission's own inspection work has been constrained by the narrowness of the Best Value performance regime, which is geared much more towards national crime reduction targets, than community safety more broadly conceived. With regard to the latter, the report criticises '... the lack of a clear national policy that includes the important role of non-police agencies in community safety' (2002: 22). There are echoes here of ACPO's (2001) complaint about the excessively narrow focus upon volume crime reduction.

It is possible that my own interpretation finds more between the lines than is actually there, but the most significant thing about the Audit Commission report appears to be the connection it draws between community safety and local government reform. Thus, the Audit Commission is enthusiastic about the idea of community safety becoming a portfolio responsibility for Cabinet members in the reformed local authority political leadership structure. It also appears to see a natural role for community safety in the LSPs established by the 2000 Local Government Act (see below), and in the general duty imposed by that Act upon local authorities to achieve the social, economic and environmental well-being of their local communities. It is these interests that move the Audit Commission to provide such a critical commentary of government policy. The poor fit between local aspirations for expansive community safety and narrow central prescriptions for crime reduction, moreover, helps to explain many of the Audit Commission's empirical findings. Thus, for example, the report notes that much local authority action in this domain is focused upon procedural compliance (e.g. the completion of audits and strategies), rather than outcomes. This echoes the point made about paper compliance in the previous chapter, and in this case this may be seen either in terms of a lack of funding to do anything much else, or a lack of commitment, or a combination of the two.

The implication of this reading of the Audit Commission's report is that, after 2002, the mainstreaming of the local crime control role of CDRPs within the local governance of crime was deeply entwined with the agendas of police reform and local government reform, themselves elements of a more broadly conceived democratic modernisation agenda. For the Audit Commission, the CDRPs ideally were to be driven by a local government-led notion of community safety, while for the Home Office, it was crime reduction. Ironically, the term community safety is often criticised for its ambiguity, but the implication of the preceding discussion is that crime reduction is no less ambiguous, because it comprises detection as well as prevention, and it is co-dependent with reassurance, as the Home Office had started to recognise (though not necessarily in its performance management regime for CDRPs – see below). Which elements of crime reduction were CDRPs best placed to address, and how could the different agendas of crime reduction and community safety be reconciled? These are questions to which we shall return after a fuller account of policy developments in New Labour's second term and beyond.

While I have identified something of an existential crisis for CDRPs, for the moment the Home Office remained preoccupied with the issue of crime reduction delivery, conceived in narrow terms despite its Damascene moment with regard to reassurance (which at this stage applied only to policing anyway). As noted above, from its perspective, experience with the Crime Reduction Programme had shown limitations in local capacity which needed to be addressed by stronger central steering, and assistance with rowing. Consequently, fulfilling an election manifesto commitment, in April 2002 the Home Office rolled out the SCI, manifestly to provide supplementary programme funding for CDRPs, although in truth without this and other sources of central funding, many CDRPs would have remained largely empty vessels, going through the ritual of the audit-consultation-strategy process without doing much else at all. The Audit Commission's (2002) criticism about the process focus of CDRPs has an obvious relevance here.

The SCI was originally envisaged as a four-year programme, providing at least £20 million each year to be distributed to all CDRPs on a formula that provided 80% of the funding according to comparative crime rates in each CDRP, and 20% on the basis of an even split, guaranteeing at least some funding to each area. In this regard, it was well received, particularly by CDRPs that had received nothing from, or that had submitted failed bids to, the Crime Reduction Programme, the competitive nature of which had attracted criticism from the Audit Commission (2002) among others, for the disincentive effect it generated.

The timing of the funding settlement, however, was unfortunate. As with the Crime Reduction Programme, funding details arrived only *after* CDRPs had put in place the second of their three-yearly crime reduction strategies, to run from April 2002 to March 2005. It is reasonable to suggest that prior local knowledge of the quantity and availability of these funds may well have influenced the content of such strategies – although the Home Office's insistence that such funds were *additional* to mainstream activity conveniently saved its blushes to some extent. Certainly, since the arrival of prescriptive BVPIs in 2001 CDRPs had been made more aware (but not necessarily more accepting) of the need to tailor their strategies to central priorities, and so the news that SCI funding was to be spent in pursuit of national strategic priorities would not have come as any great surprise at this time.

Having learnt some of the lessons of the Crime Reduction Programme, the Home Office channelled decision-making about the approval of SCI plans, which each CDRP was obliged to produce, down to the Crime Reduction Teams operating out of the government offices, and the latter were also made responsible for monitoring the spend. The expectation was that CDRPs would devise plans for evidence-based crime reduction, based upon a thorough analysis of the local crime problems to be tackled, and a careful selection of what works. One obvious problem, however, was that contrary to expectations, the Crime Reduction Programme had thus far failed to identify a substantial evidence base for what works, and thus it was envisaged that a number of projects initiated under the SCI might be subjected to a thorough evaluation to aid such a purpose.

In line with its second aim of raising local capacity for crime reduction work, the Home Office made it clear that a proportion of

SCI funds could be spent on capacity-building. However, another funding source had been established at the same time for this same purpose, namely the Partnership Development Fund (PDF). The PDF had emerged out of the second of New Labour's comprehensive spending reviews, in 2002, and it was perceived by some as a response to the lobbying of local government bodies for central funding to support the financial burden of CDRP infrastructures. Like the SCI, funding which amounted nationally to £20 million over each of three years was allocated to all CDRPs, and again it was dispensed through the Crime Reduction Teams in the government offices. The Home Office's expectation was that the funding would be used especially to support technological developments, such as GISs, that could be used to facilitate data collection and analysis, as essential elements of an evidence-based approach. In practice, while funding was used for such purposes, it was also used to support personnel who populated the CDRP infrastructure, such as CSOs. This helped to address the Audit Commission's (2002) finding that some 10% of CDRPs lacked a specialist community safety coordinator post – something that had not helped the impression in some areas that community safety was effectively a 'bolt on' to the 'day job' – an additional rather than a core responsibility.

The additional funding could be seen as a means of enhancing the local capacity to 'row', but other things were done in pursuit of this end too, such as enhancing the local knowledge base about what works. This included attempts to improve the training of local CDRP practitioners, using the resources, for example, of the now-abolished National Crime Prevention College. It also followed a long-established approach to disseminating good practice that first started with the Home Office Crime Prevention Unit's demonstration projects back in 1982, and continued under New Labour, albeit in a modernised form, in the shape of internet-based toolkits, made available from the Home Office's crime reduction website.

As ever, though, the enhancement of local rowing was accompanied by measures designed to facilitate a central steer, although in practice steering was devolved down to the Crime Reduction Teams in the regional government offices. To assist them, the Home Office had devised a cunning plan to put CDRPs into broadly similar 'family' groupings, as a basis for comparing like with like (Leigh et al. 2000). Using demographic information, police crime statistics could then be converted into crime rates, and put into 'family' league tables, allowing the Home Office and regional Crime Reduction Teams to identify 'good' and 'bad' performers in each CDRP family league, just as the Home Office had been able to do with police BCUs. Given the Treasury-imposed pressure upon the Home Office to meet its PSA targets, this meant in turn that pressure was exerted upon the regional Crime Reduction Teams to raise the performance of the 'bad' performers, which in practice tended to mean those that fell within the lowest 'performance' quartile of CDRPs in each 'family' grouping, which accounted for the greater proportion of all recorded crime.

There are a number of difficulties with the use of this kind of performance measurement that are relevant to consider at this point. Firstly, the crime statistics that are available to facilitate comparisons are limited, not only because of the lengthy delays in producing them, but also because they relate only to a relatively small number of crime categories – generally those such as burglary or vehicle-related crime that constitute the volume crime categories. Consequently, they encourage the sort of narrowing of the crime reduction agenda that undermines the importance of reassurance (as discussed above), and that neglects the wider frame of community safety. Performance management in this way only comes to measure what is measurable, and what is measurable then constitutes the field in a narrow way.

Secondly, the use of crime rates to measure 'performance' is crude because the causes of variations in crime rates may have little to do with the 'performance' of CDRPs as such. In this regard, Irving and Bourne's (2002: 12) point that 'BCUs for geographical, demographic, historical and social reasons that are not under police control, face idiosyncratic performance advantages and disadvantages' applies equally to CDRPs. Indeed, to underscore the point they go on to describe the kind of performance regime that the Home Secretary intends to use to identify 'poorly performing' BCUs as depending upon a 'facile statistical definition of failure' (ibid.: 13), and again the point applies equally to CDRPs. The Home Office's organisation of CDRPs into comparable 'families' offers some defence against this charge, in so far as such a governmental technology seeks to compare like with like, but in all honesty the construction of questionable 'family' groupings represents a very blunt instrument to inform what should be very finely calibrated judgements of performance.

Thirdly, and related to the above points, performance management cast in these terms tends to blur the distinction between process and outcome. Thus, it may be presumed that a good performing CDRP (based only on the evidence of a low crime rate) operates very effectively as a partnership, whilst a poorly performing CDRP operates ineffectively as a partnership. Yet such a presumption is nonsensical, and even if effective partnership working is a necessary condition of good 'performance' judged by crime rates (which is deeply questionable), it would be very far from being a sufficient condition for such performance. Performance management cast in these terms will inevitably set a number of false trails for the understanding of good practice, and the resolution of bad practice.

Although the SCI was originally envisaged as a four-year project, within a year it had undergone a name change, to the Building Safer Communities (BSC) fund. The name change may have been done in part to avoid confusion with the Street Crime Initiative, which was also launched in 2002 and which, carelessly, shared the same acronym. Alternatively, the BSC fund also represented something of a re-packaging job, necessitated in part by the need to incorporate drugs programme funding (as a result of the expected merger of CDRPs and DATs after the 2002 Police Reform Act), and in part by the need to simplify funding arrangements, in response to widespread criticism that the government's bad case of 'initiativitis' had caused confusion and unnecessary duplication of effort for local practitioners. Thus, rather than having to apply for, and account for the spending of, the SCI, the PDF and Communities Against Drugs (CAD) funding, after April 2003 CDRPs only had to apply for funding from a single BSC pot. What a relief.

In other respects, BSC kept to the same path as SCI, although Home Office *Circular 34/2003*, which announced the changes in the funding stream, did emphasise that Crime Reduction Teams would 'challenge' CDRPs if their crime reduction targets were not met. It also noted, perhaps suggesting that the Home Office had started to take note of the criticisms made by the Audit Commission (2002), that local crime reduction strategies needed to be linked into the LSPs that were now supposed to be up and running in unitary, borough and county council areas. This was not necessarily good news for county councils, because they included several borough council CDRPs within their geographical areas of responsibility, and thus several strategies to be linked to the county's LSP, a task akin to herding cats. The circular also provided a good opportunity to remind CDRPs that their strategies needed to fit with the Home Office's PSAs, as well as the Home Secretary's National Policing Plan.

In fact, in each of the three years of the BSC fund a Home Office circular was published (circulars *34/2003, 14/2004* and *21/2005*), and this annual process provided the Home Office with an opportunity to 'remind' CDRPs of changes in its list of priorities. Thus the 2004 circular (Home Office 2004a: 5) suggested that 'partnerships will want to consider the benefits of addressing alcohol-fuelled violence, both in addressing volume crime and reducing anti-social behaviour'. Also, perhaps as evidence of the Home Office's growing interest in civil renewal, which was a matter close to David Blunkett's heart, the same circular noted that CDRPs might want to consider spending some of the funding they were receiving on community engagement projects.

An examination of annual circulars such as these provides the reader with relevant details of policy development, but more importantly it provides an insight into the way the Home Office sought to manage – some might suggest *micro-manage* – CDRPs. Here is strong evidence of New Labour's dirigism, which was not always welcomed by local CDRPs, partly because the annual changes disturbed the three-year cycle set in motion by the 1998 Crime and Disorder Act, and partly because the annual funding created uncertainty that made it very difficult for CDRPs to plan for sustainable local crime control interventions. As many local practitioners pointed out, it was a far from satisfactory situation.

Dissatisfaction was not only expressed from the CDRPs upwards. In 2002 there was considerable media-induced panic about an apparent explosion in street robbery – due in the main to a growth in the use and theft of mobile phones among young people. The increase in such robbery threatened an otherwise good government record on crime reduction, and it moved the Prime Minister himself to launch the Street Crime Initiative, which was managed as a national emergency through a central inter-departmental Street Crime Action Group, and through local delivery teams based in each of the ten worst-affected police force areas. The importance of this initiative was that for the government it provided an opportunity to test the capacity of CDRPs to respond to a specific crime problem that, in theory, their problem-oriented methodologies and ongoing monitoring of local crime problems should have alerted them to. In this regard it was a bit like being tested in a fire drill. However, the perception from the centre was that it was a test CDRPs failed. The initiative was subjected to a thorough joint review by central inspection bodies, led by HMIC (2003: 44) which noted that '… in some areas, the introduction of SCI was perceived by partners as "enforced", working against locally-consulted priorities and as displacing effort intended for existing or fully endorsed local activities'. More damning, albeit with some faint praise, it added that

> … the inspection team found examples of good partnership activity and general confirmation of the view that SCI had

invigorated otherwise often dormant partnership initiatives. In particular, the largely ineffective nature of Crime and Disorder Reduction Partnerships (CDRPs) was, once more, highlighted.

Thus CDRPs were cast in the mould of recidivist offenders, being both resistant and ineffective in the face of an initiative that some local CDRPs, and police forces, were convinced was unwarranted, because the scale of the problem was not as great as the centre had portrayed it. Needless to say, despite these difficulties, the initiative was deemed a success, achieving a 17% reduction in street robbery in its first year of operation. But it left a dark shadow hanging over CDRPs.

At the end of 2003, the Home Office released a consultation paper, entitled *Building Safer Communities Together* (Home Office 2003), which set out the next stages of police reform. Significantly, in view of the previously expressed dissatisfaction with the performance of CDRPs, the paper talked of the need to strengthen existing partnership arrangements, although it did not offer more detail than this. Even more significantly, there was a noticeable shift in the language used. Although the paper was ostensibly about police reform, there was frequent mention of the term community safety, as if the Home Office had begun to take on board some of the criticisms that the Audit Commission (2002) had levelled at the Home Office's existing, restrictive performance regime. The title of the paper, moreover, matched the name of the rebranded funding stream for CDRPs. It seemed clear from the tone of the paper, moreover, not only that police reform and the future of CDRPs were inextricably linked, but also that the linkage was conceived fundamentally in terms of community safety.

Although the paper still identified effectiveness as one of the key themes of police reform, such effectiveness was expressed less in terms of narrow crime reduction targets, and much more in terms of adding to police powers with regard to anti-social behaviour, and making structural reforms to police forces to encourage greater specialisation, and a greater capacity to deal with organised crime and terrorism, concerns that obviously grew in prominence after the watershed moment of 9/11. As a key theme, furthermore, effectiveness was relegated to third place behind community engagement and accountability, both issues that lent weight to the growing importance of reassurance, except that, by the time of this paper, reassurance policing was being reframed as neighbourhood policing.

Innes (2005: 158) notes that neighbourhood policing was '... adopted by political actors within the Home Office and the Labour

Government to try and bring together and give a sense of cohesiveness to several different reform-oriented projects'. He suggests that the idea of neighbourhood has become a key signifier in late-modern governance because, whereas community has lost much of its implied homogeneity and spatialised focus, neighbourhood reclaims this in its territorialised emphasis. For our purposes, neighbourhood effectively pulls together policing and community safety, and provides its own institutional reform agenda, which is a strong theme in the Home Office paper. Innes (ibid.), however, regrets the passing of the concept of reassurance policing because it accurately drew attention to the symbolic nature of policing, but arguably the conjoining of neighbourhood policing with community safety restores the focus upon the symbolic, since it is this symbolic orderliness, and the sense of security that it generates, that lies behind much of the community safety ethos.

Interestingly, Innes (ibid.) describes the outcome of an evaluation of the large-scale PSU and ACPO-funded National Reassurance Policing Programme, which demonstrates that reassurance policing's key principles, namely visibility, accessibility and familiarity, by themselves were not enough to address local crime and security concerns. This is not greatly surprising if these principles are solely symbolic – at some point the police or others have to act decisively too: in Innes's terms, they have to get the balance right between 'hard' and 'soft' policing. Reassurance, then, may only be half the story, but as Innes (ibid.: 162) correctly observes, it '… makes space for the co-production of security by encouraging partnership working between police, local agency partners and the public'. Again, therefore, one can see the potentially smooth fit between reassurance/neighbourhood policing and community safety.

This is very much the tone of the consultation paper, which begins with a foreword from David Blunkett in which he writes that '… we must transcend our traditional notions of policing by consent, and establish a new principle of policing through cooperation' (Home Office 2003: i). This requires the police to go back to their roots, recalling that the office of constable was originally a civic position, and that in the new agenda of civil renewal the police need to work with the community, which, in familiar communitarian terms, has rights (to safety), but also responsibilities (to co-produce it). This means, amongst other things, drawing the community where possible into the extended police family, and giving them a stronger voice through bodies such as neighbourhood panels, which focus upon both policing and community safety, and which might link to contemporary developments in neighbourhood management within local government.

This consultation paper implied that it was now time to review the structure of local policing and community safety. It is difficult to avoid the observation that such a view contrasts sharply with the statutory guidance that accompanied the 1998 Crime and Disorder Act and that required CDRPs to focus upon delivery rather than structure. Structure, after all, turns out to be an important political question – as if it hadn't been all along!

The strong neighbourhoods focus of the consultation paper came through also in the subsequent White Paper *Building Communities, Beating Crime* (Home Office 2004b). This White Paper also brought the not entirely unexpected news that the government was to institute a formal review of the CDRPs. The rationale is worth quoting at length, stating that while some CDRPs appear to work well,

> ... some CDRPs are demonstrably less effective than others. For example, partnerships sometimes struggle to maintain a full contribution from key agencies. Lack of clarity about roles and responsibilities and blurred lines of accountability can lead to some agencies abrogating their responsibility for crime reduction. Furthermore, under present arrangements, CDRPs are neither fully visible nor properly accountable to the communities they serve, nor are they fully embedded in the local democratic framework. These issues lie at the heart of the Government's reform programme. (Ibid.: 158)

The points made here relate very strongly to the structural instabilities institutionalised within the bodies of the CDRPs, and referred to in the previous chapter. They mark a significant departure away from an obsessive narrow focus upon the delivery of crime reduction, even though the theme of 'driving performance up' is never far beneath the surface of governmental concern. However, since the proposal for the review refers to the local democratic framework, and goes on to state that the review will link with wider developments in public sector reform, including local government reform, it is time in a moment to switch our attention to local government. But firstly, as a way of accounting for where we have been and where we are going, it is worth briefly summarising the gist of the argument so far.

Through the 1998 Crime and Disorder Act, New Labour sought to make crime reduction the dominant ethos underpinning the local governance of crime, shifting it from the position of marginality previously occupied by crime prevention. In its first term of office, despite the statutory creation of CDRPs, it failed to do this, in part because of the structural instabilities that the above quote alludes to, and in part because of its continued and often clumsy meddling that undermined and exposed the fragility of those partnerships. But also, it pushed CDRPs down a crime reduction path that the Audit Commission (2002) in particular thought was too narrow. This criticism chimed with the emergent reassurance policing agenda, since both implied that public concerns – expressed particularly in the fear of crime and insecurity – had not been met, either in local policing or in crime reduction. Attempts to address the problem through a new public management paradigm, geared to strengthening central steering and the local capacity to row continued, and continue still, but they miss the point of the criticism, which really relates to the lack of local influence and voice over the direction of local policing and crime prevention. In other words, there has been a failure to deliver on the original promise of *local solutions for local problems*.

Beyond the new public management approach, one response of the government, not considered here, but investigated in Chapter 5, has been to open up a new front against anti-social behaviour, providing a range of new powers and an institutional structure through which they can be exercised. While these new powers can potentially address some of the problems from which the public often requires reassurance (as Innes [2005] observes, many of the 'signal crimes' that have such a disproportionate impact upon public concerns are instances or series of anti-social behaviour), they do not of themselves deliver the localism that has been missing in the government's crime reduction policy. This localism, symbolised here in the language of neighbourhoods and community safety, requires a restructuring of CDRPs that must necessarily take into account the wider restructuring of policing and local government, both of which remain, for good reason, the key players – if not the only ones – in local partnerships. We have looked above at police reform, so to complete the picture it is necessary now to consider the case of local government reform.

Local government reform

To understand where local government reform is going, it is best first to appreciate where it has been – although this does not require an unduly long travelogue, the reader will be relieved to learn.

The Conservative governments of the 1980s and 1990s were not renowned for the strength of their support for the institution of local government. Fundamentally, they subscribed to a public choice critique of public bureaucracy, which meant that local government was not trusted as a service provider, because it was presumed to be profligate, inefficient and characterised by bureaucratic self-interest. The fact that much local government throughout most of this period took on a distinctly red political hue – including the high-profile media-labelled 'loony left' urban socialist authorities – certainly did not help its cause, and under the Conservatives' neo-liberal agenda, consequently, local government endured a sustained political and economic assault. Amongst other things, for example, it had its fiscal powers limited; it lost responsibility for certain aspects of service delivery; other service delivery responsibilities had to be put out to tender; and in areas like urban regeneration it was effectively by-passed as central government preferred to work through appointed quangos. By the time New Labour had taken power in 1997, then, local government found itself operating in an environment accurately characterised by Stoker (2004) as one of multi-level governance, in which weakened local authorities shared governmental space with European, central and regional government, alongside a vast array of quangos, and business, voluntary and community group interests. In such an environment, questions about the appropriate role of local government loomed large, with many starting to conceive of local government more in an 'enabling' (Leach and Davis 1996) than a providing role.

In the run up to the 1997 general election New Labour had appeared to be a good deal more local government-friendly than the Conservatives had been. As Stoker (2004) ironically observes, at least New Labour had a vision for local government, even if it was not necessarily one that was shared by local government practitioners themselves. This vision was classically third way: pragmatic rather than ideological, looking for improvements in service delivery, to be achieved through the familiar themes of modernisation and reform. This was evidenced, for example, in New Labour's penchant for developing joined-up policy via partnership initiatives across a wide array of local service areas (including local crime control, of course), which suggests that it recognised the complex governmental terrain that had been the Conservatives' legacy. In this particular area, however, New Labour went too far, with its 'initiativitis' ultimately adding to this complexity, rather than successfully managing it.

Another strong theme of New Labour's approach to local government is performance management, which belies a more mistrustful approach, based upon the tenets of new public management. In Chapter 3 we have already seen how an element of this performance management regime, Best Value, was founded upon a sceptical view that provider interests might once again run rampant were local government ever to be 'let off the leash'. It was concerned about the ability of local government to 'perform', and to deliver quality public services. Consequently, Best Value, which was introduced after the 1999 Local Government Act, although it had been piloted in a few local authorities before this date, was a means of getting rid of the highly unpopular CCT regime whilst maintaining a degree of 'market discipline'. It also added a performance management regime that allowed central government to determine core objectives and standards through BVPIs, which in turn related to the PSAs that central government departments such as the Home Office had signed up to in return for Treasury funds. However, the inspection regime that backed up Best Value was extensive, cumbersome, expensive and a diversion of staff time away from the core business of delivery (Wilson 2004).

Some of this was acknowledged in a 2001 White Paper entitled *Strong Local Leadership, Quality Public Services* (DTLR 2001), which proposed to loosen some of the controls to encourage more entrepreneurial government, although some questioned whether this rhetoric could be matched by reality (Wilson and Game 2002), given New Labour's apparent penchant for dirigism. The vehicle for such change was comprehensive performance assessment (CPA), which has now modified, but not replaced, the Best Value regime. CPA is an inspection regime that offers a 'whole authority' approach to inspection, examining the package of local government services and giving the authority an overall rating, on a five-point scale, that ranged from poor to excellent. Apart from being simplified, the stated advantages of CPA are firstly, that good performers are given degrees of 'earned autonomy' which means that their services receive a 'light touch' and are spared from burdensome reviews and inspections; and secondly that some others will only have to perform Best Value reviews on those services that the CPA identifies as being in need of a review. For those deemed poor performers, however, there is the prospect of intervention from special management teams to improve their performance. Critics, however, suggest the CPA offers only a crude and potentially misleading assessment of local authority performance (Wilson 2004), and that it fosters a league table mentality that can be counter-productive, encouraging fatalism at the bottom, and complacency at the top. Nevertheless, the Audit Commission believes that CPA has helped to push up standards, so that over time a greater overall proportion of authorities have now been rated as good or excellent, and fewer languish in the weak or poor categories (Mulholland 2004). It has also recognised, however, that the process is still very burdensome, and in more recent years modifications have been made to make it less so.

The examples of Best Value and CPA are relevant to the themes of this chapter because they show that local government as a whole has been subjected to the same sorts of performance and delivery concerns that were extended to CDRPs, particularly after 1999, and that the performance management regime that has been used in local government overlaps with that applying to CDRPs. In addition, as with the performance management of CDRPs, the performance management of local government has suffered limitations, and while these can be presented as being partly technical (i.e. that performance management has yet to find the best tools for the job), they also speak to more fundamental difficulties that arise from the attempts of central government to steer the business of local government in an era of complex networks of governance, and equally complex 'wicked issues' such as crime. These difficulties are alluded to by Stoker and Wilson (2004: 251) when they say that central managerialism is unsustainable '... because the centre gets seriously stretched in setting numerous targets. It cannot calibrate the interventions that are required to meet the needs of different local authorities.' This is the problem of power-dependence.

Stoker (2004) says that the centre suffers certain inherent weaknesses that will always mark the limits to its governmental capacity. These weaknesses include information overload (too much to process), communication failure (too much to know) and an inability, despite its rationalistic aspirations, to really learn what works because of the culture of defensiveness that inevitably accompanies central performance pressure, which reflects local agencies' unwillingness, as information gatekeepers, to pass on information that does not show them in the best light.

As with CDRPs, then, the focus upon delivery and performance tells only one part of the story of local government reform. Interestingly, among the more recent modifications made to the CPA, were the requirements that in future the corporate assessment part of CPAs also would be considering the qualities of *partnership working* and *community leadership* (Mulholland 2004). These criteria point to much bigger and more fundamental issues about the role and structure of local government, that even the performance management agenda cannot ignore. These issues highlight the unresolved question of local government's appropriate role in an era of governance. As noted above, the centre may face fundamental limitations when attempting to steer localities, but local government also suffers major limitations, particularly when it comes to questions of its own legitimacy. Partly because its provider role has diminished, and partly because what it has left to provide it sometimes provides poorly, with seemingly little regard for locally-expressed need, and little citizen engagement, there has been a growing disillusionment with local representative democracy (Daly and Davis 2002), reflected, for example, in very low levels of voter turnout at local elections. Consequently, a third theme in the New Labour government's approach towards local government, and the strongest in terms of 'the vision thing', has been democratic renewal (Stoker 2004), which chimes also with developments in neighbourhood policing, discussed above.

The idea of democratic renewal covers a broad spectrum of ideas, some of which remain rather ill-defined. For our purposes, however, two key elements stand out. The first of these relates to the attempt to strengthen local government's political leadership of its communities. Thus, for example, the 2000 Local Government Act has given the higher tiers of local government a responsibility to reform their structures of political leadership by creating an executive style of government, with Cabinet membership and clear portfolio responsibilities. They were also given an opportunity to make provision for directly elected mayors to head up local executive government, although few have taken up this opportunity thus far. This part of the reform programme is reminiscent of the reassurance or neighbourhoods agenda in police reform, since both place a strong emphasis upon local *visibility*, albeit for rather different reasons, although both ultimately are connected to the value of accountability.

Along with clearer leadership structures, local authorities were also endowed with a community leadership duty to prepare a *community strategy* to promote and improve the social, environmental and economic well-being of their communities. Advocates of local government had been lobbying for a long time for local authorities to possess more than just delegated powers from the centre, and at first sight this general duty looks like a positive response to such lobbying. But as Keith (2004) observes, this duty is in fact a very conditional one, because it relates not to local government's provider role, but rather to its 'creature of influence' or enabler role, as a major stakeholder in the locality. Hence the community strategy is supposed to be devised not by the local authority, but by a new body also given legislative life by the 2000 Local Government Act, namely the LSP. The establishment of the LSP gives recognition to the local governance reality, that local fortunes are the business of a plurality of interests, and not just the local authority. Thus LSPs are conceived as forums where this plurality of interests can come together to develop a community strategy. The LSP is, as Keith (2004) describes it, an 'über-partnership', or in less trendy terms an overarching partnership that in theory sits on top of all other local governmental structures (including CDRPs), thus potentially rationalising or simplifying the local governance map and providing a cure for the initiativitis that characterised New Labour's first term of office. But importantly they are also vehicles through which local government can pursue its local political leadership role.

The LSPs are not without their problems. Like CDRPs, they suffer a structural instability, because the responsibilities of LSPs do not fall evenly on all potential members. Rather, the statutory responsibility for the community strategy falls upon the local authorities, just as the responsibility for CDRP audits and strategies falls upon the local authority and the local police commander. Consequently, as Sullivan (2004) observes, there is the perpetual risk of local authorities being seen to dominate LSPs – again just as there was a risk, subsequently borne out by evidence from the first two three-yearly crime reduction cycles, of the police and local authorities dominating the local crime reduction audits and strategies, essentially because the buck stopped with them, even if they did not want to be seen to be the dominant partners. For present purposes, however, our concern lies less with LSP structural weaknesses, and more with the influence that the LSP exercises over CDRPs.

As an overarching structure, the LSP appeals to the principle of holistic governance (Wilkinson and Appelbee 1999) – that is why the local authority's community leadership role is enhanced through it (in theory at least). Thus, the idea of bringing a whole range of different service areas and governmental interests under one roof is based on the aspiration that the process of bringing these different areas together will spark up a series of synergetic connections that, to use that dreadful term, will result in 'added value'. This aspiration can be seen in two quotes from the government guidance that accompanies the launch of the LSP idea (DETR 2001: 16):

Individual partners will remain responsible and accountable for decisions on their services and resources. Delivering an LSP's common goals will depend on its ability to demonstrate to individual partners that *it can help them* to achieve their individual goals. (Emphasis added)

Where an individual partner has goals set primarily by central government, the LSP should identify *the appropriate contribution that other members of the partnership can make* to achieving those goals. (Emphasis added)

The crucial point is that this focus on holism, synergy and added value, when applied to the case of CDRPs provides a counter-weight to the pull from the Home Office's performance management regime in the narrow direction of volume crime reduction. In other words, it can (though not necessarily *does*) lead to a stronger focus, at this level, upon community safety, which is something the Audit Commission (2002) recognised in its report on the partnerships and the implications presented by the arrival of LSPs. Consequently, whilst Home Office policy has sought to tie CDRPs down to a relatively narrow vision of crime reduction, the policy of the Department of the Environment, Transport and the Regions (DETR) (which in 2002 transmogrified into the Office of the Deputy Prime Minister [ODPM], only to change again in 2006 into the Department for Communities and Local Government [DCLG]) has provided a potential escape route back towards the local government vision of community safety. The word 'potential' is important here, because CDRPs have not necessarily become firmly embedded within LSPs since the latter's creation, and the power of the Home Office's performance management regime can still reach deep down into the collective consciousness of the LSPs.

Nevertheless, the potential remains, as can be seen from the parallel that can be drawn with Conservative crime prevention policy in an earlier period. Just as New Labour has, through the Home Office, pushed a strong crime reduction agenda, so the Conservatives sought to do the same, but this time around the theme of situational crime prevention. But the Conservatives were thwarted because the partnerships that were set up as necessary structural conditions for local crime prevention brought together, from the different agencies involved, a more holistic view of crime prevention, that tempered the 'proximate causes' approach of situationalism with the 'distant causes' aetiological approach of social crime prevention (e.g. Sutton 1996). LSPs might do the same for New Labour's crime reduction policy that local partnership's did for the Conservatives' failed hegemonic project with situational crime prevention.

The second important consequence that the connection with LSPs holds for CDRPs derives from the mandate that LSPs have been given to complement their strategic, authority-wide role with a focus upon governance at the neighbourhood level. Government guidance (DETR 2001: 27) elaborates upon this and is worth quoting at length:

> All LSPs will need to complement their strategic activity with a focus on its [sic] activity at neighbourhood level. One model for this is neighbourhood management, which is already being supported by local authorities. ... Neighbourhood management involves devolving power down to an individual, team or single neighbourhood organisation. Neighbourhood managers will be responsible for co-ordinating services at the very local level (a single estate or a few thousand homes), including negotiating with service providers about the services they run and feeding the neighbourhood's views into higher tiers of government.... LSPs offer an obvious route through which neighbourhood managers can exercise influence over main programmes which impact upon the neighbourhood level. The partnerships will be in a position to ensure that partner agencies prioritise key neighbourhoods, participate in neighbourhood renewal and perform in terms of achieving agreed neighbourhood goals.

This neighbourhood focus can be regarded as a part of the broader project of democratic renewal, which seeks a stronger connection between local government and its citizen residents. It also connects to what has been referred to as the *new localism* (Stoker and Wilson 2004), which was an emergent, albeit slightly unclear feature of New Labour's second term of office, combining an emphasis upon neighbourhoods with partnership working to deal with complexity, associative democracy and building social capital. It is too early to map out the precise direction this new localism is taking. In some ways it can be seen as an updating of the model of community governance that was promoted by Clarke and Stewart in the 1990s (see Sullivan 2004), and it can also be seen as an expression of New Labour's communitarianism, particularly in its enthusiasm for active citizenship, and its balancing of rights with responsibilities.

The required neighbourhood focus of LSPs is strongly reinforced in the National Strategy for Neighbourhood Renewal (NSNR), which was launched in 2001 following extensive preparatory work by the SEU, which is considered in more detail in Chapter 6. Importantly, the NSNR action plan sees LSPs as the vehicle for delivering neighbourhood renewal, which is based upon the idea of identifying priority neighbourhoods – effectively the most deprived neighbourhoods – and ensuring, through careful monitoring, that service delivery is improved in those same areas, as a means of 'closing the gap' with less deprived areas.

For CDRPs, there are a number of significant implications that fall out of the LSP's required neighbourhood focus. Firstly, it connects with neighbourhood policing and suggests that CDRPs need to reorient their activities towards the same neighbourhood level, although some evidently do this at present. Secondly, such a reorientation would, however, push CDRPs more in the direction of addressing local priorities, rather than centrally-determined priorities, and this would introduce more of a tension or strain than currently exists, particularly within CDRPs that have largely been disciplined into pursuing central priorities locally. Thirdly, while there may or may not be a tension between central and local priorities, it is very likely that the neighbourhoods focus would significantly alter CDRP ways of working, so that they would have to accommodate community engagement, civil renewal and community cohesion much more centrally than they currently do. They would, in other words, have to adopt a more holistic approach that accommodates the agenda of the ODPM (now the DCLG) alongside that of the Home Office if, indeed, such an accommodation is possible. Given such implications, the decision to review the structure and operation of CDRPs announced in the 2004 White Paper on police reform (Home Office 2004b) was timely, as the tensions of the status quo were becoming increasingly untenable.

Towards the new localism

Having briefly examined contemporaneous developments in police reform and local government reform, it is now time to return to the developmental account of crime prevention policy in New Labour's second term. We left the story somewhere around 2004, when CDRPs were coming towards the final year of their second three-yearly crime reduction strategy, being led by an increasingly interventionist Home Office, which used the BSC fund, and the 'policing' role of Crime Reduction Teams in the regional government offices to steer CDRPs in the direction of centrally-determined crime reduction priorities. Further examples of such interventionism included, firstly, the requirement in the 2002 anti-social behaviour White Paper (Home Office 2002b) for CDRPs to nominate anti-social behaviour coordinators (in return for an addition to the BSC funding allocation) and to ensure than anti-social behaviour featured prominently in their 2005 crime reduction strategies. A second example is provided by the launching in 2004 of the prolific and other priority offender (PPO) strategy, with the requirement that CDRPs use the NIM to find an average of 15 to 20 such offenders in their areas that they can help to catch and convict. The PPO strategy had three elements, namely 'prevent and deter', 'catch and convict' and 'rehabilitate and resettle', and it is interesting that of these three elements, CDRPs were deemed most relevant for the middle element. It shows, perhaps, how in the Home Office's master narrative CDRPs were moving out of prevention (a space occupied for the PPO primarily by YOTs), and more clearly into the policing domain.

From 2004 onwards, there has been an important change of emphasis in government policy. Following central government's spending review in that year, a decision was taken to replace the BSC fund with a new Stronger and Safer Communities Fund (SSCF), which became operational from April 2005. The SSCF is significant for a number of reasons. Firstly, as the name suggests, it represents the merging of the agendas and concerns of the Home Office (for safer communities) and the ODPM (for stronger communities) thus responding to the clear overlaps, noted above, between local government reform, police reform and the review of CDRPs, and suggesting the beginnings of a more joined-up approach to local governance from the centre. Secondly, the SSCF is part of a much larger ten-year strategy for local government (ODPM 2004), namely local area agreements (LAAs), that requires us to engage in another minor diversion.

LAAs were launched by the ODPM in July 2004 as a radical new approach to local governance. Broadly speaking, their manifest purpose is to weaken central government's dirigiste tendencies by handing over central funding to local agencies in one large pot, rather than via a complex array of funding streams, as had hitherto been the case, all with their own different accounting and accountability arrangements. In doing this, central government reduces many of the 'unnecessary' bureaucratic requirements previously placed upon local agencies. More specifically, under the LAA regime, funding – including mainstream funding – is passed initially to the local authorities, which in two-tier areas actually means county councils, rather than districts, where CDRPs are currently based (but see below). This is important because it enables local authorities to have a more instrumental role in local decisions about how to spend the funds. Thus, it is another means by which local government's community leadership role can be enhanced, although the expectation is that LAAs will actually be expressed through LSP community strategies, as the latter's delivery arm, and thus locally agreed across a mixed economy of agencies involved in the business of local governance.

While LAAs may reduce the bureaucracy involved in central government's funding of local agencies, in theory they should also mean that local agencies are freed from the 'silos' of central government department funding streams, thus enabling them to use their resources more flexibly. This is not just about reducing transaction costs. It is also about allowing local agencies to become more responsive to local need, and possibly also more innovative in how they meet that need, including the ability to work across boundaries that should become more permeable as a result of the changed funding methodology. With regard to crime prevention, this change would appear to increase the prospect of local areas pursuing an agenda characterised more by community safety than crime reduction. As discussed above, to some extent this had already been set in motion through the arrival of LSPs.

However, while LAAs offer the prospect of greater localism, and may therefore be supportive of the new localism discussed above, this localism is still conditional, because, as their title suggests, LAAs require agreement, not just among local agencies, but also between the localities (in practice, the LSPs) and central government, through the body of its agents in regional government offices. Thus, LAAs are about the pursuit of local and national outcomes, where it is the centre that specifies the national outcomes through the PSA framework, that remains very much intact; and the local agencies effectively sign up contractually to those outcomes, but acquire greater flexibility in deciding exactly *how* these outcomes should be met, as well as being able to set supplementary local outcomes. This conditionality calls into question the radicalism of the LAA framework: to what extent is this latest reform a smoke and mirrors trick, that repackages the highly prescriptive, interventionist and dirigiste modus operandi of New Labour in a more consensual and palatable form? Given that LAAs are only a recent reform it may be too soon to answer this question with any significant degree of confidence, but the finer details of the SSCF may provide some clues.

As noted above, the SSCF is an element of the LAAs. More specifically, in keeping with the ethos of the LAAs, it merges together a wide range of funding streams from both the Home Office and ODPM into a single pot, although not all funding streams were necessarily available to all local areas (see ODPM/Home Office 2004). Stronger and safer communities constitutes one of the three priority areas of LAAs, the other two being children and young people, and healthier communities and older people. LAAs have been rolled out slowly, from a few pilot sites in 2005/6 onwards. However, the SSCF element of LAAs was made mandatory across all local authorities from April 2005, and this in effect meant, as the prospectus (ODPM 2004) indicated, that this element acted like a 'mini-LAA' for each locality – an opportunity to try out this new, looser regulatory regime before applying it to other policy areas. It is interesting that local crime control should have been chosen as the first policy area for this LAA experiment, given that hitherto it had been one of the areas of local governance over which central government had been most prepared to ride roughshod (Stoker 2004).

In seeking to establish whether LAAs really do represent a genuine concession to localism, the key issue remains the nature of the performance management regime to which CDRPs will be tied. And within this regime, it is the guiding PSA framework that is of importance. This framework has changed, as the SSCF's implementation guidance (ODPM/Home Office 2004: 4–5) makes clear:

The four national outcomes are as follows:

1. To reduce crime, to reassure the public by reducing the fear of crime and anti-social behaviour and to reduce the harm caused by illegal drugs
2. To have cleaner, safer and greener public spaces
3. To increase the capacity of local communities so that people are empowered to participate in local decision-making and are able to influence service delivery
4. To improve the quality of life for people in the most disadvantaged neighbourhoods and ensure service providers are more responsive to neighbourhood needs and improve their delivery.

These outcomes form a framework within which partners can state local priorities and develop outcomes that address the needs of their area.

Of these four outcomes, numbers 1 and 3 are mandatory in all areas, while outcome 2 is only applicable to areas in receipt of liveability or neighbourhood funding, and outcome 4 is applicable only to areas in receipt of neighbourhood funding. Outcomes 3 and 4 evidently speak to the emergent neighbourhoods agenda which has been discussed above, while outcome 2 provides an ODPM 'take' that links safety to physical regeneration. Outcome 1, meanwhile is the most recognisable as a Home Office PSA, but of considerable significance, it is cast at a much more general level than earlier PSAs that focused on specific volume crimes, and specified the percentage reduction they wanted to see local CDRPs and police forces achieving in each of the specified volume crimes. This change in the PSAs, therefore, gives greater discretion to local areas to decide which crimes they decide to tackle, and indeed how they tackle them, and thus bodes well for those looking for signs that central government is committed to greater localism.

The changes that have been effected by the introduction of the SSCF and LAAs are currently being played out in local practice. Local CDRPs that have been used to operating under a prescriptive performance management regime may need to make a cultural shift if they are to 'perform' the localism imagined in the LAAs, and much may also depend upon how tightly the regional government offices police the SSCF element of the LAAs. In the meantime, however, the long-awaited review of the 1998 Crime and Disorder Act, specifically of the role of CDRPs, was finally published in January 2006 (Home Office 2006b), and those elements of the review's recommendations that required legislative action have been incorporated into the 2006 Police and Justice Act. Protracted discussions about the future role and functions of CDRPs meant that by the time that Act was passed, the precise new requirements for CDRPs had yet to be fully resolved, and thus the 2006 Act made allowance for these 'enabling provisions' to be brought in once they had been clarified. The changes to CDRPs are due to take effect from the summer of 2007.

In many ways, the changes introduced by the SSCF, which were made between the announcement of the CDRP review in 2004 and the completion of that review process, have pre-empted or set the agenda for many of that review's recommendations, that fall under the three main themes of structure, delivery and accountability.

In terms of structure, the review recognised the need for CDRPs to fit into the new local governmental structures represented by LSPs and LAAs. While the present structure fitted arrangements in unitary areas, in two-tier areas there was a disjunction, with CDRPs operating at the tier below the LSP and LAA. The review considered the possibility of merging district-level CDRPs to overcome this problem, which many local practitioners had forecasted, but in the end opted to recommend that the strategic and operational elements of CDRPs be split, in order to preserve (operational) localism in two-tier areas. Merger was only to be an option where there was strong local pressure in favour of it. There were other advantages in effecting this strategic/operational split. Firstly, it brought DATs and CDRPs together at the strategic level in two-tier areas, because while the 2002 Police Reform Act required closer working relations between CDRPs and DATs, and mergers where wanted, it had stopped short of compulsion, and thus many CDRPs and DATs remained separate bodies. Secondly, it meant that CDRPs did not so much sit underneath the umbrella of the LSP, as actually become part of the LSP, at least at the strategic level. Thirdly, it also facilitated the further development of the community leadership role of local authorities, by locating the strategic element of CDRPs on LSPs, where local councillors with an executive portfolio for community safety could conformably sit.

The review also recognised the structural instability that meant that CDRPs had had difficulty enlisting the support or contribution of local agencies that were not responsible authorities. On the basis of such a recognition it argued the case for the Home Secretary to be given powers to nominate more responsible authorities if necessary, and for this to be given more 'bite' through a provision that would extend the coverage of Section 17 of the 1998 Crime and Disorder Act from crime to anti-social behaviour, behaviour affecting the environment, and substance misuse, and that would make this reformulated requirement applicable to more local agencies.

In terms of delivery, the review (Home Office 2006b: 15) noted that:

> ... three year audits are ... resource intensive and often now seem to be a distraction from delivery, tying up key partnership staff for up to a year in their production. The reality on the ground is that many partnerships are becoming increasingly performance focussed and intelligence-led, informed by real-time information and community intelligence.

Consequently, it recommended radical changes to the three-yearly strategy-setting cycle, so that in future CDRPs would link in to the NIM to produce six-monthly strategic assessments that would also tie in with the six-monthly progress reporting required by the LAA.

CDRPs, it suggested, should still produce three-yearly plans, but on a rolling basis, updated annually by the strategic assessments rather than by three-yearly audits, as had hitherto been the case. Rather than 'talking past' one another, as had hitherto often been the case, the three-yearly rolling plans would fit with the new requirement made on police authorities to produce three-year rolling policing plans, with both also able to respond to the new strategic policing priorities that the Home Secretary has been empowered to issue following the 2006 Police and Justice Act. To facilitate the strategic assessments upon which these plans are to be based, moreover, the review proposed amending Section 115, the information-sharing provision of the 1998 Crime and Disorder Act, so that rather than being permissive, anonymised information-sharing was now a duty placed upon all responsible authorities.

Finally, in terms of accountability, the review borrowed the idea of visibility from reassurance policing to suggest that CDRPs should become more visible to the local community, firstly by being required to provide regular progress reports to the community as part of the LSP's communication strategy, and secondly by requiring senior members of CDRPs to attend public question and answer sessions that are reminiscent of police community consultation bodies, as originally recommended in the Scarman Report (Scarman 1981), and implemented in the 1984 Police and Criminal Evidence Act. Following the suggestion of the 2004 White Paper on police reform (Home Office 2004b), the review also recommended that the community should be given some 'teeth' to call CDRPs to account through a 'community call-to-action', that might be instigated by local authority ward councillors, requiring CDRPs to account for alleged failures to address specific local community concerns.

Lastly, in terms of accountability, the review recommended embedding CDRPs more firmly within the local democratic process, partly by putting executive portfolio holders onto the strategic part of CDRP business on LSPs, but partly also by placing CDRP business within the ambit of revamped local authority backbench overview and scrutiny committees, that perform a similar role locally to that performed nationally by parliamentary select committees at Westminster, and that, following the 2006 Act, are to include also police authority members – another means through which local policing and crime and disorder reduction are being joined up. In this way, then, CDRPs, and implicitly therefore their constituent parts, could be held to account through local authorities to their local communities, and while this stops short of the accountability arrangements proposed by Loveday (2005), it does at least provide an indirect channel through which the local authority might hold the local police commander to account, although this depends, of course, upon coterminosity between the BCU and the local authority, which does not exist in all cases. Yet.

Chapter summary

This chapter has charted the progress of crime and disorder reduction, through the vehicle of CDRPs, from 2001 to the end of 2006. Prior to 2001, barring the intervention of the not insignificant Crime Reduction Programme, CDRPs had been left largely to themselves, and the result was, in many cases, a degree of 'paper compliance' with the legislation, in terms of doing audits and producing strategies, but little in the way of action 'on the ground'. The problematic nature of such inaction had been covered to some extent by a favourable economic climate under which the crime rate followed a downward trend, thereby averting any sense of impending crisis. After 2001, however, the pressure placed upon CDRPs to deliver effective crime reduction increased in line with the additional central funding that started to flow their way, but so did the understanding that in many cases they were not up to the job. They were implicated, for example, in many of the 'implementation failures' of the Crime Reduction Programme (Hedderman and Williams 2001), although as those such as Hough (2004) observed, such 'failures' may also have had something to do with too reductionist a view of local practice which assumed that 'what works' was all that occupied the minds of local practitioners. They were also criticised by the Audit Commission (2002), and for their limited contribution to the Street Crime Initiative. Consequently, one line of policy taken by the Home Office was to drive up 'performance', no matter how narrowly and problematically that was conceived, through New Labour's familiar tools of evidence-based policy and new public management, which together served to strengthen the steering role of the centre, and its regional government representatives, whilst simultaneously enhancing the local capacity to row, through the provision of various funding sources and tools for capacity-building. Inevitably this drew crime reduction policy further and further away from the original premise of local solutions for local problems.

However, in the midst of this process of driving up performance, CDRPs became entwined in the much bigger agendas of police reform and local government reform, which should come as no surprise as the police and local authorities played the lead roles as responsible authorities on the CDRPs. The problem in all this was that the scripts for police reform and local government reform did not tally so well with the Home Office's preoccupation with crime and disorder reduction. The police service and local government may well have both confronted problems related to their effectiveness, but they also confronted problems linked to a more worrying democratic deficit, which required both to make stronger connections to their local populations, for reasons of both legitimacy and accountability, and to become more embedded within structures of local governance represented by bodies such as the LSPs. But in addressing this democratic deficit and the problems posed by the transformation from local government to local governance, these agencies, and through them the CDRPs, were simultaneously drawn away from the Home Office's crime reduction agenda, and closer towards a neighbourhood approach that reflected the more progressive agenda of the ODPM (now DCLG), which chimed with a large part of the theme of civil renewal, which was championed by David Blunkett during his time at the Home Office. In some ways, civil renewal could be seen as the Trojan Horse that threatened to pull CDRPs away from crime reduction and towards a line of practice which was more consistent with features of community safety.

In many ways, many of the policy changes that have occurred since 2001, culminating in the 2006 Police and Justice Act, have served to correct the structural instabilities that were put in place in the original 1998 establishment of CDRPs, and there is probably now greater scope for more localism and more local joined-up policy. It is important to emphasise, however, that there has been no decisive break away from crime reduction and towards community safety. Rather, the policy domain contains dynamics that can pull in both directions, which is likely to create strain for CDRPs, or opportunities, depending upon the degree of agency they aspire to possess (some CDRPs undoubtedly tend to follow the line set by the centre, while others may be more inclined to chart their own course, albeit with various constraints). As local crime control policy enters the terrain of police reform and local government reform, so the Home Office's relationship of power-dependence with other central government departments and agendas comes more to the fore, and it may be that community safety provides a more palatable vision of local crime control as far as the DCLG, or for that matter the Audit Commission, is concerned.

As this chapter has identified, crime reduction can combine both (situational) crime prevention and detection through law enforcement, both generally targeted towards volume crimes such as vehicle-related crime and residential burglary. By contrast, as noted in Chapter 1, community safety demonstrates a stronger interest in low-level crimes and disorders that particularly tend to feed public anxiety about, or fear of, crime. It is also prepared to countenance more 'social' approaches that do not simply look to block criminal opportunities, but seek also to address the more entrenched social causes of criminality, located particularly in families and neighbourhoods. Consequently, if we are interested in exploring the extent to which local crime control has moved more firmly in the direction of community safety, it makes sense to assess the extent to which it is now addressing such low-level disorders, and such social causes. The next two chapters, hopefully, do exactly that.

Chapter 5

Getting tough? Anti-social behaviour and the politics of enforcement

Introduction

In the previous two chapters we have examined the unfolding of New Labour's crime reduction policy from the centre downwards. Running parallel to this development, there has emerged a whole new infrastructure for the governance of anti-social behaviour (hereafter ASB), and it is this infrastructure, in which CDRPs are heavily involved, that forms the focus of this chapter's efforts. In practice, just as we found in the last chapter with regard to the links between crime reduction policy and police reform, it is difficult to disentangle the development of this infrastructure from developments in other fields. Squires and Stephen (2005) make this point with regard to the link between ASB policy and youth justice, but it applies equally to other domains, such as housing policy, policing and of course crime reduction. I have chosen to separate out ASB in part because it makes the whole thing more digestible, but in part also because the low-level problems that the label ASB represents are in theory a distinctive feature of community safety, and our interest in exploring them is motivated by an interest in establishing to what extent ASB policy does indeed 'drag' local crime control in the direction of community safety, and with what consequences.

As in the two previous chapters, the discussion is ordered in a broadly chronological way, so that we can see the developments and transformations that have taken place over time, and particularly so that we can isolate the pressures that have led to them. The chronology, however, is laced through with a sometimes wandering commentary that addresses broader issues that it is hoped will illuminate and help to make sense of this fascinating but deeply troubling new policy domain, and the various dilemmas and contradictions that it leaves in its broad wake.

The rise of the ASB problem

Official attempts at defining ASB often acknowledge the difficulty of the task, and then go on to list a range of putative ASBs, sometimes grouped into thematic categories. In reality, ASB covers a divergent array of problem issues that have been grouped together into a category that, like crime itself, unites these issues by virtue of the societal reaction against them. Thus, while crimes are acts united by legal sanctions taken against them, ASB is united, according to the Home Office at least, by reactions of 'harassment, alarm and distress', although evidently we are not all harassed, alarmed or distressed by the same things – just as we may disagree with the central state's definition of certain acts or behaviours as crimes.

The official label of ASB, as a description of these various problem issues, is relatively recent in origin, but there is a rich modern history of formal responses against such issues. Burney (2005), for example, links the current policy domain back to nineteenth-century measures taken against a 'breach of the peace', as well as to more specific pieces of legislation such as the 1824 Vagrancy Act. Revisionist historians, meanwhile, give the permanent police an instrumental role in the social and moral regulation and taming of the Victorian working classes (Cohen 1979), whilst Squires and Stephen (2005) connect contemporary developments with post-war concerns with relatively minor juvenile delinquency, although the welfarism underpinning those concerns (see also O'Malley 2005) stands in stark contrast to the enforcement orientation of contemporary policy, at least as directed from the top. Others (Burney 1999) connect ASB to developments in the administration and management of tenant behaviour in social housing, which has developed apace since the residualisation of the council housing stock following the enactment of the 'right-to-buy' legislation in the 1980 Housing Act – a 'triumph' of Conservative anti-welfarism.

The catch-all nature of ASB raises the possibility that the whole is somehow greater than the sum of its constituent parts. In other words, it gives a name to divergent concerns that renders them, somehow, more grave, in the same way that, say, the decline in the numbers of garden birds takes on a much more portentous aura once such a decline is linked to global warming. ASB, as a concept, describes but also simultaneously seems to amplify that which it constitutes.

If ASB is a new label but not a new problem, the obvious question to ask is why it has emerged as a new policy domain now, or more specifically over the last decade since the mid-1990s. One possible explanation is that the problems that constitute ASB may have worsened. This is certainly an impression that the Home Office has not tried hard to discourage. Indeed, the wave of ASB reforms from around 2002 onwards were largely justified by reference to the finding that, while officially recorded crime, and particularly volume crime, has fallen steadily since the mid-1990s, the public has failed to recognise this fact because ASB has got worse through this same period. The 'evidence' for this is found in BCS data that shows a high proportion of respondents perceiving crime to be still rising, which correlates with the date that shows increases in the proportion of respondents finding various forms of ASB (although they were not called that when the questions were first asked in earlier surveys) to be a problem in their residential areas. This is the 'reassurance gap', deemed to be caused in one way or another by ASB.

There is an obvious problem, however, in claiming that ASB has worsened by reference to BCS survey findings, because the survey measures perceptions, rather than the actuality of ASB, whatever that may be. For obvious criminological reasons I am not advocating here the objective measurement of 'harassment, alarm and distress', or conceiving that such a thing is even possible, but it is possible to compare ASB with crime on this point. For all their flaws, police crime statistics do have the merit, as far as policy-makers are concerned, of making crime governable, in a Foucauldian sense. But in the mid-1990s ASB was not governable in a similar way, because its diversity inevitably meant it appeared on to the radar screens of an array of governmental agencies, all with their own recording systems and practices, or, equally likely, the lack of them. This was brought to light to some extent by the infamous and methodologically questionable 'day count' (of which more below) in late 2003, which also threw up problems of double-counting, when complaints of ASB were reported to more than one agency, or when more than one complaint about the same phenomenon was registered with the same agency. Things may have improved to the extent, for example, that agencies have improved their recording practices, and importantly the police now have a recording standard for categories of incidents other than recordable crimes, but we are probably still some way from being able to make ASB governable in the same way that crime currently is.

In the absence of 'hard data' about the number of ASB incidents, we are left with 'soft' perceptions. These perceptions have become far more 'governmentally acceptable', as the BCS has evolved into an annual survey aimed at a much larger sample of the population (some 40,000 respondents), to set alongside police crime statistics, but they do remain vulnerable to environmental influences. It would hardly be a surprise, for example, if the amount of governmental 'noise' about ASB did not feed through into BCS respondents finding ASB to be more of a problem in recent years, particularly given the high media profile that New Labour has given to its ASB campaigns (although admittedly that profile has grown especially subsequent to 2002), and given the media's penchant for lurid headlines in their reportage of ASBO cases, which has provided their demonisation of youth, in particular, with a new lease of life. Furthermore, perceptions are also vulnerable to measurement error. Hunter (2001) compares the findings of the BCS, that indicate a general perception of ASB problems getting worse between 1994 and 2000, with the Survey of English Housing, which over the same period of time registered a *decline* in the perception of disorder problems. And even within the BCS there have been quite marked but possibly unlikely annual changes in perceptions, including – ironically – perceptions of ASB problems *improving* in the year *before* the launch of all the new ASB initiatives in 2002 (Squires and Steven 2005).

As we have seen, the community safety paradigm prioritises the fear of crime as a problem in its own right, and in so far as perceptions of disorder feed fear, concern and anxiety (as is generally presumed to be the case), then perceptions remain important regardless of their basis in factual or objective measures of ASB. Consequently, while we cannot be certain whether ASB problems have or have not worsened, we can say that it has nevertheless been problematised. The statistics may be shaky, but politicians have also been able to fall back on traditional readings of the nation's preoccupations, such as those emanating from doorstep canvassing at election times, or the alleged contents of MPs' postbags. On both less than scientific or verifiable counts, the message is that ASB is a big national concern. This is what Field (2003) says, it is what Labour Party canvassers found in the local and European elections of 2004 (Squires and Steven 2005), and it is probably what persuaded New Labour to put ASB at the heart of their 2005 general election campaign (Cummings 2005). But then, if the label draws such a wide boundary around itself, it is bound to constitute a whole that is much larger than the sum of its constituent parts. It is a very effective way of transforming private troubles into public issues (Mills 1959).

The ASB edifice

So, we know that ASB has been put on to the political agenda, and that New Labour politicians have played an instrumental role in this. Evidently, through ASB they have perceived an opportunity to pursue the twin imperatives of office-seeking and policy, and in pursuit of such ends they have constructed a coalition of interests around the issue, by building up the edifice of ASB in such a way that it incorporates a range of other policy areas, issues and interests. In particular, in this section I want to look at how the ASB edifice has been built to incorporate the fear of crime, nuisance neighbours, zero-tolerance policing, youth justice and, latterly, alcohol-related disorder.

Firstly, the ASB edifice incorporates the issue of the fear of crime. Fear of crime may have more to do with the ontological insecurities of late-modernity (Sparks 1992), but for New Labour it was, in the mid-1990s, a valuable motif for making sense of the Conservatives' failures in government. Before the mid-1990s they failed to stem the rise in crime, they risked creating a 'fortress mentality' out of a crime prevention policy based upon privatised prudentialism (Gilling 1997), and their social and economic policies established 'sink estates' and urban wastelands that provided plenty of environmental cues for fear and anxiety. As noted in Chapter 1, moreover, greater fear and anxiety may paradoxically be an unintended consequence of neo-liberalism's valorisation of freedom, which comes at the expense of security, and therefore induces such anxiety (O'Malley 2004), which may be easily directed at 'anti-social others'.

If citizens have been imprisoned within a climate of fear, New Labour has staked a claim to becoming their saviour, proposing without a hint of irony that 'securing people's physical security, freeing them from the fear of crime and disorder is the single greatest liberty government can guarantee' (Straw and Michael 1996: 6). For a left-of-centre political party, such a statement comes as a surprise, and tends to support O'Malley's (2005) claim that at the heart of the New Labour political project there is a disturbing lack of vision.

To what extent has New Labour cynically exploited the fear of crime? O'Malley (2005) opines that the focus on the fear of crime fills a void created by the political elite's abandonment of a more socially integrative and inclusionary vision of the future. In other words, New Labour's abandonment of social democratic aspirations for social justice, which as we saw in Chapter 2 was deemed a necessarily 'pragmatic' response to the constraining forces of globalisation, left it with little to offer except to assuage people's fears, as if the state has been reduced to a role of little more than precinct policeman (see Bauman 2000). O'Malley (2005: 19) contends that a 'society with no vision of a better world soon becomes hostage to its fears', and he compares such a (contemporary) society unfavourably with a welfarist era when crime was far less of a political issue because political elites subscribed to a vision of the good society. In such a society, crime's role was residual, not central, and there was no political need for elites to accentuate the fear of crime. Rather, crime policy was conjoined to social policy, as both pursued inclusionary ends. By contrast, the problematisation of fear, with no positive vision, fuels exclusionary responses, as we shall see below when we explore the range of ASB measures that New Labour has brought into existence.

O'Malley may be a little harsh on New Labour, because it is apparent (see below) that tackling the fear of crime is part of a communitarian political project that *does* offer something by way of an inclusionary vision, even though, as we have seen from Chapter 2, their particular brand of communitarianism is unlikely to deliver such a vision. Nevertheless, in attaching ASB to the fear of crime issue, New Labour was dressing in the right kind of clothes to attract the interest and support of left-leaning local community safety practitioners, many of whom had been inspired by left realist criminology's 'discovery' of the apparently rational links between incivilities and the fear of crime.

A second part of the edifice of ASB has been constructed around the issue of 'nuisance neighbours', which has brought those responsible for the management of social housing – particularly but not exclusively council housing (see Burney 1999) – more into the domain of local crime control. Nuisance neighbours might not be considered a particularly 'hot' criminological topic, but its place in popular consciousness is attested to by the array of voyeuristic 'neighbours from hell' programmes that have graced television screens over the last few years. In terms of social housing, as council housing has become increasingly residualised as a result of right-to-buy legislation and expenditure constraints that have ruled out any serious new building, so the problem of ASB in the neighbourhoods of the remaining stock has apparently worsened. This problem prompted the establishment in 1995 of the Social Landlords' Crime and Nuisance Group (SLCNG), specifically with the purpose of lobbying central government for additional powers to deal with ASB (SLCNG 2004). The Conservatives responded to this lobby with provisions in the 1986 Housing Act, such as introductory tenancies and extended grounds for property repossession from troublesome tenants (see Burney 1999). But this was a nettle New Labour was also keen to grasp, and prior to the 1996 Housing Act they issued their own policy document – *A Quiet Life* – which advocated 'tough action on criminal neighbours' (Labour Party 1995). It was in this document that New Labour first publicly floated a proposed 'community safety order' (later to be renamed as the ASBO), along with a 'parental responsibility order'.

The proposed new community safety order trumped the Conservatives' later response because in theory it extended the ASB crusade from areas of social housing to all tenure categories, thereby recognising that ASB was not a problem confined to council housing – so at least *exclusion* was going to be distributed more equitably under New Labour. This proposed new order, together with the changes in housing legislation that made repossession a more straightforward task, ensured New Labour's appeal to the SLCNG, which represented authorities that were responsible for in excess of three million tenancies across the UK.

A Quiet Life did not include any substantial evidence about the scale of the ASB problem, but instead relied upon the assertion that '[e]very citizen, every family, has the right for a quiet life – a right to go about their lawful business without harassment, interference or criminal behaviour by their neighbours' (Labour Party 1995: 1), before going on to examine two illustrative case studies of extreme ASB, one drawn from Jack Straw's own Blackburn constituency. And it is this moral claim, rather than any objective evidence, that really justifies the problematisation of ASB. The claim, moreover, is lent greater weight in the document by a critique of the criminal law because 'criminal procedures have never been designed to curb chronic and persistent anti-social criminal behaviour and so, as they stand, are themselves defective' (ibid.). This attack upon the alleged inadequacies of criminal procedure, and thus upon due process, became an increasingly significant theme once New Labour entered office.

Before we move on to consider the next part of the ASB edifice, the case of nuisance neighbours merits a few other relevant observations. Papps (1998) reminds us that ASB has always had a strong connection with social housing. Indeed, social housing, whether provided philanthropically in the nineteenth century, or by local authorities in the twentieth, was once regarded as the solution to the 'bad' and 'immoral' behaviour of the working classes. Slum clearance was as much an exercise in social hygiene as physical reconstruction. But from the 1960s onwards, the solution increasingly became the problem, and as the cracks in social housing literally started to show, so the focus of attention was directed more and more strongly on the problem estates.

As in other areas of social policy, the interventionist dialectic switches between explanations that individualise and pathologise housing problems, and explanations that are more structurally informed and conceive of tenants more as victims of circumstance, and of deprivation, in particular. While pathologising discourses have never been far from the surface, as evidenced in part by the persistence of the idea of a *culture of poverty*, there were a number of interventions between the 1960s and 1980s that sought to address some of the structural problems of social housing. These included attempts to correct the chronic under-provision of neighbourhood facilities; to improve housing management and tenant participation; and to facilitate local economic development and the provision of employment opportunities in depressed areas. However, as we moved into the 1990s, the discourse of nuisance neighbours and ASB started to shift the focus from problem areas to problem tenants (Papps 1998), and in so doing it consolidated a more individualising and pathologising approach that has fed the exclusionary dynamic that informs contemporary policy. In other words, in its pursuit of the ASB issue New Labour has served to undermine the pursuit of more structurally informed measures to address the problems of social housing, although their 'success' in this endeavour depends upon the extent to which the ASB agenda is challenged by competing agendas elsewhere within central government (e.g. in what is now the DCLG), and the extent of local resistance to such agendas.

A Quiet Life associated ASB strongly with residential neighbourhoods and neighbour relations, but the problem was not confined there for long. Alongside the fear of crime and nuisance neighbours, the third part of the ASB edifice took it out more decisively into wider public space, and connected it with contemporaneous developments in policing. In particular, in the mid-1990s certain parts of the police service were seeking to reassert sovereignty in the face of criticisms of police effectiveness that had surfaced during Kenneth Clarke's period in office as Home Secretary, although much of his intended reform programme was ultimately shelved. This was the time when the idea, if not the wholesale practice, of zero-tolerance policing crossed the Atlantic from the USA, and from New York City in particular.

A theoretical rationale for zero-tolerance policing may be found in Wilson and Kelling's (1982) broken windows theory, which is so well known that it does not require much in the way of elaboration here. The theory justifies the idea of 'nipping crime in the bud' by attending to minor disorders and incivilities that, if left unattended, would tip neighbourhoods into a spiral of decline resulting in the commission of much more serious crimes, although not necessarily by those responsible for the original disorders and incivilities. The validity of the theory has been questioned by many, as has the effectiveness of its expression through zero-tolerance policing (see Burney [2005] for a useful review), but these issues do not concern us at this point. For present purposes, the important point is that zero-tolerance policing arrived at a timely moment for New Labour. Both Jack Straw and Tony Blair visited New York to witness the zero-tolerance 'miracle', and both were seriously impressed by the claims made for it effectively to reclaim the streets from a list of social undesirables and outcasts who, after two decades of harsh neo-liberal social and economic policies, had made their uncomforting presence felt on the streets of towns and cities across the UK. Where a welfarist discourse might have spoken of the casualties of neo-liberalism, including the workless, homeless, de-institutionalised and unsupported, zero-tolerance policing provided us with a discourse that enabled such people to be represented as the enemy within, whose presence threatened a spiral of decline, presaging more serious crime. The 'winos' and 'squeegee merchants' that so upset Jack Straw were to New Labour what the striking miners had been to Thatcherism in 1984, and while welfarism might have sought inclusive measures to bring such people, often literally, in from the cold, zero-tolerance offered a tough, punitive, enforcement-oriented approach. Batons may have been the weapon of choice for the mounted police officers charging the pickets at Orgreave, but for these disorderly folk devils, the weapon was more 'civil' (no hint of irony here), arriving in the shape of what was to be the ASBO, and a range of other sanctions.

The point here, then, is that the emergent ASB agenda provided a means through which US-style zero-tolerance policing could be prosecuted in the UK, because the agendas fitted, and it required no great leap of imagination to see how remedies for nuisance neighbours could be taken out onto the streets not just of residential neighbourhoods, but also of town and city centres, leisure and retail districts, to address what came to be described in many places as 'quality of life' offences. The ASB agenda thus fitted the interests of those parts of the police service that wanted to reassert police sovereignty on the streets, although zero-tolerance was by no means welcomed by all sections of the police service (Pollard 1997), and the idea of re-directing police effort to 'low-level' disorder is not something that chimes well with the police occupational culture, or that fits with a performance management framework that prioritises volume crimes such as burglary and vehicle-related crime.

With its emphasis upon the quality of life, the ASB agenda also brought on board those who connected crime and disorder to broader economic fortunes. Back in 1988 the Safer Cities Programme had been launched in part to make cities places where enterprise could flourish (Gilling 1997), but now in the mid-1990s the ASB agenda promised to sweep the streets clean of those groups whose presence was offensive to enterprise and to business, and thus it garnered the support of urban growth coalitions, particularly comprising local authorities and business interests, and particularly manifested in the concerns and actions of a growing cadre of town centre managers.

The fourth part of the ASB edifice is largely the subject of Squires and Stephen's (2005) book. Their argument is that it has become increasingly hard to separate youth justice policy from the management of ASB because the latter has provided a further 'enforcement opportunity' to target problematic young people. Thus while in the 1980s an effective but relatively low-profile policy of non-intervention with troublesome young people had taken root, exemplified in particular by a liberal cautioning policy, in the 1990s this was ultimately reversed. The reversal was started by the punitive official response to the murder of Jamie Bulger and the 'discovery' of 'feral' and out-of-control youths on a number of housing estates across the country, but Squires and Stephen make special mention of the contribution of the Audit Commission's (1996) report, *Misspent Youth*. In the report, the Audit Commission took a critical swipe at youth justice policy, and seemed to accept that the idea of young people growing out of crime, that had informed the policy of non-intervention, was no longer applicable to young people in the 1990s. Quite to the contrary, the Audit Commission argued the case for swift intervention, and for 'nipping crime in the bud' with a much stronger preventive orientation. This rekindled interest in the identification of risk factors for youth criminality, and in the idea of the anti-social personality. Once again, New Labour was well placed to make the connections, this time between youth justice and ASB, and subsequently it undertook a reimagining of the youth justice system. This eventually saw life with the establishment of YOTs after the 1998 Crime and Disorder Act, and with the introduction of a number of measures, most notoriously the child curfews, that pushed the emphasis more from justice to prevention, in the management of troublesome young people. *A Quiet Life* had foreshadowed this in its suggested idea of a 'parental responsibility order'.

It would be wrong to suggest that the attachment of youth justice to the ASB agenda has brought with it the enduring support of youth justice professionals, since many of them demonstrate considerable disquiet about the problematisation of ASB, and the measures devised to tackle it, and there is often a manifest tension between local YOTs and CDRPs over the practice of local ASB policy. However, since many of the measures do not require the active involvement or support of YOTs, their support has not been vital to the construction of a broad ASB agenda such as the one described here. While most youth justice professionals would not identify themselves amongst the coalition of interests pushing the ASB agenda, the implied 'toughening up' of youth justice that is achieved by aligning it with the ASB agenda certainly plays well to the gallery of public opinion, and accords with the model of 'populist punitiveness' identified elsewhere by Bottoms (1995).

The fifth and final part of the ASB edifice was put in place some time after the other parts, but the fact of its inclusion bears testimony to the exceptional versatility of the concept of ASB. This part, which Burney (2005) suggests was only added from around 2002, is alcohol-related disorder, and particularly that associated with town centre disorder in the night-time economy, typically at its worst on a Friday and Saturday night, typically involving young adults, and typically involving interpersonal violence, with a liberal measure of vandalism and urination. While it may be the case that this alcohol-related crime in public has become worse over recent years, the delay in its inclusion in the ASB edifice may also have something to do with the fact that the night-time economy, which has assisted in the 'regeneration' of a large number of urban areas, currently contributes around 3% of the UK's gross domestic product (Hobbs 2004), and thus constitutes an economically powerful interest bloc against which government may be relatively reluctant to act – hence it remains relatively poorly regulated. The extension of the ASB label into this area, however, conveniently constructs the problem as one of individual misbehaviour, thus side-stepping the structural dynamic, in which the profitability of the night time economy is based on the active promotion of excessive drinking – although some ASB measures, it should be noted (see below), do target licensed premises as well as the more inebriate of their consumers.

To summarise this section, then, as New Labour approached office in 1997 it had managed to fashion a broad ASB agenda by attaching ASB to a range of divergent issues, namely the fear of crime, nuisance neighbours, zero-tolerance policing and youth justice, and since 1997 it has extended this label further, to incorporate alcohol-related disorder. This does not mean that New Labour was guaranteed the unconditional support of the likes of CSOs, managers of social housing, the police and youth justice professionals, but it does mean that such groups had an interest in an emergent ASB agenda. They were, as it were, a coalition of interested parties, and in so far as the agenda had yet to take firm shape in policy, at this stage there was neither full support nor complete opposition. Connecting ASB with these other issues, however, promoted it as something about which something should be done, and in the next section we will explore what exactly was done when New Labour took office.

ASB policy in practice

True to its word, on reaching office New Labour moved quickly to bring its ASB proposals into force. In September 1997 the government issued a consultation document on the proposed community safety order, and following the consultation, when the proposals were incorporated into the Crime and Disorder Bill, the name was changed to the anti-social behaviour order – one can only speculate why. Interestingly, while *A Quiet Life* had noted that the order's principal aims were punitive and preventive, the 1997 consultation document specified that, while the order was preventive, it was there mainly 'for the protection of the community from future anti-social conduct' (Home Office 1997), a subtle but significant change of emphasis that linked it to the strongly emergent theme of public protection in penal policy. There was also a shift from 'the neighbourhood' in the 1995 document, to 'the community' in 1997, which perhaps supports the argument above, regarding the encroachment of ASB into the wider public sphere, beyond residential areas.

The centrality of ASB to the New Labour mission is perhaps indicated by its positioning – as Section 1 – in the 1998 Crime and Disorder Act. The Act borrowed the wording of the 1986 Public Order Act to define ASB in terms of a person acting 'in a manner that caused or was likely to cause harassment, alarm or distress to one or more persons not of the same household as himself [*sic*]', and it restated the order's purpose by requiring 'that such an order is necessary to protect persons in the local government area in which the harassment, alarm or distress was caused or was likely to be caused from further anti-social acts by him [*sic*]'. In a legislative sleight of hand, therefore, 'the community' had suddenly grown to become 'the local government area'. ASBOs became operational from April 1999, and in anticipation of this, in the preceding month the Home Office issued procedural guidance to all local agencies involved – principally the local police and local authority, who were required to consult one another prior to applying for an order.

Although it was not tenure-specific, the ASBO had been presented in particular as an offering to social landlords, who had been impatient for more effective powers to tackle troublesome tenants. Perhaps not unreasonably, therefore, the Home Office expected to see something of an ASBO deluge after April 1999, but none materialised. By the end of 2001, 518 orders had been granted, a number the fell some way short of the 5000 anticipated by the Home Office. This was particularly surprising given that the 1999 guidance had, in another sleight of hand, made it clear that ASBOs could be used against young people, when previously it had been understood that young people were unlikely to form a major target of the ASBO (Burney 2004a) – although *A Quiet Life's* reference to an intended parental responsibility order suggests that young people were perhaps never far from policy-makers' minds.

As early as October 1999, Jack Straw wrote to local agencies requesting them to make more use of the ASBO powers that they had been granted (Burney 2005), seemingly confirming in the process that as far as the government was concerned, enforcement was all-important. Indeed, in many ways in this area it was, because ASB provided New Labour with an opportunity to deliver on both sides of the 'tough on crime, tough on the causes of crime' soundbite. This is because the early intervention discourses both of the new youth justice and of broken windows theory enabled ASB policy to be 'sold' as preventively addressing a cause of more serious crime, while the enforcement side of the ASBO was toughness personified, because a breach of the civil order was an imprisonable criminal offence. Yet this opportunity to deliver was being spoiled for New Labour because of local inactivity – local agencies did not appear to be 'playing ball'. In many instances, the view persisted that the ASBO was a measure of last resort, and in fact such a view had been promulgated in *A Quiet Life*, only for New Labour in office to perform something of a U-turn. Jack Straw also felt it necessary to allay concerns – presumably from the 'Hampstead liberals' that troubled him as much as the 'winos' and 'squeegee merchants' – about the potential infringement of human rights contained in the discretionary and wide-ranging conditions that could be attached to ASBOs.

Overall, it was not entirely clear whether local inactivity was attributable to resistance or problems with local capacity. At roughly the same time as ASBOs were *not* being applied for in the numbers anticipated by the government, the Crime Reduction Programme was *not* being implemented in the way the Home Office had expected, as we saw in Chapter 3. The latter was explained in terms of capacity issues, such as poor project management, information exchange and the like, and it is plausible to suggest that since CDRPs were the prime suspects in both instances, then the ASBO problem was likely to have been interpreted in a similar way. The response from the Home Office was to set up an action group under Lord Warner, and the main product of this action group was guidance about local protocols that would hopefully result in more effective local working relations, and more effective use of the ASBOs than hitherto. This guidance was issued in mid-2000, just after the publication of a more thorough review of ASB conducted by the SEU (2000) Policy Action Team 8 (PAT 8).

The SEU's interest in ASB was attributable to the identification of ASB as one of the contributory factors to social exclusion, because of its putative impact upon the fear of crime and neighbourhood decline, and because analyses of the BCS consistently showed that various indicators of ASB were perceived to be more of a problem in the most deprived and excluded neighbourhoods, as identified by the ACORN classification. This explicit recognition of the part of ASB in social exclusion would seem to support a community safety orientation to the problem. Significantly, moreover, ASB was a problem that was perceived to threaten the success of urban regeneration initiatives (Hunter and Nixon 2001). Like the 17 other PATs that had been set in motion by the SEU, therefore, PAT 8's work was to feed into the emergent NSNR (see Chapter 6), and as a cross-cutting theme, ASB fitted well into the SEU's wider brief to seek 'joined-up' solutions at the level of central government.

There were obvious and probably not coincidental overlaps between the guidance issued by Lord Warner's action group and some of the conclusions of the PAT 8 report, which, it was claimed, had been fully endorsed by the government (but see below). In particular, the PAT 8 report echoed a number of capacity themes that will be more than familiar to those who have read the numerous reports on cross-cutting policy issues where partnership working is required. Thus, there was no clear responsibility for ASB either at the centre or at the local level, and ASB was not a clear priority or 'core business' for any one agency. Hence it did not feature as a measure in any performance management regime – not surprising, given what we have said above about measurement difficulties. In terms of local practice, there was a lack of effective joint work, manifested in poor information collection and exchange, divergent practice across different areas, and ideological differences between partner agencies. Such problems can be made to fit an essentially managerialist diagnosis that in turn prescribes a number of measures for improving performance. However, as is so often the case (Gilling 2005), such managerialist approaches to best practice badly underestimate the contested politics that frequently underpin these cross-cutting problems. However, while this part of the PAT 8 report was essentially an orthodox managerialist account, other parts were more challenging to New Labour's growing obsession with enforcement.

To be more specific, the PAT 8 report offered a welfare liberal reading of the problem of ASB, consistent with a progressive community safety orientation to local crime control, and noting (SEU 2000: 8) that '[a]nti-social behaviour is often fuelled by wider problems of social exclusion and deprivation such as poverty, unemployment, family breakdown and school exclusions, drug dependency and community disorganisation', going on to add that '[t]he deep-seated problems need to be tackled for new measures to be effective'. This welfare liberal diagnosis is hardly radical, and on closer inspection it turns out to be not dissimilar to the list of social causes of crime identified by Straw and Michael (1996) only a year before they came to occupy the key hot seats at the Home Office. But now that New Labour was in power, the official hymn sheet had been changed, and unreconstructed talk of social causation had been largely expunged from governmental discourse. The SEU, however, evidently did not share the same inhibitions as New Labour's political leadership, and the PAT 8 report went on to argue the case for a three-pronged attack on ASB based upon the principles of prevention, enforcement and resettlement. Prevention was conceived as being primarily situational, using measures such as better street lighting, CCTV, and more sensitive housing allocation policies that did not lead to the concentration of a 'toxic mix' of local authority tenants. But there was also some space for social crime prevention measures that would help to build local communities, or that would provide school children with citizenship education, for example. Enforcement, meanwhile, was conceived in rather less punitive terms than those normally used by the Home Office. While ASBOs and injunctions were appropriate measures for the small 'hard core', enforcement was also recast as early intervention, relying more on 'softer' measures such as mediation, warnings and case conferences, which hinted at some form of family support. Resettlement, finally, was premised on the need to avoid 'perverse outcomes', where enforcement merely led to greater exclusion. Thus the report argued the need for oversight and support so that a small number of ASB hard cases could be reintegrated into society rather than being excluded from one neighbourhood after another in the fashion of some latter-day Vagrancy Act.

As already noted, the PAT 8 report makes the claim that its recommendations were accepted by the government, one of whose then junior ministers – the future Home Secretary Charles Clarke – was a member of the reporting team. But how credible is this claim, given Jack Straw's apparent enthusiasm for the enforcement option, and his relative neglect of both prevention and resettlement? The Home Office's news release that reported upon Jack Straw's launching of a new ASB action plan in 2000, to put the SEU's recommendations into effect, makes reference to the PAT 8 report '… which links effective prevention with tough enforcement' (Home Office 2000). The measured enforcement just described above, therefore, is recast as 'tough' enforcement, and resettlement is as good as airbrushed out, like the image of Trotsky from a Stalinist era photograph. The news release certainly makes no specific mention of a three-pronged attack, and in so far as resettlement gets a look in, its meaning becomes adjusted to '… preventing perpetrators repeat their behaviours in new accommodation or different neighbourhoods' (ibid.), which is not quite the same thing.

A comparison of the PAT 8 report with the Home Office news release provides a fascinating insight into the operation of the New Labour 'spin machine', but we are left with the problem, as is so often the case with New Labour, of separating the spin from the substance. Was this news release, and Jack Straw's incipient ASBO-mania, an opportunity to 'talk tough' to an imagined middle England that is presumed to be insecure and intolerant of anything with the slightest whiff of welfare liberalism, and to erect a clever smokescreen around what really could have been 'softer' policies that were less uncompromising and less punitive in their orientation? Or had New Labour adopted this neo-conservative moralism with some relish, as evidenced by David Blunkett's helpful suggestion that local practitioners who refused to make use of the ASBO should be sacked (Burney 2005)? These questions are difficult to answer, in part because between New Labour's political intentions and representations lies a local practice that mediates central policy with a local politics that inevitably diverts the course of any central policy stream. Thus we will never be able to deduce 'real' political intentions from 'what really happens' on the ground. But then opportunities for local practice are still set by a central policy steer, even if it is not quite the masterful steer imagined in the discourse of new public management, and for this reason it is necessary for us to examine the course taken by the centre as a response to the PAT 8 report.

One obvious difficulty with the PAT 8 report, from the government's point of view, was that it restricted its attention to ASB in residential neighbourhoods, and particularly deprived ones. This, perhaps, made a welfare liberal diagnosis more likely, as ASB was heavily entwined with other aspects of social exclusion, as the SEU had indeed recognised. But in line with the argument set out earlier in this chapter, the limitation here was that government policy in the area of ASB had moved from its earlier focus upon residential neighbourhoods, to a broader and more inclusive definition of ASB – although not the kind of inclusion that the SEU was keen to promote. In particular, as ASB policy moved into the youth justice sphere, and as it moved from the residential neighbourhoods and into town centres and other temples of consumption, so government's unwillingness to entertain a welfare liberal discourse grew. The PAT 8 report was undoubtedly an important moment in the development of ASB policy, since it launched a government action plan to take policy forward. But in which direction did such policy finally flow?

ASB policy developments since 2001, like those in the field of crime reduction, have been fast and furious, and it is not possible to provide a finely detailed description of them all without deviating too far from our purposes in looking at them. Broadly speaking, however, it is possible to characterise the policy developments that have occurred under two general themes. Firstly, a number of developments have worked to build up an ASB infrastructure, or perhaps more accurately a structure for the local governance of ASB. Secondly, policy developments have served to provide this structure with the tools to exercise its purpose of governing ASB – thus we have seen the emergence of a number of different measures for tackling ASB, many but not all of which have been oriented quite strongly towards enforcement. We will look at these two themes in a bit more detail over the pages that follow.

An infrastructure for the local governance of ASB

In terms of the structure for governing ASB at the national level, one of the most significant developments, following the recommendation of the PAT 8 report, has been the identification of the Home Office as the lead central government department on matters relating to ASB. In theory, this resolved a 'turf war' between the Home Office and what was the ODPM (and before that the Department of the Environment, Transport and the Regions [DETR]) over which central government department led policy developments (Burney 2005). In practice, however, because ASB, like crime, does appear to disproportionately affect deprived neighbourhoods, it is not so easy to shake off the interests of other government departments such as the ODPM (and now the DCLG) and their neighbourhoods agenda, which we previously encountered in Chapter 4. The question of which central government department takes the lead is an important one because these departments have different cultures and different discursive traditions. The Home Office may well have a much stronger enforcement orientation than, say, the DCLG, which may operate with a more welfare liberal perspective on the links between deprivation and ASB. Whichever department leads, therefore, it is bound to leave its distinctive mark on the domain, even if its influence is not finally determining on outcomes at the local level.

Following its nomination as lead central government department, the Home Office responded by establishing, at the beginning of 2003, the Anti-Social Behaviour Unit (ASBU), headed by Louise Casey who had previously had the distinction of being the government's 'homelessness tsar'. Just as, two decades earlier, the Home Office Crime Prevention Unit had been set up to spread the crime prevention message and to encourage the adoption of best practice at the local level, so broadly speaking the ASBU sought to do a similar thing with ASB, albeit through a more sophisticated political communications machine. Following the 2003 Anti-Social Behaviour Act, which consolidated and introduced a range of measures for tackling ASB (see below), the ASBU was heavily involved in leading the high profile Together Action Plan, which was an attempt to publicise the new range of ASB measures to local agencies, and to local communities. Publicity has continued to play a prominent part in ASB policy, and the Home Office appears to have operated on the assumption that strong publicity will put increased pressure upon local practitioners to use the ASB remedies that have been made available to them, because it provides local communities with a stick with which to beat local agencies that do not appear to be doing enough to tackle the problem locally. A cynic might see such publicity as an opportunity for the Home Office to bludgeon reluctant local agencies into submission, to accept the Home Office's essentially enforcement-oriented agenda.

Publicity, of course, is also an important part of politics and office-seeking, and at the beginning of 2006, following the high profile given to ASB in the previous year's general election, New Labour staked considerable political capital on the launching of a new Respect Action Plan. In many ways, Respect has provided little that is new in terms of concrete measures, involving instead the minor alteration of existing measures, and their repackaging into a cross-departmental initiative that emphasises, in particular, the value themes of good parenting; school discipline; pro-social activities for young people; active communities; and, last but by no means least, a heavy dose of enforcement for those who do not take to such values. But while Respect may not have much that is new in the policy cupboard, it may be regarded as being particularly significant for the moral agenda that it endeavours to prosecute, and with which the Prime Minister Tony Blair is closely, and personally, identified. It could even be regarded as his equivalent of John Major's ill-fated *back to basics*, and where the latter ran aground on the rocks of 'cash for questions' and the sexual indiscretions of government ministers (not to mention of the Prime Minister himself, as Edwina Currie later revealed); the former hit troubled waters in the 'cash for honours' affair, not to mention the sexual indiscretions of the former Deputy Prime Minister. Plus ça change.

Moving from the centre to the localities, the structure for governing ASB has developed in a number of different ways. Again following the recommendations of PAT 8, CDRPs have been obliged to nominate named individuals to coordinate local ASB action, although a carrot for this was provided in the form of a 'top-up' to each CDRP's BSC funding allocation from 2002. Following a commitment made in the 2001 Labour Party election manifesto, localities have also been under pressure to organise their responses to ASB through multi-agency ASB units, and many have indeed done this. Given that local housing authorities have been building up their enforcement machinery for ASB since the mid-1990s, the obvious option in many cases was to base local units around the activities of local authority housing departments (Papps 1998). However, given the necessary focus of such departments on areas of council housing, the danger here has been that ASB policy has been pursued much more vigorously in areas of council housing than elsewhere, thus contributing to the problem of justice by tenure category, although this problem is a long-standing one, and is certainly not attributable only to ASB policy. As any criminology student will be able to tell you, nevertheless, such discrimination is likely to result in a self-fulfilling prophecy.

Having been required to nominate local ASB coordinators, CDRPs were also put under pressure to include ASB in their crime reduction strategies from 2002 onwards, although it is likely that many would have been doing this anyway, given that ASB had been mentioned in the statutory guidance that many CDRPs effectively used as a template for their local audits from 1999. Following the 2002 Police Reform Act, moreover, ASB was placed within the radar of the first of the three-year rolling National Policing Plans, and it was made clear to the police that HMIC inspections would be looking to see how well local forces and BCUs were doing in tackling ASB. The pressure placed upon local agencies to address ASB has continued more recently, moreover, with 'building respect and tackling ASB' both included as mandatory outcomes expected for the LAAs that have been operating since 2005 in some localities and that are due to have been rolled out nationally by 2007. In addition, the 2006 Police and Justice Act amended the general crime prevention duty of Section 17 of the 1998 Crime and Disorder Act to cover also ASB, alcohol-related crime and the misuse of drugs; it also required police authorities to include ASB as an issue on which they were obliged to consult their local populations; and it also empowered local residents to invoke a 'community call-to-action' to their local councillors, and possibly through them to a committee of the local authority charged with scrutinising the performance of CDRPs, in cases where there was sufficient local feeling that local responsible authorities had failed adequately to address local concerns about ASB. In this way, then, 'steering' under New Labour can be seen in terms of exerting pressure from the top down, but also from the bottom up.

In the past, one problem with efforts to prioritise ASB was that there was no good measure to include within a performance management regime, to which local agencies could then be held to account. However, after 2002 the Home Office decided to use BCS questions on feelings of public safety as a performance measure for ASB, and this measure was incorporated both into a revised set of PSA targets, and BVPIs, which applied both to local police services and local authorities. Judging local police and CDRP performance on local perceptions, however, brings its own dangers, since increased activity against ASB – its increased local problematisation, often involving increased local media reportage – might actually enhance perceptions rather than diminish them. Perhaps for this reason, performance measurement also falls back on annually surveyed counts of the use of various ASB measures by local agencies. It is a count, in other words, of enforcement activity.

ASB policy provides a good example of the much-noted shift from government to governance, or for that matter from police to policing. Thus while the police service remains an important local agency in ASB policy, particularly because it has to initiate or be consulted over some of the ASB enforcement measures, in recent years there has been a clearly discernible shift towards dispersing ASB powers across a range of other agencies. The following agencies (and possibly some others) are all involved in some aspect of policing ASB:

- district, borough or unitary councils;
- county councils;
- town and parish councils;
- the British Transport Police;
- other social landlords such as housing associations or Housing Action Trusts (HATs), and Tenant Management Organisations (TMOs);
- YOTs;
- schools;
- PCSOs; and
- 'community safety accredited' non-police employees, such as neighbourhood wardens, park rangers, and private security guards.

These bodies may acquire certain enforcement powers, such as the ability to issue PNDs or fixed penalty notices (FPNs), but more generally they may also be involved in various ways in the surveillance of public space, with their presence either acting as a deterrent, or facilitating the gathering of information and the communication of risks to agencies that may be formally empowered to tackle ASB, such as the police service. Most of these bodies are public, and thus publicly accountable for their actions, although since many may not be regarded as normally accountable for the policing of ASB, it may be that there are certain gaps in the accountability process. Not all of the bodies are publicly accountable, however, and it must be a cause for concern that private security guards, operating in a sector that is not renowned for the quality of its self-regulation, could in theory be empowered to enforce ASB measures that could, if not complied with, result in criminal sanctions.

The ASB policy toolbox

Moving now to the measures that have been devised to tackle ASB, it is important to recognise that some are not new: there was widespread suspicion that the 2003 Anti-Social Behaviour Act, and the White Paper that preceded it, involved a fair amount of window-dressing to create something that would make the necessary 'splash' demanded from high political expectations – just as, in 1998, there was a concern that ASBOs were unnecessary given changes that had already been made to housing legislation (Burney 1999). Some measures, moreover, are designed to be used in concert with others, and for this reason their likely effect needs to be considered in combination, rather than in isolation. And some measures have been piloted in select parts of the country, rather than being more generally rolled out. Thus, with these provisos in mind, it is possible to put together the following list of ASB measures which again is probably not exhaustive, but which does at least convey a sense of the general tenor or orientation of the changes that have taken place (the focus here is only on new measures, but Burney [1999] provides a good account of the extant ones):

- revisions to ASBOs, generally making them easier to process, and more widely applicable, particularly as they may now be attached to come into effect subsequent to criminal convictions (so-called 'CRASBOs');
- the introduction of on-the-spot FPNs and PNDs for a range of ASB issues including unauthorised absences from school, cycling on pavements, littering, graffiti, public nuisance, public disorder, and, of course, dog fouling;
- powers to regulate the consumption of alcohol in public places, including powers of confiscation;
- powers to close 'crack houses';
- powers for the police and local authority to designate specified areas as the subject of a dispersal order, with attendant powers to disperse problematic groups (i.e. more than one individual) from that area;
- powers for police officers to arrest those found in possession of an air weapon or imitation firearm; and
- powers for environmental health officers to close licensed premises where a public nuisance is being caused by noise.

Most of these are predominantly punitive and enforcement-oriented measures, whilst some facilitate the police tactic of disruption, which has moved to the fore in recent years as a sometimes more efficient alternative to detection (see Innes and Sheptycki 2004). But there are some measures that may be regarded as somewhat more supportive or preventive, at least in theory. These include mediation, which is a preferred course of action for a number of local agencies. They also include a number of measures included in the Respect Action Plan, including the use of a Youth Opportunities Fund to support pro-social activities amongst young people; the employment in 77 local authority areas of 'parenting experts' to work with families with young people 'at risk of' ASB; and the establishment of 50 family intervention projects to provide intensive work with particular, prolifically anti-social 'problem families' (Home Office 2006a).

They also include parenting orders, although they are not often regarded as being especially supportive, and the implied responsibilisation and 'conditional inclusion' (Hughes 2006), rather than support, is sometimes criticised for straining relations between family members, rather than helping to build them. Also, under the 2003 Anti-Social Behaviour Act it is possible for YOTs to obtain parenting orders where young people have committed anti-social or criminal 'offences', but where they have not actually been convicted of them. In future perhaps young people should think twice before being asked by criminologists to fill in a self-reported offending questionnaire! Furthermore, since parenting orders are often combined with ASBOs, the supporting side of the sanction may easily be undone by the punitive and prohibitive aspects of the ASBO.

The same basic point applies to the individual support order (ISO), which was created for 10 to 17 year olds by the 2003 Criminal Justice Act as a means of addressing the causes of ASB in a more positive way, such as through counselling for behavioural problems. Its combination with an ASBO, however, does not necessarily provide the ideal conditions under which such positive work can be undertaken.

Acceptable behaviour contracts (ABCs), which were first pioneered locally by the London Borough of Islington, and picked up and promoted by the Home Office since 2000, have been presented by many as a less draconian measure than the ASBO, but as the enlightening research of Squires and Stephen (2005) shows, appearances can be deceptive. The ABC cases that they examined offered little or nothing by way of support for compliance, which is remarkable given that the scheme they researched was part of a New Deal for Communities (NDC) scheme, which should have been comparatively awash with social support for such relatively deprived communities. Furthermore, it was found that the ABCs were effectively backed up by threats of lost tenancies or ASBOs in cases of non-compliance, leaving parents of what were often difficult young people, with sometimes severe behavioural problems, too scared to let their children out of the house. In such situations, it is difficult to see ABCs as anything more than a pitifully thin velvet glove concealing an iron fist.

Concluding discussion

If we compare the progress of government policy against the direction envisaged in the PAT 8 report it is difficult to avoid the conclusion that, despite apparently accepting these recommendations, New Labour has selected those recommendations that have fitted its own vision, which we shall come to in a moment. Rather than PAT 8's imagined three-pronged attack, we have the construction of a governmental structure which has been made far more accommodating of an enforcement-oriented approach, and less accommodating of a welfare liberal approach, based on social prevention and resettlement or rehabilitation. In other words, and with reference to the central theme of this book, if this is community safety it does not look like a particularly progressive version of it: it is more about the enforcement of a moral authoritarian 'tough love' agenda, which probably too frequently propels those unwilling or unable to comply towards custody.

Hughes (2006) is quite right to stress that we should be careful not to mistake central government rhetoric for local practice, because localities have their own distinct geo-histories and cultures. This is ably demonstrated, for example, by Burney (2005) in her comparison of differences between practitioners in Nottingham and Milton Keynes, and it is quite likely that the rather harsh approach to ABCs observed by Squires and Stephen (2005) is not necessarily repeated in all other locations. However, nor can we ignore the pressure that has been put upon localities to adopt an enforcement approach towards ASB: central government has undoubtedly succeeded in pressurising local areas into applying for more ASBOs, while the use of other measures is also increasing. The unevenness in the take-up of ASBOs and other sanctions suggests that some local areas are less receptive to this central pressure than others, while others such as Manchester have been so enthusiastic that they have barely needed any such pressure to reach for the ASBO. Similarly, it is apparent from the figures cited in Burney (2005) that some police force areas have been particular enthusiasts for CRASBOs, while others have used them hardly at all.

If the local take-up of ASB measures is one indicator of New Labour's 'success' in driving forward its ASB agenda, another may be the way ASB as an issue has crept up the political agenda. As noted earlier, it figured prominently as a doorstep issue in the local and European elections, and it was prominent in the general election of 2005. Given that ASB is defined so broadly, it is perhaps unsurprising that ASB has figured so prominently, because its breadth is such that it is likely to be encountered, and indeed possibly even stepped in, in virtually anyone's daily routine activities in public space. But its political prominence probably also bears testimony to the high profile publicity campaigns, such as the Together and Respect Action Plans: the message transmitted is that 'ASB is a problem' (albeit a particular kind of individualised, behavioural problem), and the message received back is 'it certainly is'. And it is this that makes the promotion of ASB policy a high-risk strategy, as Tonry (2004) has noted.

But if this is all a success, it comes at a cost for those on the receiving end. Roughly half of those receiving ASBOs are young people under the age of 18 years, and according to Campbell's (2002) Home Office study, nearly two-thirds of recipients have mental health problems or have problems with drug or alcohol misuse. Like many other campaigning groups, ASBO Concern (2005) also draw attention to the vulnerability of ASBO recipients. The needs of such vulnerable people remain unmet when ASBOs are used primarily to exclude or for reasons of public protection or reassurance (see Hughes [2006] for a brief discussion of some local case study research). When evidence suggests, furthermore, that ASBOs are more vigorously pursued in areas of council housing because this is where most of the local governance structures are most likely to be located (Burney 2005), then a picture builds up of ASB policy having the very same perverse effect that the PAT 8 report warned about, where exclusionary measures are applied to already excluded people – a criminological double whammy if ever there was.

Indeed, one irony may be that where it was once thought that ASB threatened efforts at urban regeneration by providing environmental cues of unsafety that were 'bad for business', that threat now comes from ASB *policy*, where through measures such as dispersal orders and ASBOs a geography of ASB is mapped out that plots urban danger zones, as the new no-go areas. More specifically, in so far as ASB policy is prosecuted more enthusiastically in areas of social housing, it may be counter-productive to *social* regeneration, rather than *physical* regeneration, which operates more comfortably with such an exclusionary dynamic. Certainly the frequency of ASBO breaches, and the almost unenforceable nature of conditions attached to some ASBOs does not serve to reassure or protect the public as much as government might like to think. It is no surprise, as recent research has suggested (Youth Justice Board 2006), that in such a context ASBOs take on the status of badges of honour: criminologists familiar with their subcultural studies would see this as a classic inversion of conventional routes to success and status, as one means of resolving the strain that excluded people undoubtedly encounter in their daily lives.

Although it is difficult not to be pessimistic, the picture is not entirely a negative one. Firstly, the worst excesses of the Home Office's enforcement-orientation can be offset to some degree by the less exclusionary approach of the ODPM, evidenced through constructive programmes of social support such as the Supporting People Programme. The recent neighbourhoods agenda, and the programme of civil renewal, both seek genuinely to empower local people to become more than passive recipients of public services, and to become involved in shaping the kinds of public services they do want, which could also mean a more welfare liberal approach to ASB, seen for example in the provision of better leisure facilities for young people, who remain ill-served by patchy and under-funded youth services (see Squires and Stephen 2005). Secondly, where local agencies have been involved, then just as local crime prevention partnerships in the 1980s and early 1990s used to challenge the hegemony of situational crime prevention with a constructive social rejoinder, so in the multi-agency case conferences that are sometimes used to review ASB cases, more constructive non-enforcement approaches to ASB may be pursued. Some localities, for example, have sought to introduce their own versions of the successful Dundee Families Project (Dillane *et al.* 2001) that provides intensive family support for those in danger of homelessness in cases of alleged ASB, and have actively resisted the ASBO route where possible. This project, it should be noted, was publicised by Crime Concern (2002) in a guide entitled *Tackling Anti-Social Behaviour*. Similar family support has also been provided by the voluntary organisation National Children's Homes (NCH) Action for Children (Burney 2005), and this has also been well received.

Burney (2005: 63) notes that '[i]t has taken the Labour government many years to come round to the realisation that there are only a relatively few such people ['problem families'], and that they need social support as well as enforcement'. To some extent this is recognised at the rhetorical level in the Respect Action Plan, where family intervention projects have followed the Dundee model, and where there is a recognition of the need for such things as pro-social leisure facilities for young people. Yet, too often this professed intent to tackle the deeper causes of ASB is undermined by the latent threat of enforcement. And this is where the broad label of ASB does progressive governmental aspirations a disservice, because it feeds a *general* discourse of enforcement against a *general* problem of moral decline and misbehaviour, when discrete issues such as 'problem families' really need to be separated out and dealt with according to their discrete causes and manifestations. At present, while there may be some recognition of the need for social support for these people, an unhappy halfway house is reached where, as in the case of parenting orders, 'support' may be combined with enforcement, with the latter providing an impossibly inflexible context in which to pursue the former. The representation of what might once have been considered social policy issues linked to questions of parenting, schooling and leisure facilities as 'the causes of ASB' is an example of the criminalisation of social policy.

This brings us to the question of what ASB policy is really all about. When it started out in *A Quiet Life*, it seemed to be primarily about addressing the inadequacies of the criminal law to reach down to problems that required some kind of authoritative intervention, but too often did not get one, because of such legal inadequacies, and because minor disorders have become neglected by the police in particular. But as the ASB edifice has grown, or as the juggernaut has rolled on, so it has taken on a more central place in New Labour's communitarian project, so that ASB policy is now conceived as part of a moral campaign to tackle social disintegration, and to rebuild 'the community', that always remains so ill-defined. It seeks to do this by providing tools, in the form of a local ASB structure and various ASB measures, that can be drawn upon *by* 'the community' to tackle the problems found *in* their community or neighbourhood. This is why active citizenship and civil renewal are so important – because they require citizens to take active responsibility for the problems they find, and to pressurise public agencies to apply the necessary ASB measures. The recipients of these measures, moreover, are responsibilised to fulfil their contractual obligations to desist from the behaviour that has been problematised, or to pay their fines and learn from the experience.

The presence of this communitarian vision, in which responsibility plays a key part, suggests that O'Malley (2005) may go too far in suggesting that ASB policy, which particularly plays off the fear of crime, offers no vision. But the problem remains as to whether the vision of building communities out of their responses to ASB is ever likely to be feasible, as if it is ASB that is holding communities back (because of the disintegrative impact of fear), and as if doing something about ASB will help to build the social capital upon which healthy communities are supposed to thrive. There are some major problems with this vision.

First, the vision of drawing communities together through their response to ASB commits the sin of defining communities only in terms of an inclusionary and exclusionary dynamic. The included only know they are the included because of their differentiation from excluded 'others', and keeping 'the community' together in this way requires a continual process of 'othering' that is far from socially integrative, particularly in a fragmented (Burney 2005) and diverse (Hough and Jacobson 2004) society where the scope for divisive othering is considerable. In such a vision, the looseness and breadth of the concept of ASB enables it to be used too easily as the basis of this othering. It may be argued in response that ASB policy is not so much about exclusion as 'conditional inclusion' (Hughes 2006), so that, for example, those that comply with the conditions of an ASBO are brought back into the community fold. ASBOs, seen in this light, are more about 'tough love'. However, given PAT 8's concerns about the perverse effects of exclusion (SEU 2000), and given the impossibilism of many of the conditions attached to ASBOs, the fact that a high proportion of ASBOs are breached, and that a high proportion of such breaches result in custodial sentences, lends support to the argument that such love is decidedly more *Joy Division* (Love Will Tear Us Apart) than *Captain and Tennille* (Love Will Keep Us Together). The former wins on quality, the latter wins on sentiment.

It is also difficult to see recipients of ASB measures being particularly happy about the prospects of this conditional inclusion. If the vulnerability of a large proportion of ASBOs recipients is not addressed, then their inclusion in 'the community' still leaves their needs largely unaddressed, and their deprivation and social exclusion still largely intact. In the same way, as Squires and Stephen (2005) eloquently argue, the 'something for something' logic of conditional inclusion does not work well for young people, who are the most likely targets of ASB measures, because young people are generally disengaged from the social policy process, and the areas of provision that are most applicable to them, such as leisure and youth services, are often poorly provided or unavailable, leaving them with little to do but hang around, generating fear and anxiety elsewhere in 'the community'.

An alternative to New Labour's communitarian vision is provided by Hughes (2006), who, as we have seen in Chapter 2, argues that even if New Labour's moral authoritarian communitarianism is highly suspect, critics should be careful of throwing the communitarian baby out with the bath water. For Hughes, communitarianism does not have to be constructed upon the inclusionary/exclusionary dynamic of a putative consensual entity, where, to put it crudely, you are either 'in' or you are 'out'. Rather, it needs to be built upon the multiple identities that are formed both individually and socially in diverse late-modern societies, which makes community membership a fluid thing, and which means that communities effectively act as checks on one another. Within such a vision there exists a possibility (but only a possibility) that communities can act as sites of resistance to neo-liberal and neo-conservative discourses, that flow so freely through contemporary crime control policy.

Central government's ASB policy may indeed be enforcement-oriented, and it is highly influential upon local practitioners, but due to central government's power-dependence it is not completely all-powerful and determining, and communities do not have to draw upon it for othering, as if that is the only way they can keep themselves together. Rather, and this is why Hughes (ibid.) places such importance upon local politics and the construction of advocacy coalitions, they can use it to pursue more welfare liberal approaches, which recognise that certain features of what New Labour calls ASB may indeed be local problems, but that addressing them does not necessitate an enforcement response. In this way, perhaps, social policy could be brought back in, but in a far less paternalistic way as it is made to serve the ends of communities, rather than being bureaucratically determined. New Labour's civil renewal agenda may be on the right tracks here, but as a challenge to populist punitiveness it is undermined by an adherence to the controlling logic of new public management, which just replaces bureau-professional paternalism with managerial paternalism, and which over-emphasises the pursuit of civility through the pursuit of a more easily measured and targeted incivility, as opposed to, say, a more normative rights-based model of welfare.

The theme of welfare takes us on to the subject of our next chapter. Although, as noted earlier in this chapter, ASB can be presented as a cause of (more serious) crime against which New Labour can present itself as being tough, more usually 'tough on the causes of crime' has been interpreted as addressing the social causes of crime, a more traditional Old Labour preoccupation. Our discussion of ASB in this chapter suggests that this area of policy, with its heavy enforcement orientation, is not addressing these causes, because of its de-emphasis of social prevention and rehabilitation or resettlement. But this does not necessarily mean that the social causes of crime are not being addressed elsewhere. Crime control is not the only home of social policy and nor, for certain good reasons that we shall begin to explore in the next chapter, is it ever a particularly desirable home. Although nearly 20 years of Conservative rule have left their mark on the welfare state, talk of the death of social policy is much exaggerated, and under New Labour there has been a renewed engagement with welfare that is of clear relevance to our understanding of New Labour's approach to controlling crime.

Chapter 6

Going soft? Tackling the causes of Labour's crime and disorder problem

Introduction

The Conservatives' populist punitiveness of the 1990s was premised upon a right realist criminology that attributed the causes of crime to the wickedness of those that John Major, in the wake of a moral panic about youth crime in the early 1990s, required us to 'understand a little less and condemn a little more', and to the 'criminals' that the then Home Secretary Michael Howard reminded us, for we had obviously forgotten, were the cause of crime. For their part, the political elite of New Labour may well have seen the office-seeking value, or even necessity, of engaging in such discourse in order to be seen to out-tough the Conservatives on the law and order issue. Yet deeper within the psyche of a political party that in 1997 was still recognisably social democratic, on the social if not the economic front, there was a tradition of left-of-centre thinking that had not given up altogether on questions of aetiology. In the 1990s, this tradition lived on in the construction of crime as a *wicked issue* that defined simple solutions, including punitive ones. This much was acknowledged even among the political elite, such as by Straw and Michael (1996), in an influential policy document published before Labour had seized the reins of power in 1997. And moving into Labour's second term, it was acknowledged too by Tony Blair in his speech launching the 2001 White Paper *Criminal Justice: The Way Ahead* (Home Office 2001b). In this speech, Blair proposed a recognisably 'social' approach to tackling the 97% or so of crime that never results in a warning, a caution or a conviction, and past which floats the tough-talking punitive rhetoric of politicians, as if it is just so much hot air.

The purpose of this chapter is to assess, critically, what New Labour has done to address the wider social causes of crime, or at least the causes of *New Labour's* 'crime and disorder problem' (for all crime problems are politically constructed), which in both policy and political rhetoric has been identified in, and sourced in large part to, the deprived urban neighbourhoods of the UK. Criminology stakes a claim for the intellectual ownership of much of this terrain, not least because criminologists have spent the last two centuries searching for the causes of crime, nearly always in towns and cities, even if all too frequently they have been looking in the wrong places, and often continue to do so. But one aspect of crime's 'wickedness' as an issue is the fact that the pursuit of crime's 'causes and cures' quite rapidly moves outside of the criminological and criminal justice domains, into the wider political, social and environmental structures that frame such neighbourhoods. Consequently, we shall be doing the same as the narrative unfolds.

Another aspect of crime's wickedness as a policy issue is to be found in the fact that its relationship to the social is one of both cause and effect. That is to say that crime may be caused by certain putative social conditions, as we shall see below, but it also can have a detrimental effect on the same, or other, social conditions. Straw and Michael (1996: 5) acknowledge this when they note: 'Poverty and lack of opportunity cause crime. But crime and disorder worsen poverty and reduce opportunity further.' This is not especially surprising, because crime is a social phenomenon, and abstracting it from other social conditions is in many ways an unhelpful and artificial, not to mention dangerous, pursuit, as we shall come to see later in the chapter. Crime is significant not only for its causes, but also for its effects on victims and social spaces, and in the above quote Straw and Michael may be offering a nod to 'the square of crime', and tacit recognition of left realism which, as Taylor (1999: 226–7) claims, was an attempt to persuade Labour '... of a more imaginative and comprehensive ... *national* project of social reform in the sphere of crime control, mobilised through the national state' (original emphasis).

Without giving away the plot, as thin as it is, I do not mean to suggest that Labour has embraced exactly the kind of social reform project envisaged by Taylor or other left realists, but it has come to acknowledge that wicked issues such as crime do indeed require imaginative responses, if by this is meant a *joined-up* response, this term having been first used by Tony Blair when announcing the establishment of the SEU in 1997. The term emphasises the fact that problems such as crime cannot be tackled alone through the institutions, procedures and practices of the criminal justice system, with such a fact being a well-established 'truth' of the crime prevention domain that rose to prominence at the end of the 1970s, partly as a response to the *nothing works* crisis (Gilling 1997). Mention of crime prevention reminds us of that policy history, and may prompt the alert reader into the thought that surely CDRPs were set up in 1998 to provide just such a joined-up approach to the problem of crime.

I do not rule out the possibility that in some geo-historical contexts (Edwards and Hughes 2005) some local CDRPs have managed to engage in just such an approach, but as the review of policy in the last few chapters has hopefully demonstrated, CDRPs have had to contend with a strong steer from the centre that has pushed them firmly in the direction of a mainly situational and enforcement-oriented crime and disorder reduction approach, which makes it harder for them to carve out an alternative social agenda, although more space has potentially been provided for this as crime reduction has become entwined in the broader processes of police and local government reform. Others might argue, however, that as government policy has increasingly addressed the local authority and the police as the two original responsible authorities, and as its intentions in the 2006 Police and Justice Act seek to embed CDRPs more within established structures of local government, so the idea of CDRPs representing any more expansively imagined joined-up approach to crime is stretched to the limits of credibility. In other words, again notwithstanding the possibility of more creative local practice, if we want to examine central government's policy in respect of the causes of crime we need to look beyond the confines of government policy with respect to CDRPs, whatever original promise they held for joined-up government.

If CDRPs, and for that matter local ASBUs, form one stream of central government's local crime control policy, then another stream is formed around a collection of initiatives that, to greater or lesser degrees of directness, seek to address the social causes of crime. There is always the possibility, of course, that these streams converge when they meet locally, and central government's aspiration is, indeed, that joined-up government should become joined-up policy (Clark 2002). This is what the establishment of LSPs and the neighbourhoods agenda may be seeking to achieve. But joined-up government at the centre does not necessarily mean joined-up policy, and in the case of the two policy streams just described, it may be, as we shall explore later, that they do not even flow in the same direction.

As one might expect from a wicked issue such as crime, while attempts may be made to tackle its social causes, such causes are not necessarily conceived in a single coherent explanatory discourse, neatly packaged up like the treatment of a criminological perspective in a textbook. However, in so far as it may be possible to impose some kind of conceptual unity on New Labour's project in this area, the idea of social exclusion has come to play a central role in accounts. Consequently, before we move on to look in more detail at the programmes and initiatives that have been directed at the local crime problem from beyond the criminal justice system, we need to explore and further unpack the concept of social exclusion which, had Jack Straw been more up on his social policy literature, he would surely have used in the above quotation, in preference to the distinctly passé concept of poverty, which is not a favourite of the New Labour lexicon.

The problem of social exclusion

Like crime prevention, social exclusion is a slippery concept, meaning different things to different people at different places and different times. The concept started to enter the vocabulary of social policy academics and governmental agents (whether practising or aspiring) in the UK in the 1990s, though it was not an idea that the Conservatives used then, just as it is not an idea that the Bush government in the USA uses now (Byrne 2005). Initially it was more familiarly, and somewhat differently, used in continental Europe, but it has now become a central focus of New Labour's policy agenda. For some, it replaces the negative term of underclass, for others it provides a more sophisticated understanding of the multi-dimensionality of poverty and deprivation, while for others it is a proxy term that conceals what Marxists call the reserve army of labour.

As the terminology implies, exclusion refers to being in some way left out or marginalised: its primary referent is its opposite, namely inclusion, which is the preferred end-state, although there might be considerable disagreement over what ideally one might be included into. Levitas (2005) suggests that the language of social exclusion tends to structure our understanding of a problem that is residual, because it conveys the impression that most of 'us' are included; and of a solution that is conceptually (if not necessarily practically) straightforward, in so far as the excluded must become included. This depends to some extent upon how the message is read, however. Policy-makers might like to convey such an impression, but this is certainly not how critical social scientists such as Byrne (2005) read it, because the problem is endemic, and the solution is one of political struggle.

The meaning of social exclusion depends very much upon the political understanding that is poured into it. The best, and best known, typology is probably that provided by Levitas (2005), who distinguishes between a redistributivist discourse (RED), a moral underclass discourse (MUD), and a social integrationist discourse (SID). Each of these is worth unpacking in a little more detail, though the reader is referred to Levitas for a fuller exposition, and is urged to accept Levitas's caution in treating the typology as ideal typical – the use of the discourses in practice is often a good deal more murky and ambiguous, and probably, in the case of New Labour, deliberately so. The different discourses operate through different linguistic usages of the term exclusion: for some, exclusion is conceived as an outcome, and the usage is adjectival; whereas for others, it is conceived more as a process, and the usage is as a verb, wherein exclusion is something *done* to others.

According to a RED interpretation, social exclusion stems from relative deprivation, measured not only in terms of income, but also in terms of aspects of social participation, so that in addition to being poor people may be effectively shut out from access to good quality public services such as housing, education, health and transport (and of course policing); may lack political voice; and may suffer from discriminatory or unfair treatment. The emphasis on social exclusion for many commentators is progressive because it usefully extends the focus here from class inequalities to inequalities based upon other aspects of social differentiation such as gender, 'race', age or disability. Inclusion, according to this interpretation, may require vertical income redistribution, and, broadly speaking the restitution of full citizenship rights (civil, political and social) to those who, in LeGrand's (1982) terms, have been victim to a 'strategy of equality' that sees the benefits of social welfare spending too frequently going to those least in need of them, but with the sharpest elbows. Byrne (2005) is less convinced that the promotion of Marshallian citizenship rights fits a progressive, redistributive paradigm because the allocation of such rights tends to be cast at the individualistic rather than the collective level, thus making it easy to fit conceptions of citizenship into the liberal 'rights and responsibilities' discourse of market society, rather than transcending this with a more collectivist vision of social equality. Although he is broadly supportive of Levitas's typology, he tends to see the redistributive interpretation more in terms of a Keynesian 'social market' position that explicitly seeks to tame the excesses of market societies that inevitably produce inequalities and exclusion, and thus require state action to regulate the economy in order to achieve social solidarity, or inclusion.

According to a SID interpretation, which is more in keeping with the French interpretation of the term, social exclusion is primarily about being marginalised from the labour market, and inclusion is therefore about 'insertion' into the labour market. This is a far less expansive, and more reductionist, understanding of social exclusion than that offered by the RED perspective. Although work might also be an inclusionary solution for those arguing from a RED and MUD perspective, the SID interpretation fits a neo-liberal position, because its emphasis is upon providing those out of work with opportunities for work that amount to supply-side measures, for example through better education, skills and training. It is not concerned about inequalities *within* the labour market; it is not overly concerned about structural problems of the labour market where, as a result of global capitalist developments, parts of the labour market – in particular spatial locations – have collapsed; and it does not entertain the idea of the functionality of a reserve army of labour for capitalism. It is, however, very much about the state providing, handmaiden-like, a 'suitable' workforce for the market, but not otherwise intervening in areas such as demand management.

The MUD discourse, meanwhile, is one that chimes with the contemporary use of terms such as a culture of poverty or the underclass, or nineteenth-century terms such as the dangerous classes, or 'the residuum'. Social exclusion, according to this discourse, is due to the individual or cultural failings of those who are excluded, who lack habits or industry and propriety. It is, in other words, a blaming discourse, focusing upon the inadequacies of individuals, families and communities: these people exclude themselves. This is the kind of discourse that finds expression in Charles Murray's imagination of an underclass. Summarising the contribution of Murray and others, Levitas identifies three indicators of a putative underclass, namely illegitimacy, crime and withdrawal from the labour market, and together these allegedly conspire to produce a culture that is transmitted inter-generationally (although it must be said that such indicators might also have fitted a ruling class rather well). It is also neo-conservative, because of its strong moralising tone, and in so far as its emphasis, in terms of inclusion, lies in enforcing order, and appropriate standards of behaviour, such as good parenting and virtuous habits of industry.

How, it may be asked, does crime fit into these different discourses of social exclusion? Broadly speaking, the RED discourse appropriately corresponds with left-of-centre political ideologies, while MUD, perhaps also appropriately, corresponds with the politics of the right. In terms of crime causation, although they are not necessarily all-encompassing, RED sits most comfortably with the structural analysis of left realism, while MUD sits with right realism. SID sits somewhere in the middle, not least because the focal point of its attention, namely paid work, is also covered in the other two discourses, albeit from different standpoints, for which SID may represent the point of intersection. For this reason, we will concentrate here on the causes of crime as perceived in RED and MUD discourses of social exclusion, which are of most direct relevance to our concerns. What follows is not intended to be an exhaustive account, but it is broadly illustrative, and necessarily brief.

According to the RED discourse, processes of social exclusion cause crime in a number of different ways. In the economic sphere, the neo-liberal project of global capitalism has generated massive and widening social inequalities that, for many of those at the bottom, and thus relatively deprived, produce a considerable and recognisable Mertonian strain. As Young (1999) points out in his familiar realist refrain, the problem here is that relatively deprived people also have aspirations, particularly as they are exposed to the voracious consumerism of late-modern market societies. But while they can look, they cannot touch, and the frustration that this induces can all too easily spill over into violent or acquisitive criminal reactions. For Young the process is the social equivalent of bulimia: relatively deprived people are ingested into the vision, but vomited out from attaining the actuality, the trophies of a consumerist age.

Crime is not just the direct cause of income inequality, however. Rather, exclusion can be corrosive of community life. Thus, for example, working-class communities that might once have been tightly bonded around the common experiences of members employed in the same industry have such commonality or solidarity ripped away from them once this industry disappears, for worklessness individualises just as work unites, particularly through organised labour, which has been so undermined by neo-liberal politics. And when work disappears we encounter what Taylor (1999) calls a crisis of masculinity, particularly leaving young males to engage in the sort of violent and intimidating 'protest masculinity', documented so well by Campbell (1993), in some of the more disadvantaged and notorious northern estates of the UK.

The excluded may then find themselves being squeezed into an increasingly residualised stock of council housing which, following right to buy legislation that has made its own distinctive contribution to exclusion, '... has shifted from housing for the working class to housing for the non-working class and those who are marginal to the labour market' (Murie 1998: 30). This involves pushing marginal, vulnerable and sometimes dangerous people into close proximity to one another, with predictable consequences both for crime and the fear of crime. Problems are then compounded, as Murie says, by the fact that areas of poor housing also tend to have poorer facilities, whether that be transport, shops, provision for youth, or other public services, including housing and environmental management, but also policing, leaving those most at risk of crime potentially the most unprotected. An important dynamic, for its detrimental impact upon community life, is mobility, as people move between the geographical and social boundaries of inclusion and exclusion (Byrne 2005), thus making it hard to generate the stability on which 'successful' community life may depend, particularly in terms of the informal controls that work to prevent crime. In this way '[t]he processes of determining what happens on council estates, as in other neighbourhoods, are the consequence of a wide range of factors and the interaction between them' (Murie 1998: 31).

If the community is one criminologically well-known insulator against crime, the family is another, although feminist criminologists have been successful in pointing out that the opposite is also likely – though this tends to be more visible (not necessarily more prevalent) amongst already excluded populations. However, whilst the relationship between family life and crime may not be straightforward (Young 1999), there is little doubt that social exclusion puts more strain on family life, and that this can have criminogenic consequences. Low pay may force all adult family members into the labour market, thus taking parents away from childcare, and away from their neighbourhoods for most of the day. And unemployment and 'protest masculinity' certainly do not provide sound bases for stable family relationships.

Young (1999) sees late-modern market society becoming simultaneously more individualised, because of its consumerism, but also more differentiated, because of the lifestyle choices of consumerism; because of the impact of immigration and large-scale population movement; and because of the effects of economic polarisation. This differentiation can generate insecurity as certain groups – among them young people and the most economically deprived – become 'othered' or demonised. In a context in which power is unevenly distributed, criminal justice and crime control can easily become tools for those with most power or influence to turn their insecurities into exclusionary practices, whether that be the over-policing of black and minority ethnic groups, zero-tolerance policing, or the effective criminalisation of anti-social behaviour. Consequently, for the RED discourse, one cause of crime is the uneven use of aspects of crime control, that operates to exclude or consolidate the exclusion of relatively powerless groups.

For the RED discourse, crime is something that requires action on a number of different fronts to secure inclusion. It requires redistribution to tackle the massive social inequalities that have arisen from decades of neo-liberalism, particularly through the greater availability of good work. It requires improvements in public services so that they do not discriminate against or reinforce the exclusion of those who are most marginalised. And it requires the rebuilding of communities, by supporting families and helping to build informal social controls, but also by encouraging greater tolerance of difference and diversity.

If the RED discourse's linguistic use of the word exclusion is as a verb, so that it is effectively something 'done to' the marginalised that can cause crime, then the MUD discourse uses exclusion – or more accurately 'the excluded' – as an adjective, to describe the characteristics of those so-labelled. As noted above, the idea here is that the excluded are morally deficient: they have learnt to be irresponsible because of their welfare dependency, which means they do not have to work, do not have to take their parental responsibilities seriously, and do not feel any compulsion to abide by normative standards of behaviour and decency. They are, therefore, fundamentally disorderly, and crime is a part of their deficient way of life. The solution is to impose order on such disorderly people. One obvious way of doing this is through tough enforcement, such as zero-tolerance policing and an assault on anti-social behaviour. But another way is by enforcing responsibility, so that, for example, individuals have no option but to work, parents are obliged to take responsibility for their children, and children are given a moral education. Consequently, the MUD discourse does not imagine the solution to crime purely in terms of criminal justice and law enforcement, but also entertains the idea of 'joined-up' solutions, that address those aspects of 'the social' in which moral order may be produced.

Having set out the broad differences between RED and MUD discourses of social exclusion and crime, we are now in a better position to assess the direction of Labour's attempts to tackle the causes of crime.

Tackling social exclusion: the contribution of the SEU

The policy focus upon social exclusion, and upon a joined-up approach to tackle it, are two of the features of Labour's political project that clearly distinguish it from its Conservative predecessors. Perhaps this needs to be qualified because the Conservatives' promotion of multi-agency or partnership approaches to crime prevention could be read as an early prototype, but while the Conservatives made a somewhat half-hearted attempt to coordinate inter-departmental activity at central government level (see Gilling 1997), Labour did it with a flourish, establishing the SEU, and initially attaching it to the Prime Minister's Office, giving it both the profile and the authority to pursue its joined-up mandate.

The SEU's (1998) first report *Bringing Britain Together: A National Strategy for Neighbourhood Renewal*, set out a diagnosis of the problem of social exclusion, as well as a proposed solution. The problem was conceived in terms of the spatial concentration of social exclusion in up to 4000 neighbourhoods across England, caused by a combination of economic changes, social changes (including rising crime), the failure of previous urban policies, and the poor quality of public services in such areas. The aim of any solution, according to such a diagnosis, was to 'reduce the gap' between these socially excluded neighbourhoods and elsewhere, thus presumably bringing the excluded across the threshold and into the ranks of the included. The solution, conceived of as a three-pronged national strategy, which stressed the importance of 'bottom-up' community involvement, was to consist of current mainstream programmes developed by Labour since taking office (particularly welfare reform and the establishment of the New Deal to effect a transition from welfare to work); a raft of new area-based initiatives (ABIs) to tackle the spatial concentration of exclusion; and the establishment of 18 separate PATs to explore and make recommendations on issues that existing policy responses had yet to properly or effectively address. These PATs were organised around five themes, namely:

1 getting people to work;
2 getting the place to work;
3 the future for young people;
4 access to services; and
5 making government work.

In different ways, PAT 4 (*neighbourhood management*), PAT 5 (*housing management*), PAT 6 (*neighbourhood wardens*), PAT 8 (*anti-social behaviour*), PAT 9 (*community self-help*), and PAT 17 (*joining it up locally*) were the most relevant of the PATs for the governance of crime.

Although crime clearly featured as one of the key aspects of social exclusion in this first SEU report, it did not receive an especially high profile. Significantly, however, where it was most prominent was in the citation of survey evidence showing that amongst residents of these excluded neighbourhoods, crime-related issues (more specifically, 'low-level' anti-social behaviour) were among the most pressing problems that they faced. This probably accounts for the selection of ASB as a focus for one of the PATs (as seen in Chapter 5), as well as neighbourhood wardens, an idea that built upon the experience of other countries such as the Netherlands, that had successfully reintroduced a number of formal occupations (such as park-keepers, bus conductors, housing block concierges, etc.) in order to exploit their informal policing and order maintenance functions for the broader purposes of urban governance. But more importantly, the survey evidence conveyed the impression of crime as a problem of victimisation, not necessarily of individuals, but of these neighbourhoods, thus according with the views of Straw and Michael (1996) set out earlier, namely that crime and disorder make these neighbourhood problems worse. Such a view encourages the idea that crime and disorder can be separated out and dealt with individually, apart from other aspects of social exclusion. Thus, what matters is not so much what causes the crime or the anti-social behaviour, but rather the effect of crime and anti-social behaviour in increasing the immiseration of those living in these 'pockets of deprivation'.

The forensic examinations of others (e.g. Watt and Jacobs 2000) have found traces of RED, SID and MUD in this foundational SEU document, but what is of particular importance here, that sets off a discursive slide towards MUD (a mud-slide?), is the separation of crime and disorder from other aspects of social exclusion. The problem that this separation causes, which will form a consistent theme throughout the rest of this chapter, is succinctly put by Byrne thus:

> The focus on specific and isolated dimensions of exclusion translates in an audit culture of public governance at the meso level into a wholly inappropriate specification of targets which is both a misrepresentation of the real processes of social change and an important method through which effective popular politics are disabled at the local level. (2005: 54)

We will turn to the question of this translation and popular politics later when we look at how the SEU's national strategy has unfolded in practice at the local level, but I think this was a key moment in Labour's approach to crime and social exclusion, in terms of the path not taken. This is when Labour's crime problem is set as the problem of its occurrence, and of its effects (particularly the erosion of community support systems [Watt and Jacobs 2000]), rather than of its causes. This does not mean that the causes are entirely ignored, firstly because there is some space for local agency to resist the thrust of central policy, and secondly because there is still a whole machinery for addressing the causes of offending behaviour through the criminal justice system. But as Allen (2006) observes, through the criminal justice system, and specifically through the National Offender Management System (NOMS), tackling offending behaviour is set within a largely individualised and psychological paradigm.

Allen (ibid.) says that while it may be the case that crime and disorder are perceived as greater problems in the kinds of deprived neighbourhoods identified by the SEU in which social exclusion is concentrated, much less attention tends to be paid to the simple fact that the vast majority of offenders emanate from such places too, and little thought seems to be given to the idea of tackling offending behaviour *spatially*, rather than *individually*. This explains why '[a]lthough one of the four aims of local area agreements is to create safer and stronger communities, strangely absent from their scope is the money spent on the punishment and rehabilitation of criminal offenders' (ibid.: 57). Allen's point is that such money often dwarfs that made locally available to regeneration schemes, and it could be put to much better use if it were spent in the excluded neighbourhoods from which offenders typically originate, on '... an approach that requires offenders to pay back to their local communities for their wrongdoing, while offering opportunities to solve their problems through a much enhanced local infrastructure of community-based services' (ibid.: 54). There go those Hampstead liberals again.

Blaming the SEU for the path not taken might be regarded as akin to shooting the messenger, because what matters is how its message is translated at the political level. As noted above, while the SEU report does contain traces of MUD, it also contains traces of RED and SID that could have led in a different policy direction. By the same token, it will be remembered from Chapter 5 that the PAT 8 report on ASB argued for a balancing of enforcement with resettlement and prevention, which, despite the more recent rhetoric of the Respect Action Plan, government policy has thus far failed to do. However, Watt and Jacobs (2000) do not want to let the SEU off the hook too quickly. Their discourse analytic approach suggests that the spatialised conceptualisation of social exclusion leads to the negative contrasting of excluded spaces with the rest of the country that is 'included'. This reading supports Levitas's (2005) view that the discourse of social exclusion simplifies the problem, and it also defines the problem in terms of 'those neighbourhoods' (just like Margaret Thatcher once problematised 'those inner cities'), thus taking attention away from the characteristics of the included. As Byrne (2005) is not slow to point out, 'the included' are not all the same, and contain within their ranks the super-rich, who can purchase their advantage, their safety and their security, and whose continued 'success' for Byrne depends upon the maintenance of the excluded, as a reserve army of labour, to deflate wages and to keep the neo-liberal project on track.

Perhaps, then, even *before* the SEU's report contributed to the surgical removal of crime and disorder as separate dimensions of social exclusion that could be tackled separately, the decisive moment may have been the identification of social exclusion as a spatial problem, because making social exclusion spatial simultaneously made it *governable* in ways that are unlikely to challenge the social structure that generated it in the first place. This is because the focus was rendered spatial, directed at excluded places and their populations, rather than at the processes that generated their exclusion. It is important to recognise, in this regard, that while the SEU links social exclusion to particular neighbourhoods, it is rather vague about precisely which neighbourhoods it is talking about (although there are apparently thousands of them), and exactly what distinguishes these neighbourhoods from others. This is not to claim that there are not neighbourhoods that are in large part excluded, but it is to make the point, as Byrne (2005) does, that spatial exclusion is *the most visible* form of exclusion, which means it is not the *only* form. The SEU's correlation of social exclusion with deprived neighbourhoods conveniently ignores other places where people may be excluded (the common criticism of area-based anti-poverty initiatives, that most of those in poverty live outside such areas, is very relevant here), just as the separation of crime and disorder risks ignoring other aspects of social exclusion.

Indeed, related to this latter point, Watt and Jacobs's (2000) analysis also shows how social housing problems are constructed in the SEU report as if the problem is one of surplus housing, due to people not wanting to live on many of the hard-to-let estates, due in turn to poor reputations fashioned to a large degree out of the crime and ASB problems found there. Thus, in terms that accord very much with the MUD discourse, the solution to the housing problem becomes one of managing and controlling difficult tenants along the lines well documented by Burney (1999), rather than, for example, addressing acute shortages in the South East; the poor quality of much of the stock; and poor housing management practices.

We will move on to explore some of these issues later in the chapter, but now it is necessary to move on to explore the different initiatives that have emanated from Labour's strategy to tackle social exclusion and crime, and to assess their contribution.

Policies for work

Work has a central place in Labour's programme of welfare reform, and it is also regarded as having a central place in Labour's strategy to tackle the causes of crime, as Tony Blair (2001) made clear in his Peel Institute speech, when he said that measures such as the New Deal for the unemployed were '... as much part of the strategy to fight crime as more bobbies on the beat and tougher sentences'. Work fights crime, according to this approach, because it is the path to inclusion.

Labour's policy in this area, as in many others, was heavily influenced by 'workfare' developments in the USA under the Clinton administration. The aim of their New Deal, funded by an early 'windfall tax' on privatised utilities, has been to effect a transition from welfare to work, by introducing an element of conditionality into welfare benefits so that eligibility is tied to a preparedness to look for and take advantage of work opportunities, or to enhance employability through training and skills development. The conditionality introduced into welfare benefit provision is a good example of Labour's 'tough love' approach (Driver and Martell 2002). Supporting this, measures such as tax credits and payments to employers have led to the government's subsidisation of work as a means of removing people from welfare dependency, and of helping to sustain low wages (despite the introduction of an ungenerous minimum wage) in what Byrne (2005) regards to be a modern-day version of the notorious Speenhamland system.

Overall, policy towards work has operated with a supply-side orientation. The assumption has been that work opportunities are available, often very close to excluded neighbourhoods (Hall 2003), and that all that is required is to responsibilise individuals to take advantage of these opportunities, sometimes with the assistance of personal advisors to facilitate the process of work 'activation'. The assumption also has been that paid work is the way out of exclusion, and thus out of crime. But do these assumptions stand up to scrutiny?

The idea of paid work having a 'natural' crime preventive effect is persuasive. Byrne portrays the idea that '[w]ages provide an income without resource to crime. People who go to work don't have the time, or energy, to be disorderly and criminal. The threat of job loss is an important order-maintaining sanction' (2005: 156). In addition, work may have a moralising effect. This is certainly an assumption of the MUD discourse, and the assumption is also found in Durkheim's sociology, where work has an integrative effect, which also helps to build self-esteem, a sense of self-worth. But there are problems.

Firstly, the promotion of the virtues of paid work is very undiscriminating. As Byrne (2005) and others have pointed out, there is 'good work', but there is also plenty of 'bad work', which may be of short duration, poorly paid, set in intolerable conditions, unrewarding and so forth. There is no interest here in a progressive approach to address labour market inequalities (Bennington and Donnison 1999), which are considerable; there is an acceptance that job insecurity is an inevitable part of global capitalism (Levitas 2005); and there is gross overestimation of labour market demand, in which there has been a long-term decline in some areas and regions (Hall 2003). While, until recently, Labour's New Deal may well have contributed to a significant drop in unemployment as it is officially recorded, it has done so in very favourable economic circumstances, and even within them, those living in areas with buoyant local economics have felt the benefits much more readily that those in areas of less buoyancy (Walker and Wiseman 2003). For many people, the New Deal has been experienced as a revolving door from benefits into short-term or poorly paid work opportunities, or training courses that many do not finish, and back again. As has been the experience in other European states, welfare to work 'activation' policies do not really work (Walker and Wiseman 2003), and in neo-liberalism's functionally necessary flexible labour market, employment can never be the road out of exclusion for more than the lucky few, whose inclusion might well be achieved by getting out of excluded neighbourhoods altogether. These lucky few might become the 'stakeholders' that New Labour's vision once sought to create (before the word was dropped because of its association with a more progressive view of stakeholders offered by Will Hutton [Levitas 2005]), but they leave behind them non-stakeholders who have badly paid work, no paid work, or who cannot, for various reasons, do paid work.

For these non-stakeholders, work is not the answer, because flexible labour markets will always generate the substantial relative deprivation that Young (1999) and others identified as a prominent cause of crime. And besides, as Young and Matthews (2003) point out, the elevation of work as the principal route out of exclusion, even if it has some beneficial impact on crime, neglects the fact that the economy is only one front on which crime can be tackled. This is demonstrated by the fact that work also provides opportunities for crime which are often well-exploited by those involved in white-collar or corporate crimes. As Taylor (1999) has observed, the market society generates crime according to different 'market positions'.

Another crucially important front for tackling crime is found within civil society, where a strong community plays a vital role in the co-production of order, just as parenting plays a vital role in the co-production of a child's education and socialisation. And as Levitas (2005) points out, Labour's heavy promotion of paid work over unpaid work, which is mostly done by women, and which forms a vitally important part of a strong community, is, to say the very least, disingenuous, not least in crime preventive terms. Overall, then, Labour's policy with respect to work has limited prospects for tackling social exclusion. In terms of discourses, it is intrinsically SID, with a strong hint of MUD in so far as the solution has been perceived as one of responsibilising people to exploit thought-to-be-available employment opportunities, as if welfare dependency had previously sapped such responsibility from them. Although paid work might make some positive impact on income inequalities, there is not much about Labour's policy that is RED, and until it locates the problem in neo-liberalism's flexible labour market, and in global capitalism's dependency on a reserve army of labour, nor is it likely ever to be so.

Childcare and the family

Labour sees the family as one of the principal means through which individuals, and young people in particular, can be insulated from crime, because the family is thought to be a source of social support, a source for the inculcation of pro-social values, and a key building block of strong communities. There are many ways through which Labour has sought to address childcare: it launched a national childcare strategy in 1998 following the comprehensive spending review of that year, which had included a review of services for young children as one of six cross-cutting policy reviews. The brief focus here, however, is upon Sure Start, an integral part of the national strategy and a new policy development that Tony Blair (2001) explicitly identifies as an anti-crime measure. Sure Start provides another example of policy transfer from the USA to the UK, because the policy is modelled on the Perry Pre-School Programme, that was thought to have saved $7 in tax for every $1 spent on the programme, because of its positive impact on beneficiaries' earnings and criminality (Schweinhart et al. 1993), which showed a 20% difference in offending for those who had had the pre-school provision, compared to a control group that had not had such provision. It was also modelled on Headstart (Byrne 2005), which was an integral part of President Johnson's 1960s War on Poverty, that, incidentally, the right-wing critic James Q. Wilson regarded as being entirely misguided.

Sure Start became operational from January 1999, and its aim was to prevent social exclusion by improving the life chances of children under four years of age, by promoting their physical, intellectual, social and emotional development, so that they would be in a position to thrive once they reached primary school (Glass 1999). This was to be achieved through the integration of core services relevant for childcare, including home visiting, play and learning facilities, primary and community health care, but interestingly it has also included training and employment advice, presumably not for the kids. The initial target was for there to be 250 separate area-based Sure Start programmes, targeting 150,000 children in the most deprived fifth of electoral wards in England, but by the beginning of 2004 six waves of the national programme had been rolled out, and there was a total of 524 schemes.

Since Sure Start is a policy targeted at the under fours, the age of criminal responsibility is currently 10 years old, and at the time of writing Sure Start is approaching only its eighth year of operation, it is a little too early to assess its effectiveness in crime control terms, although given Labour's track record in shifting *doli incapax* downwards, perhaps it is never too early. While some successes have been claimed for Sure Start, generally in terms of outputs rather than outcomes, Ormerod (2005) questions its impact upon social exclusion. While Sure Start is targeted upon the most deprived electoral wards, its services are made available to all local residents with young children, so that it is perceived to be non-stigmatising. The result of this, however, has been that, just as with education and health services, the best use of such services has been made by less deprived groups, and those such as teenage parents, lone parents and workless households have been less well equipped to take advantage of the available services. In relative terms, therefore, the most deprived may have become *worse off* as a result of Sure Start.

Ormerod (ibid.) puts the weaknesses of Sure Start down to the obsessive desire of central government to micro-manage its policy interventions, which results in complex interventions that often end in failure, and he draws parallels with other interventions, such as the £1 billion spent on anti-truancy measures that have resulted in a 30% increase in truancy, the payment errors made in the administration of family tax credits, and the £1 billion in uncollected maintenance payments, thanks to the well-publicised inadequacies of the Child Support Agency. Ormerod may be a little harsh and a little premature in writing off Sure Start, and there is the hint of a Hayek-style critique of the limitations of any government action, but there is also some mileage in the complaint about micro-management, which chimes with Byrne's (2005) criticism of the 'audit culture of public governance', to which we shall return later. For now, we might just acknowledge that despite a hint of the RED discourse in the design of Sure Start, to support childcare for the most socially excluded, the provision of employment advice also carries shades of SID, while underpinning it all is a MUD discourse because '... it is still founded around a rectifying deficits model of the parenting practices of the children who engage with the scheme' (Byrne 2005). However, since the most deprived are not necessarily the greatest beneficiaries of Sure Start, this MUD is often slung at the wrong targets, though perhaps its discursive presence may be enough to act as a deterrent to those who suspect Sure Start to be the modern-day equivalent of the nineteenth-century child-savers. In terms of crime control, meanwhile, the relative absence of the most deprived and excluded children plausibly suggests that those most likely to be actuarially assessed as delinquent-prone are least likely to be touched by the programme.

Neighbourhood renewal

Although there are many other examples of initiatives that have been introduced by Labour to tackle aspects of social exclusion, such as health action zones or education action zones, there is not the space here for a full exploration, and our time may be better spent examining the key theme of neighbourhood renewal, which has been something of a meta-narrative around which a lot of the SEU's main work has been focused and organised. This became clear after the public spending review of 2000, when the way was cleared for the SEU to launch its *New Commitment to Neighbourhood Renewal* (SEU 2001), accompanied by the creation of a new Neighbourhood Renewal Unit (NRU), based in the DETR, the forerunner of the ODPM, and now the DCLG. Neighbourhood renewal as a policy agenda broadly consists of what was set out in *Bringing Britain Together* (SEU 1998). There are five thematic domains within the strategy, namely employment, housing, education, crime and health. These could perhaps be regarded as the late-modern revision of Beveridge's *five giants* (want, ignorance, disease, squalor and idleness) that originally inspired the formation of the post-war welfare state. The five domains are tackled through a combination of mainstream policy programmes and ABIs such as the NDC scheme, which are then 'joined-up', in theory at least, by localised structures of neighbourhood management, for which NDC Boards have served as a blueprint, and/or authority-wide LSPs, which we previously encountered in Chapter 4. In the most deprived 88 local authority areas, LSPs have had their budgets topped up with additional resources from the Neighbourhood Renewal Fund (NRF), to develop and support services in the most deprived and excluded areas. In this way, then, the intention has been to use the additional funding not just for new initiatives, but also to effect the 'bending' of mainstream services into these areas, on the assumption that such services in the past have been inadequate (SEU 1998), and with the aim of *closing the gap* between these neighbourhoods and the rest of the country, so that nobody 'loses out' simply by virtue of where they live (Hall 2003).

As a consequence of its predominantly urban focus, neighbourhood renewal places itself in a stream of nominally distinct urban policy developments that can be traced back to the 1960s. But what is distinctive about New Labour's approach is that it is founded upon a different model of governance because, in theory at least, it is based upon a joined-up approach that is incorporated in the very notion of social exclusion, which unlike poverty is multi-dimensional, and therefore agencies operating in the different domains can be made to see that they 'own' a little slice of social exclusion. The services they collectively provide constitute what Wallace (2001: 2165) refers to as '… the joined-up needs of individuals'. Another feature of this joined-up approach, moreover, is that it connects vertically to 'the community', so that local residents are required to participate in a number of different ways in the processes of governance, thereby helping to *co-produce* neighbourhood renewal, where renewed neighbourhoods become included neighbourhoods, presumably. This joined-up approach may indeed be Labour's 'big idea' (Clark 2002), but it does require something by way of qualification, because in the 1990s Conservative policy was also to some extent joined-up, although the terminological currency in those days was *partnership*. However, as Byrne (2005) points out, Conservative policy was joined-up in a different way, as *urban regimes* that often sidelined local authorities and put business interests very much in the driving seat of regeneration, as in the case of the Urban Development Corporations (UDCs).

While the UDCs may have gone, the urban regimes have not necessarily disappeared (see Coleman *et al.*'s 2002 account of Merseyside), but they were implicitly the target of the SEU's progressive criticism that previous approaches to excluded neighbourhoods had tended to be property-led, based upon investment in bricks and mortar (more like steel and smoked glass) rather than investment in people. This bricks and mortar, property-led approach never brought the much-anticipated 'trickle down effect' that was to benefit people in deprived communities, and thus New Labour's joined-up approach is one that professes to be recentred on the social fabric (although it certainly does not ignore the physical fabric – see below), and one that brings the public sector, particularly in the shape of local authorities, and 'the community', back into sharper focus.

In terms of discourses of social exclusion, neighbourhood renewal at first sight appears to pick up on a RED discourse that identifies the structural causes of exclusion in the economic restructuring that has resulted in considerable disinvestment and job losses in most urban areas (Levitas 2005), and this may be one reason why the neighbourhood renewal agenda has been broadly welcomed among progressives (Watt and Jacobs 2000). But this structural analysis soon gives way to one grounded more in the MUD discourse (Levitas 2005). Thus, the requirement for 'the community' to be involved in the co-production of urban governance rests upon an implicit assumption that excluded communities are deficient and pathological, which chimes, criminologically speaking, with the earlier formulations of Chicagoan urban ecology, as expressed in social disorganisation theory. In addition, endowing the MUD discourse with something of a new twist, neighbourhood renewal does not only pathologise 'the community', but also it pathologises the providers of public services whose 'provider interests' have somehow conspired to let down residents by providing poor-quality services in these same areas.

With regard to this, Emmel's (2005) research provides an illuminating account of service providers in one perhaps typical excluded neighbourhood, in so far as there is such a thing. These service providers, for example, were wary of making bids for new initiatives in case the bids failed, because failure would impact negatively upon the hopes and aspirations of residents who already carried more than their fair share of demoralisation and low aspirations. Is this the self-interest of 'provider interests', which makes them reluctant to play the role of New Labour's neo-liberal enterprising souls, or is this, rather, their considered realism, in the face of the structural disadvantages faced by such neighbourhoods? And while these service providers could see the multi-dimensionality of social exclusion, they too frequently lacked the resources to do anything positive about it, in terms of tackling its underlying causes. The overwhelming sense from residents was of public services being in decline not because of provider interests getting in the way, but rather because resources were always being taken away from the locality. The only area of urban governance that was relatively well resourced was that concerned with the management of anti-social behaviour through enforcement, which is ironic because of the perverse exclusionary impact that such enforcement can have on already excluded neighbourhoods. This accords with Levitas's (2005) observation that the strongest theme running through the neighbourhood renewal agenda is that of social order, seen particularly in terms of the policing of anti-social behaviour and tackling truancy through the enforcement of parental responsibility. It also illustrates the SEU's misguided approach of separating out crime and disorder from other aspects of social exclusion.

As an element of urban policy, it is difficult to disentangle neighbourhood renewal from the wider focus of that policy, which in recent years, and in contrast to much of the pessimism of the 1980s and 1990s about urban decline, speaks to a vision of urban renaissance. As an example of Labour's investment in people, neighbourhood renewal addresses the social fabric whilst a parallel stream of physical regeneration has been informed by the 2000 White Paper *Our Towns and Cities* (DETR 2000), which emphasises design (Johnstone and Whitehead 2004), and which is premised upon the imaginary of an urban idyll (Hoskins and Tallon 2004). In this imaginary, the city stands as a cathedral to consumption, comprising the gentrification of residential spaces around notions of a dynamic cultural melting pot; the commodification of urban arts, culture and heritage; and the commodified 'naturalisation' of green space, parks and features such as waterfronts. Byrne (2005) offers a characteristically good, critical reading of attempts to realise this idyll in North East England, where the culture that has been commodified is always a culture that is some way removed from the lived experiences of real, deprived urban dwellers.

Such deprived people become the 'others' who do not fit the idyll, and this is one reason why it becomes impossible in practice to keep physical and social regeneration on separate tracks. Perhaps somewhat ironically, they effectively become joined-up, but in different ways depending upon the different urban spaces that may be involved. Thus, for example, in something that particularly fits the case of gentrification, Hoskins and Tallon (2004: 33) suggest of the policy focus that '[r]ather than addressing the needs of residents, the residents are instead replaced with more affluent citizens who better fit the popular image of a cosmopolitan bohemia'. In areas of mass private property such as shopping malls, meanwhile, 'undesirables' such as groups of youths hanging around, street drinkers and homeless people are kept under surveillance by CCTV schemes, and moved on by policing agencies so that they may be cleared from view, allowing others to indulge in the free exercise of uninhibited consumption. In both cases, then, the regeneration is primarily physical, and so is the exclusion, although by denying access, and thus participation, the effect is also felt on the social variant of exclusion. The city may not be as polarised or divided as Mike Davis's (1990) *City of Quartz*, but it is not immeasurably better.

Clearing deprived people from mass private property and gentrified residential areas still leaves them in neighbourhoods that require renewal, but here one still finds the conjoining of the physical with the social, as the moral reform of the inhabitants of excluded neighbourhood is combined with the improvement of the physical fabric, perfectly captured in the nomenclature utilised to describe a 'cleaner, greener and safer' funding stream alongside the SSCF. In this way, New Labour betrays a vision of itself as a latter-day wild west sheriff, moving in to clean up the town. This is, as Whitehead contends, a moral geography in which certain normative standards of appropriate conduct prevail, flowing discursively through policing bodies such as neighbourhood wardens who provide '… a moral blueprint of the 21st century neighbour' (2004: 64). This is the MUD discourse in full flow, and in such an admittedly pessimistic scenario, the idea of neighbourhood renewal seems strangely apposite, because as the likes of Raco (2004) and Byrne (2005) remind us, capitalism requires the renewal of processes of polarisation, to provide low-paid workers who can service the demands of the consuming middle classes, and to provide a reserve army of labour that keeps the low-paid low paid, and that keeps many of the rest of us insecure. Urban policy facilitates this polarisation spatially, while neighbourhood renewal, with its emphasis upon social order maintenance, keeps the urban poor in their place through a moral geography that some have likened to a process of spatial apartheid.

Why, one might legitimately ask, has this been allowed to happen, when the SEU started out from a progressive, RED diagnosis of urban problems, and when New Labour's approach to urban governance marked a clear shift away from private sector-dominated urban regimes, to joined-up policy? The New Labour government may well have sought to impose its MUD discursive stamp on the neighbourhood renewal agenda from above, but surely the vehicle for developing policy locally, namely a joined-up, community participative approach, has been able to pull policy in a more progressive direction? Unfortunately, however, the joined-up approach, and community participation have both suffered major limitations, which means they have not been able generally to tame the excesses of Labour's moralising mission. We will now look at both areas in more detail, in order to identify these limitations.

Joined-up government

The premise underpinning joined-up government is that 'wicked issues' such as crime are interconnected: concepts such as community safety or social exclusion, which reflect more holistic understandings of social problems, effectively attest to this. But while joined-up government may indeed be Labour's 'big idea' that distinguishes its approach from that of the Conservatives, the problem is that the idea is only an aspiration, that has yet to be realised. It refers to a normative ideal of what governing should be, where the architecture of joined-up government results in joined-up policy on the ground. Its aspirational quality is recognised by Mulgan (2005), who along with Peter Mandelson has been one of Labour's strongest advocates of a joined-up approach. He accepts that the departmentalised traditions of government, both central and local, have been better suited to the goal of efficiency in operation, rather than effectiveness in outcome. This departmentalism leads to a silo mentality that manifests itself in a protectiveness over 'turf', an inclination to offload problems – often perceived as 'costs' – onto others; and a disinterest in prevention because the benefits of prevention may often accrue elsewhere. These features, it is argued, are replicated further along the implementation chain, amongst local authority departments and the different professional and semi-professional constituencies that they represent, and between different public services such as, for example, the police and health services.

While tradition might not provide favourable conditions for joined-up government, Mulgan contends that a number of factors have conspired to provide these favourable conditions, including:

- improvements in information technology, which facilitate better information exchange; and
- a growing understanding of the interconnectedness of social problems; and
- examples of successful local joined-up working that could be replicated elsewhere.

Central government, Mulgan contends, has set about its own reform in the direction of joined-up government by establishing various cross-cutting roles and units (such as the SEU and NRU) to coordinate the actions of different government departments across Whitehall, as well as by creating newly joined-up central government departments such as the ODPM. It has encouraged similar joined-up action at the local level, through the provision of joined-up budgets for initiatives such as Sure Start, and through newly-established structures such as CDRPs or, at a higher level of abstraction, LSPs. But Mulgan (ibid.) concedes that while progress has been made, much of the old 'vertical culture' remains, and stands in the way of the full realisation of joined-up government.

Mulgan's account may be broadly accurate, in so far as New Labour has genuinely sought a more joined-up approach to public policy, but it may be that the one step forward of structural reform has been accompanied by the two steps back of an obsessive adherence to a culture of new public management which he cites, ironically, as one of the features of Conservative governance that creates the very silo mentality that joined-up government seeks to transform, and others have been similarly critical of this impact of managerialism (see Crawford 1997). Mulgan suggests that Labour's use of PSA targets has encouraged an outcome orientation that facilitates the pursuit of joined-up policy, but others would suggest that these PSA targets are merely an aspect of Labour's own version of new public management, with the same, or even an intensified, disabling effect in terms of the frustration of joined-up policy. These PSA targets have spawned an industry of performance measurement and management that pushes agencies into a narrow focus upon their own 'core business' that makes the realisation of joined-up policy more rather than less difficult.

In the case of neighbourhood renewal, the outcome orientation is encouraged, in a classic case of central steering, by the use of *floor targets* to secure improvements in absolute standards across a range of service areas, and *convergence targets* to secure a relative improvement, and thus to narrow the gap, between deprived areas and elsewhere (Lupton and Power 2005). But these targets operate to undermine the joined-up policy that they are manifestly seeking to create. Central government's defence of its use of targets generally falls back on the claim that targets specify outcomes, but they do not specify exactly how the outcomes are to be achieved, but this is not necessarily how they are experienced from below. Thus, for example, in his meta-analysis of the progress of all NDC schemes operating across England, Lawless points to '… a subtle managerial tightening of the reins' (2004: 396) which was experienced by NDC Boards that had originally been under the impression that they had considerable freedom in their ten-year mission to regenerate pockets of deprivation. In Chapter 3, moreover, we saw how CDRPs were originally set up to find 'local solutions for local problems', only for a tighter performance management regime to be put in place, particularly after 2001. And Sullivan (2004) writing about local government, identifies a similar problem in his depiction of what he calls their 'regulated autonomy'. Much the same point about the strong regulatory steer from the centre and its constraining effect, in forcing members of local partnership bodies into silos, is made by Hall (2003) and Skelcher (2004).

Lawless (2004) identifies one of the problems of a tight performance management regime in terms of the pressure such a regime places on in this case NDC Partnership Boards to seek 'quick wins', rather than looking for long term change. In his example, this means a de-emphasis upon longer-term policy change agents such as education, but in the case of crime control it might mean an over-reliance on situational and deterrent measures such as CCTV schemes and concentrated policing patrol presences, which, by chance, happen to figure quite prominently in NDC policy repertoires. It could also mean a heavy reliance on measurable achievements, such as crack house closures, the number of ASBOs and ABCs issued, or the number of dispersal orders taken out. In this way, while targets for crime reduction or reassurance might be met, there is no joined-up policy as such, no attempt to address the underlying causes of problems that, as noted above, exclusionary measures such as ASBOs can actually make worse. The problem often lies with the nature of the targets themselves and with the audit culture that informs their creation. As the quote from Byrne (2005) (previously cited above – see page 170) suggests, the problem is the 'misrepresentation of the real processes of social change'.

What I think he means by this is what Emmel (2005) finds in his research. Targets tend to be directed at the most severe symptoms of social exclusion, and focusing upon them runs the risk of decontextualising them from the causal or mediating processes that created them. These severe symptoms, problems like crime, anti-social behaviour or even ill health, are constructions that are taken as symbolic representations of exclusion. Their use, when expressed as targets, is to make social exclusion governable, effectively by imagining it, in Whitehead's (2004: 64) words, '... as local bundles of educational, health, employment, crime, transport and housing problems'. But this imaginary runs counter to the imaginary of joined-up policy, where such problems cannot be so neatly separated, and nor can they be spatialised in the way they are, as if by crossing the road out of a neighbourhood renewal area all the problems of exclusion are left behind. The emphasis upon targets gives conceptual priority to these symptoms of exclusion, and effectively forecloses that which policy-makers claim to actively seek, namely joined-up policy.

This is exactly what happened in the case study explored by Emmel (2005), where partly for reasons of plentitude, as noted above, priority was accorded to enforcement activities against anti-social behaviour. Emmel points out that where these symptoms are targeted, they are targeted at an aggregate level that does not necessarily relate to the real problems that joined-up policy seeks to address. Thus, for example, a statistical reduction in residential burglary says nothing about what has happened to those who commit the burglaries in the area: have they stopped, have they got a job, have they diversified into street robbery instead? These are never easy questions to answer, but Emmel's point is that it would be more useful, and more conducive to joined-up policy, if there could be more of a focus upon 'soft outcomes' such as building the self-control and self-confidence of excluded people so that they might become empowered in ways that ease their exclusion. This view connects with Byrne's (2005) advocacy of a social pedagogy approach which cannot be confined to excluded areas in some over-simplistic community development model because, as Hall reminds us in his critique of third way supply-side spatial policy, '… the key structural changes in the economy and society that create disparity and disadvantage are national, indeed global, in scope and have prevailed for generations' (2003: 276). Or as Ian Taylor (1999) would have said, the problem is market society, and this is ultimately where joined-up policy needs to connect.

If targets provide one major barrier to joined-up policy, another barrier comes in the shape of the 'initiativitis' which the SEU (1998) had identified as a limitation of previous attempts at tackling social exclusion, but that Labour has perpetuated, perhaps as an inevitable corollary of the 'permanent campaigning' of contemporary politics, which requires the continual re-invention of policy, despite efforts to rationalise it. Initiativitis is thus more of an addiction than a disease. The proliferation of different initiatives and the creation of sometimes temporary partnerships, or ones like CDRPs that are subjected to frequent structural reforms, introduces complexity to a policy environment that was nicely conceived of by Lord Rooker as a bowl of spaghetti. The complexity makes joined-up policy logistically difficult to organise, particularly since many partnerships run parallel to local authorities and it is often unclear whose responsibility it is to organise things anyway. This makes local governance a highly politicised affair. Lawless (2004), for example, explains that some local authorities have used NDC as an excuse to withdraw resources from mainstream services in NDC areas, thus deepening the hole more than narrowing the gap. Others have witnessed local authorities trying to hijack NDC funding for their own specific housing agenda (Dinham 2005). And then, of course, there is the politics that operates within partnership bodies, where there may be competition for resources, competition over different definitions of the problem and its putative solution, and difficulties bringing prospective partners on board when the regulatory framework from above pushes them firmly into their own silos (for a fuller discussion of partnership politics in the case of CDRPs, see Gilling [2005]).

The establishment of LSPs as the 'über-partnership', and the requirement for them to prepare community plans using LAAs as the delivery plan, may be intended to bring everything together at the local level, but given its subjection to the centre's performance management regime, it still falls a long, long way short of joined-up policy. LSPs might look impressive as diagrammatic representations of the way everything can be knitted together, but the truth is that they are no less of a fantasy than building castles in the air. The point is that the *cultural* shift, that others such as Mulgan (2005) have identified as a necessary condition of joined-up government, has not occurred and cannot occur in the present structural context.

Community participation

Joined-up policy is a vertical as well as a horizontal phenomenon. In its idealised vision it is about connecting public agencies with 'the community', so that both may be involved in the co-production of policy. Given that such co-production is promoted through government policy, the idea is that it is 'a good thing' that, in this particular instance, will in some way help to draw disadvantaged people out of their social exclusion, which includes their vulnerability to criminality, to criminal victimisation, and to the disabling effects of fear. For this to happen, the process of joining up requires some element of community participation. But what exactly does this mean, and how has it been operationalised in practice under Labour's spatialised approach to tackling social exclusion?

The prominence accorded to 'the community' in neighbourhood renewal, broadly conceived as Labour's strategy to tackle social exclusion, should come as no surprise to students of criminology or urban policy. In both these areas, community – generally imagined spatially – has figured prominently in diagnoses of the problem to be addressed, and in putative solutions. But as several other commentators have ably demonstrated (see, for example, Little [2002] or Delanty [2003]), community is such a notoriously ambiguous term that its usage in governmental discourse marks not the end point but the starting point of analysis. Community may be '... a symbolically constructed reality' (Delanty 2003: 47) that, when used governmentally, maps out normative expectations for the way non-state actors should conduct themselves, but this obviously leaves unanswered the question of what these normative expectations are in practice, and our concern here is particularly with New Labour's normative expectations. By the same token, if community is ambiguous so too is participation. Arnstein's (1969) famous ladder of participation shows that there are strong and weak versions of participation that afford, respectively, more or less power and influence to 'the community'. And critics of Arnstein have emphasised that the situation may be further complicated by the fact that different parts of 'the community' may occupy different rungs on the ladder at any one time; that different positions on the ladder may best fit different stages of the policy process; and that the ladder, with its progressive dynamic, carries its own normative assumptions about the participative ideal that forecloses political debate about the scope and desirability of participation (for a fuller discussion see Taylor [2003]). In short, then, the introduction of the idea of community participation brings with it considerable ambiguity, which requires unpacking if we are to understand the character of New Labour's political project in this area. Inevitably, however, we should not expect this unpacking to resolve the ambiguity, because ambiguity is itself a feature of the third way political project, and in this particular instance it means that there is no single, coherent vision of community participation, but rather certain discernible tendencies, which we shall explore below.

Perhaps the clearest tendency in Labour's vision of community participation is the one that equates with the moral authoritarian communitarianism of Etzioni, which has proved to be so influential in the formation of Labour's political project since 1997. Etzioni's community, as we saw in Chapter 2, is one that speaks with a single, consensual moral voice. It is an idealised vision where individuals take responsibility for their own behaviour, where parents take responsibility for their children, and where neighbours take responsibility for their neighbourhood. In this vision, participation is conceived narrowly in terms of social control (Levitas 2005), though one might also add self-control. Consequently, when residents of socially excluded neighbourhoods are called upon to participate, such calls are implicitly predicated upon a 'community deficit' model (Taylor 2003), which supposes that residents of these neighbourhoods have failed to exercise the requisite control that is, also implicitly, a characteristic feature of the non-excluded 'normal' community, comprising the rest of us. For these people, then, as Levitas (2005: 91) observes, '... the agenda is the remoralisation of social life'. This moral authoritarian communitarianism therefore fits snugly into the MUD discourse of social exclusion.

In terms of social exclusion, this discourse says that these people have excluded themselves. They have not acted as archetypal stakeholders, playing out good habits of industry and responsibility, primarily through work and family. With regard to crime, they may themselves be criminal or disorderly; they have not controlled their children's behaviour; they have not acted to protect their neighbourhoods; and this is why excluded neighbourhoods are also high crime neighbourhoods. Such a discourse offers a convenient reading, for example, of why it is that neighbourhood watch, symbolising as it does the quintessence of good neighbourliness, has failed to take root in deprived, high-crime neighbourhoods to anything like the extent that it has taken root in other areas. It is, of course, their fault. The solution, therefore, is to bring morality and civility to residents of deprived neighbourhoods, so that they may become active citizens and social entrepreneurs, as symbolised in the role of the neighbourhood warden (Whitehead 2004), and so that collectively they may become the 'entrepreneurial community' (Imrie 2004).

The community imagined in this vision is not, however, a community without government. Rather, in seeking to realise this vision of social control (Cohen 1985), community is envisaged as a conduit through which central governmental power may flow, through an array of instruments that may be designed to induce conformity to the vision. These include both carrots and sticks. Thus, for example, in terms of carrots parents can be taught the art of parental responsibility through Sure Start programmes, and young people can be responsibilised through the Youth Inclusion Programme, or through their contact with Connexions personal advisors. And this can all be measured, as of course it has been, through such things as reductions in teenage pregnancy rates, school exclusions and truancy. Community action, in the form of self-help and mutual support, meanwhile, can itself be supported through the Community Chests that have been allocated to each of the 88 NRF areas, to encourage a vibrant voluntary and community sector in these areas. The sticks, meanwhile, can include the likes of ABCs, ASBOs, PNDs and dispersal orders, and the enforcement of parental responsibility through orders and fines.

There are a number of problems with this moral authoritarian vision that seeks to correct the deficits of deprived communities. Most obviously, the vision and the capacity to realise the vision do not match up. As Hughes and Edwards (2002) have made clear on a number of occasions, the centre is heavily dependent upon local agents for the delivery of its vision – it displays considerable power-dependence. Consequently, it is vitally important to recognise that New Labour's vision of social control, based essentially upon the co-option of 'the community' into its own self-policing, is not the actuality of social control. It may be its ambition, but the ambition can not easily be realised, because there is considerable capacity for local resistance, as well as unintended consequences. A good example of the former can be found in the initial reluctance of local practitioners to make use of the ASBO, much to the annoyance of elite politicians like Jack Straw. Consequently, while it is correct to identify this vision as an integral part of Labour's political project, we should not assume that it has been able to progress that far beyond the drawing board.

One reason for the lack of substantial progress beyond the drawing board may be found in the flawed conceptualisation of 'the community' that is found in Etzioni's communitarianism. New Labour's vision is of a single community – hence frequent reference to 'the community' into which excluded neighbourhoods need to be included or integrated. This presupposes the existence of consensus, denies conflict, and, where the latter is encountered it cannot help but slide into authoritarianism to suppress it (Levitas 2005), which means in practice that attempts to realise the vision are likely to depend considerably more upon sticks than carrots, although even the carrots, when they are attached to notions of conditionality as they often are, have a certain woodiness to them.

If the vision is of a single community, with a single morality, the obvious question to ask is *whose* morality? Byrne (2005) suggests that Etzioni's communitarianism operates on the assumption that morality can be cut off from other spheres of social life and treated as an undisputed absolute to which we should all demonstrate a happy compliance. But in late-modern societies, with their characteristic diversity and fluidity of identities, the idea of a single dominant morality is anachronistic, and quite probably dangerous. For some critics this may be enough to justify dismissing any attempt to govern through communities, because in the Etzioni model the result is authoritarianism, and exclusion, which is the unavoidable flip side to the inclusivity that makes community imaginable in the first place. But the abandonment of aspirations to govern through communities does not necessarily produce a better vision if the alternative is the unrestrained polarising dynamic of a globalised, market society, the values of which tend to be destructive of non-instrumental values such as loyalty and trust on which community cohesion may depend (Little 2002), and towards which governments such as New Labour's appear to be profoundly submissive.

Consequently, as we have discussed previously, it may be better not to throw the baby out with the bath water, but rather to follow the advice of those such as Little (ibid.) and Hughes (2006) in pursuing a more progressive, radical pluralist model of communitarianism, which imagines *communities* rather than 'the community'. This means accepting that late-modern communities consist of people with multiple cross-cutting identities, rather like Rooker's analogy of a bowl of spaghetti, except that what is a vice for government policy with regard to too many initiatives becomes a virtue for civil society that government should seek to support, and to provide a forum for airing and hopefully resolving the conflicts that are an inevitable part of late-modern society, that cannot simply be wished away as they are in Etzioni's vision. Unfortunately, however, the northern town riots in 2001 and other signs of post-9/11 urban unease have not encouraged the Labour government to venture down such a radical pluralist path, and although there may well be space for the emergence of a more progressive politics at the local level, Labour's response, conceived in terms of community cohesion, which has also been a strong governmental theme within the European Union since 2000 (Levitas 2005), has been to reassert its moral authoritarian communitarian agenda.

A second discernible tendency in Labour's agenda for community participation reflects a more conventional understanding of participation as part of the policy process. While its MUD-inspired communitarianism may be preoccupied with questions of social order (Levitas 2005), this tendency in Labour's political project plays more to the SID and RED discourses of social exclusion, depending upon the extent of its radicalism. In terms of a relatively conservative SID discourse, community participation in the policy process is about being integrated into structures of governance, and perhaps into the body politic, in recognition that modernist bureau-professional ways of working have previously tended to leave communities very much on the outside. Broadly, this accords with Taylor's (2003) characterisation of 'system failure' as a theme of community policy. In terms of RED, meanwhile, participation provides communities with an opportunity to find a voice and to challenge existing constructions and responses to both themselves and the social conditions that they endure, rather in the way imagined by Hughes's (2006) radical pluralism, or in Byrne's (2005) advocacy of a social pedagogic approach. This roughly accords with Taylor's (2003) characterisation of 'structural failure' as a theme of community policy.

So, how have New Labour's overtures to participation in the policy process panned out? Raco *et al.* (2006) place New Labour's efforts at enhancing community participation within the wider context of a policy shift from representative democracy to participatory democracy.

Representative democracy, in the shape of local government, has undergone a period of decline in which its legitimacy has suffered as a result of a perceived democratic deficit, evidenced especially in low electoral turnouts, but also given expression in the public choice critique, which New Labour has indulged, that sees local government services as being dominated by bureau-professional provider interests. One policy response has been to attempt to 'cut out the middle man' by developing a more direct, participatory style of democracy where local people can become more directly involved in the governance of problems such as neighbourhood renewal or social exclusion. Such participatory democracy fits well with the neighbourhood management approach that has been tested in NDC areas, and which has now become a part of the more extensive neighbourhoods agenda being pursued by New Labour, and it also fits the authority-wide approach to governance reflected in the establishment of LSPs.

Another element of New Labour's approach, however, has been to strengthen and breathe new life into representative government as part of a new localism in local government (Stoker 2004), evidenced in the emphasis upon a community leadership role for local authorities, and the shift to Cabinet-style government, headed where wanted by a continental-style local mayor. This simultaneous pursuit of developments in representative and participatory democracy is contradictory. It is plausibly attributable to the pursuit of different agendas within the New Labour government elite, but its effect is to create complexity, confusion and almost certainly tension.

Raco *et al.* (2006) researched the community strategies of two different LSPs with an eye to examining how the tension between representative and participatory democracy is played out in practice. Their findings suggest that this is likely to be contingent upon local political circumstances, but a common finding across the two case studies was that local community engagement tended to be relatively minimal, and that local authority interests tended to dominate, through the bodies of elite officers and members in the urban case, and through elite officers and members of the local 'squirearchy' in the other rural case. 'Hard to reach' groups generally were not sought out, and in one case the limited effort was 'justified' by a concern that their views might conflict with those of local elites. Consequently, although LSPs appear to provide a conduit for participatory democracy, and there is even a Community Empowerment Fund to support such an end, in practice they empower not 'the community', but elite officers and members who are able to engage in strategic capacity-building, serving as the 'guiding hand' of LSPs. Thus representative democracy remains generally dominant, but accommodates participatory democracy of a very limited kind, that allows elite officers and members to build strategic capacity with others, certainly not those who may be numbered amongst the socially excluded. Raco *et al.*'s findings support Byrne's (2005) concern that the authority-wide focus of LSPs does not prioritise the participation of socially excluded people, and consequently there is the ever-present danger that the community participation that does take place is vulnerable to elite capture, as the strongest voice is given to the best organised and most strategically placed community interests. Others either might not be involved at all, or their involvement can be dismissed because their generally parochial concerns do not fit the authority-wide, strategic focus of the LSPs.

Community participation at the neighbourhood level is potentially a different kettle of fish, because here the parochialism is not likely to be out of place. Lawless's (2004) overview of the experiences of NDC areas does not suggest that participation has fared much better here, however. The research, which included extensive surveys of residents, suggests that there has been a general failure to engage with black and minority ethnic groups, and that residents tend to hold mistrustful views of NDC Boards, in part, Lawless suggests, because residents might confuse them with local authorities, that are evidently not held in high esteem either. Dinham (2005) provides more detailed research into community participation in a single NDC area in London. In his research he found that community participation tended to favour the most organised and well-established groups that did not reflect all interests within the neighbourhood. But even these participants found familiar problems in fitting in with the demands of the highly bureaucratised structures and processes of NDC Boards, which have often been constructed in a way that looks 'upwards' to the demands of central government's silo-based performance management framework, rather than 'downwards' to the neighbourhood. Ironically, the participants were often treated as representatives, as if they were councillors, and thus another layer of the bureaucratic process, rather than having their presence seen as an expression of direct democracy. Finally, while there was a considerable amount of informal community activity or participation occurring outside of the NDC structures, little attempt was made by the NDC Board to engage with or tap in to it, as if it was not 'proper' participation. In Dinham's view, the fundamental problem he found was a lack of emphasis upon community development, or of 'starting where people are', so that participation tended to be conceived '... as a technical device for delivering active citizens within a prescribed polis of "stakeholders" whom, having glimpsed government's vision, opt into it with energy' (2005: 304). Without community development, participation becomes more about incorporation (Byrne 2005), which probably speaks more to the control agenda of the MUD discourse than to any progressive, empowering politics that is genuine about providing neighbourhoods with the opportunity to participate in ways that would seriously challenge their social exclusion.

If the prospects for community participation at this level of policy-making do not look especially good, perhaps there has been more space for participation at earlier stages in the policy process. It is important to remember that some degree of participation gives a gloss of legitimacy to public policy, and thus, in some form at least, it is desirable as a governmental objective. With regard to crime, participation as consultation, cast in Arnstein's (1969) terms somewhere towards the bottom rungs of the ladder, has a history that preceded New Labour's accession to political power in 1997. Particularly noteworthy were the police community liaison panels (CLPs) that were first recommended by Scarman as one of a range of community policing measures intended to counter the police's urban legitimacy crisis in the 1980s, and that were given legislative force in the 1984 Police and Criminal Evidence Act. Research into the operation of such panels suggested that their influence on local policing policy was negligible; that they rarely engaged those such as young people and black and minority ethnic groups with whom relations had become most strained; and that the direction of the flow of communications tended to be more from the police to the public than vice versa. Consequently, from the police point of view, CLPs often took the form of an irritating but necessary public relations exercise.

Despite its obvious limitations, the police CLP took on a renewed sense of importance after the 1994 Police and Magistrates' Courts Act, which made such consultation an integral element of the police's annual planning cycle, and after 1997 Labour maintained the emphasis upon consultation by making it a requisite feature of the strategic planning of the newly-created CDRPs, although the positioning of consultation within this process was somewhat vague, and in addition to consulting the public the statutory guidance identified a range of other agency 'stakeholders' with whom responsible authorities were supposed to consult. The guidance also made it clear that the responsible authorities should make an effort to consult 'hard to reach' groups, and that the process should connect with other established methods and processes of consultation, thus establishing a possible bridge between CDRP consultation, police CLPs, and the consultation duty that had been placed upon local authorities following the 1999 Local Government Act, and that was subsequently built into the Best Value performance regime for both the police and local authorities.

So, what are the prospects for community participation afforded by the provision of all these consultation opportunities? The first point to note, perhaps, is that as with participation on LSPs, the scope of these consultation opportunities is wider than excluded or high-crime neighbourhoods, and while one might imagine that a number of so-called 'hard to reach' groups may be concentrated in these neighbourhoods, the injunction to seek out the views of such groups does not necessarily mean this is what will happen. As with the LSPs, there is a chance that consultation will prove more responsive to the views of others. Who these others are might depend upon the consultation method adopted. Although it is something of a stereotype, promulgated in part by police officers themselves, there is a kernel of truth in the observation that police CLPs tend to be populated by the likes of neighbourhood watch coordinators and people who fit the profile and conservative 'mindset' of those most likely to volunteer, namely white, male, middle-aged and middle class. Such a mindset is usually thought to be well-tuned to the exclusionary discourse of populist punitiveness, which therefore does not make it a promising basis upon which to fashion an approach to crime control that fits its twin objective of tackling social exclusion. And such a method of consultation, if it does not actively seek out those who are excluded, cannot further the cause of participation that is in itself seen as a part of the solution to exclusion. That does not mean, however, that other methods cannot offer better prospects for such participation.

Newburn and Jones (2002) have conducted research for the Home Office on the use of consultation by CDRPs in the first round of strategic planning in 1998/9. Although this first round was perhaps a more hurried affair than subsequent rounds, and although practice has probably changed somewhat in the intervening years, the research is still relevant, particularly as there are grounds for thinking that changes in practice are unlikely to have been substantial, because the stronger central steer on the content of strategies from 2002 onwards provides a disincentive for investing heavily in more expansive approaches to consultation. What, after all, is the point in consulting 'below' when the contents of the strategy are largely set from 'above'? Of course this point also casts a heavy and dark shadow over the prospects for consultation evolving into the kind of influence that makes participation fulfilling and worthwhile (and thus inclusionary), although as previously noted we must be wary of assuming that the centre always gets its way, or that localities do not possess a genuinely inclusionary 'will to consult' that can override this central steer.

The research was based upon a national survey of local community safety coordinators, and a small number of follow-up case studies where issues were explored in greater depth. What may be particularly important for present purposes is the fact that, while CDRPs had in mind a number of different aims for consultation, most of them, and certainly the most common ones, were highly instrumental, using consultation effectively to identify local issues and strategic priorities. Generally, when the consultation is used for such instrumental purposes, it ends up confirming the picture of local crime problems that is painted in the crime audit, which relies heavily on police recorded crime and incident data. Thus, usually, the consultation does not result in a profound change to the list of strategic priorities that 'fall out' of the audit, and thus its impact is limited (Newburn and Jones 2002). This instrumentalism has subsequently become institutionalised in a consultation *toolkit* provided for CDRPs on the Home Office's crime reduction website. But the problem with this instrumental view of the uses of consultation is that it is not a firm basis upon which to build an inclusionary form of participation, though the extent of the problem may depend upon the method of the consultation and the results it yields. If the consultation is instrumental but yields only what is already known, then what is the point, particularly when the data collection capacity of state agencies is continually increasing, so that, for example, there is now far more extensive information about disorder and anti-social behaviour than used to be the case, when police incident data remained largely a 'closed book', and when the BCS was just a twinkle in the Home Office's eye? And if it yields new information, there is always the danger that it will be dismissed, either because it is 'too parochial' (complaints about dog fouling and illegal parking frequently fall into this category); or, ironically, because the claim is not backed up by those self-same 'facts' gathered by the police, that put the police service in a position of almost unchallengeable power in being able to define the nature and scale of 'the local crime problem', or because the identified problem is not of sufficient magnitude to justify it becoming a strategic priority. If the results of consultation are dismissed, then this is likely to feed disillusionment and a sense of exclusion, particularly if there is no 'debriefing' following the exercise.

My own understanding is that practitioners are rightly wary about consulting with the public about sensitive issues such as crime and anti-social behaviour for instrumental reasons. While such consultation might be premised upon the idea of either lending weight and thus legitimacy to formal agency perceptions, or of exposing the local 'dark figure' of crime, the danger that certain voices remain unheard, or that the exercise brings forth the list of usual suspects, is very real, and it is interesting that in all the advice and guidance about consultation there is little discussion of how to deal with the conflicts and contradictions that may emerge from the process. But it is not all bad news. Newburn and Jones (2002) cite positive examples, for example, where efforts to reach homosexual people have shed light and detail upon local problems of homophobic violence, which but for such consultation would remain a largely hidden crime; and where seeking out the experiences of young people has brought to light the extent of their often inter-group victimisation, to set against the usual demonisation of them as offenders. Such examples show that careful consideration of appropriate targets and methods of consultation (the most widely used methods are not necessarily the most productive), and of the most appropriate stage at which consultation should occur (consultation aimed at revealing hidden crime problems, for example, might not occur at the same time as consultation intended to shed further light on the nature of problems already brought to light), can result in a positive role for consultation in giving a voice to those who might not otherwise have one.

Yet while consultation will always be there for instrumental crime control reasons, more consideration should be given to its wider social purpose, if it is to be a vehicle for enhancing the participation and inclusion particularly of excluded people. This requires more attention to the method and frequency of consultation, and in this regard, before we leave the subject of consultation, a couple of other points need to be made. Firstly, when consultation is framed by spatialised conceptions of crime and disorder, it is likely to give conceptual priority to the crimes that typically occur on the streets, in public space. This means that crimes and harms that occur elsewhere, for example within the private spaces of the home, the office or the factory, may well be overlooked, and thus the whole consultation exercise becomes implicated in a process of neglect that is in itself a part of the exclusionary dynamic. Why not have a consultation exercise, for example, that conveys information about local employers – many of them now just as likely to be found in the public sector – that systematically exploit, bully and intimidate their own workforces?

A second point concerns methods such as public surveys, which Newburn and Jones (2002) found to be the most common form of consultation, used by 90% of their survey respondents. Particularly because these surveys may also be used to fulfil Best Value requirements, they are quite likely to borrow questions from the BCS about fear of crime and perceptions of disorder, because these form the subject of certain BVPIs, and because while the BCS provides a national picture, it cannot be analysed at a level of resolution below police force area. From a governmentality point of view, this survey data makes crime governable by imagining it from a collective victim or witness perspective: it tells us, for example, how great a problem 'youths hanging around' is in a respondent's local area. But it does not tell us why respondents perceive 'youths hanging around' to be a problem (the question's phraseology marks it out as an archetypal leading question), nor why, indeed, youths may be hanging around in the first place. It casts these problems, then, as problems of order, that support late-modern tendencies towards 'othering' (Young 1999), and that are most likely to be tackled through a heavy dose of law and order and/or surveillance.

This survey data is often geo-coded, so it can be spatially mapped by a growing army of GIS-savvy analysts, who can produce beautifully designed maps that can mark out, for example through red-shaded hotspots, the areas where problems are perceived to be at their worst. The outcome of consultation drawn in such narrow terms, can be a geography of trouble that can feed approaches to crime control that are exclusionary, simply because while the problems have been mapped, no attempt has been made to explore their constituent features or wider causes. In excluded neighbourhoods, these disorder issues tend to be regarded as more of a problem than in other neighbourhoods, and these surveys may be administered more frequently, as they are done, for example, in all NDC areas. The ironic consequence, then, is that people in excluded neighbourhoods may be asked for information that is then used to justify exclusionary tactics that become targeted at those same neighbourhoods – hardly a case of inclusionary participation. This does not render these surveys scientifically invalid, but it does problematise the use of these surveys, which should be used as the precursor to a consultation process, rather than as an excuse for it.

Overall, as the examples of participation that have been reviewed in this section have hopefully shown, the aspiration for a vertical joined-up approach to governance that draws people from excluded neighbourhoods or elsewhere into the policy process in a genuine participative way, has not been realised, and much of the participative effort, such as it is, can actually work in the opposite direction, to intensify exclusion. Although this is not widely acknowledged by policy-makers, there has been some recognition that something is amiss in civil society that requires more fundamental attention. Thus, while the problem of social exclusion might have started out as one of neighbourhood renewal, it has since transformed into the issue of civil renewal, and accompanying this, the discourse has shifted from social exclusion to social capital. It is to this transformation, that started in Labour's second term in office, and that was pursued with some missionary zeal by David Blunkett in particular, that we now devote our attention.

Social capital and local crime control

During Labour's first term of office the solution to wicked issues such as social exclusion and crime was framed in terms of the need for joined-up policy, conceived as the vertical linking of central, regional, local and neighbourhood-based structures of governance, combined with the horizontal linking of public services both with one another, and with others in a mixed economy that also included the private, voluntary and community sectors. The role ascribed to the community sector in the resultant complex network of multi-level governance demonstrated some continuity with the past, in so far as community had always been a thematic current of urban policy (Imrie and Raco 2003), and particularly since the national evaluation of the Action for Cities initiative by Brian Robson and his colleagues in the mid-1990s, community involvement has been placed at the heart of urban policy discourse (Wilks-Heeg 2003). Yet the precise nature of the role that communities were supposed to play remained unclearly articulated. The discourse of joined-up policy implied that the different and dispersed elements of multi-level governance could be fitted together like pieces of some governmental jigsaw, to offer a more holistic approach to policy, but there was no clear indication even of what the community piece (or pieces) of the jigsaw looked like, let alone of where it (or they) fitted.

As New Labour moved into their second term of office, however, the theme of community participation started to gain more theoretical coherence. Just as Old Labour had struggled in the past to find or cultivate the communities upon which its urban policies in the 1960s and 1970s had been inscribed, so New Labour had similarly struggled in its first term, although it is a moot point whether the problem lay in the absence of such communities, or the inability or unwillingness of public services to look for, find or work with them. As we have seen, for example, notwithstanding the odd exception, CDRPs generally had not gone out of their way to engage with their local communities in the first round of strategies, with such consultation as was done often having little or no bearing on the ultimate shape of those strategies. But moving into their second term, New Labour's approach towards communities began to take on a coherence around the theme of capacity-building, to cultivate communities to the point where they were in a position to play their full part in joined-up policy. Capacity-building as an idea demonstrates some continuity with community development, which had been a theme of Old Labour's approach to communities, evidenced particularly in the infamous Community Development Projects (CDPs). But into the new millennium, the capacity to be built was identified specifically as that of social capital, a concept that had been absent from the neighbourhood renewal discourse of the SEU until around 2001, when '... the dialogue seemed to shift away from social exclusion and economic development to social capital' (Kearns 2003: 39). A little later, according to Faulkner (2003) by 2003, Labour was clearly seeking to reposition itself in a reform project that crystallised around the notion of civil renewal, with important intellectual contributions being made on this theme by the likes of David Blunkett, Tony Blair and Hazel Blears. Overall, then, the idea was that for communities to participate in Labour's communitarian-inspired vision of a third way, civil society first needed to be renewed (just as the SEU had previously identified the need for deprived neighbourhoods to be renewed), and the route to such renewal was through the building up of what in deprived and high-crime communities were conceived to be depleted stocks of social capital. The themes of building social capital and civil renewal thus gave Labour's policy a distinctive theoretical coherence, not to mention something of an evangelical mission.

The concept of social capital holds a particular salience for criminology, because if it is about enhancing the capacity of communities to participate in joined-up local governance, it is also about protecting neighbourhoods from crime. Thus the empirical research of Sampson *et al.* (1997) demonstrates that localities that register high on measures of social capital also register low on measures of property and violent crimes, while the same is also true vice versa. They prefer to use the term collective efficacy rather than social capital, but the meaning is much the same and the understanding is that stocks of social capital translate into a greater likelihood of pro-social attitudes and behaviours, and a greater propensity to exercise the kinds of informal social controls that keep delinquency largely at bay. Social capital is a concept that has arrived at the right time. As governments seek variously to activate communities, to reduce crime and disorder, to improve social cohesion, and even to strengthen economic performance and competitiveness, so social capital fits the bill on all counts (Kearns 2003). Its alleged cure-all qualities make it a desirable commodity for those seeking to govern in late-modern times under a global neo-liberal economic and political order, particularly because the focus is upon civil society rather than state action, and particularly for those third way governments that adopt such a fatalistic response to the alleged constraints of globalisation on state action. Cynics may suspect that social capital is some kind of latter-day snake-oil, but the concept has been cautiously welcomed by many within criminology (Hope and Karstedt 2003).

Inevitably social capital is a slippery concept. The Organisation for Economic Co-operation and Development (OECD) definition identifies it as 'networks together with shared norms, values and understandings that facilitate cooperation within and among groups' (cited in Faulkner 2003). Trust is seen as having a key role in sustaining these networks of cooperative relations, just as it is seen as being central in the formation of inter-organisational partnerships (Gilling 2005). And rather like the horizontal and vertical dimensions to joined-up policy, social capital has two different forms: a *bonding* social capital that cements networks *within* communities, and a bridging social capital that consolidates ties or connections between communities and the external environment (Taylor 2003). Bonding social capital fixes the sense of community that many sociologists of modernity have bemoaned the loss of, and it is based upon a similarity of interests (Taylor 2003) and an 'inward-looking' quality to neighbourhood life (Hastings 2003). Bridging social capital, meanwhile, makes these neighbourhoods 'well-connected' to significant others, such as local political actors, and it is thus inherently more 'outward-looking' (Hastings 2003). Individually, bridging social capital can give the possessor access to commodities such as paid work, through a connection to 'the right people', while collectively it plugs local communities in to political opportunity structures, so that along with public bodies they may be fully involved in the co-production of local governance.

As a consequence of its putative benefits, Labour has valorised the building of social capital, so that civil renewal can be achieved, as well as the more specific benefits already identified above. Yet this normative support for building social capital does not translate unproblematically into policy action, in part because social capital is largely a property of civil society, and thus not something that direct government action can simply 'make'. Rather, social capital may be thought of more as a naturally-occurring social phenomenon, the formation and sustenance of which government action might be able to indirectly influence, but never control, thus making policy outcomes rather less certain or predictable than in other areas of public policy. Yet while social capital may indeed be a 'naturally-occurring' social phenomenon, like other forms of capital it is unevenly distributed, with its distribution structured according to the power relations that exist between groups and areas. Consequently, government policy has been to concentrate efforts to build social capital upon those groups and areas from which it has been most noticeably absent – typically the deprived and high-crime neighbourhoods that have always formed the focus of urban policy.

It is possible to identify a number of means by which Labour has sought to build social capital. Firstly, it has made significant efforts to support or strengthen the voluntary sector, on the understanding that volunteering and a vibrant third sector are good expressions of social capital, evidencing high degrees of cooperation and mutuality. At the national level, governmental bodies in each separate country of the United Kingdom have signed strategic compacts with bodies representing the voluntary sector at this level, and local authorities have been encouraged to do likewise at the local level, though many have yet to do so. Furthermore, the voluntary sector has been drawn more and more into a service delivery role, being contracted to provide services at arm's length from the government, and often with a lot more local credibility (than statutory services). But as Fyfe's (2005) research shows, the contracting of voluntary service provision can end up creating a 'shadow state', where state funding supports those voluntary agencies that are most compliant, 'conventional', managerialised and professionalised, leaving others that may have a more campaigning or radical edge to them out in the cold. Thus, while manifestly seeking to build social capital by engaging with and activating the voluntary sector, state action ends up using voluntary agencies for their own service delivery ends. Those that make themselves useable may thrive, and may become better connected, thus enhancing their own organisational social capital. But those that are left out are relatively neglected, with their active citizenship being effectively discouraged, and treated as unwelcome. Fyfe's findings are supported by Hodgson's (2004) research into the experiences of those working in voluntary agencies in Wales. Here, again, certain voluntary agencies were favoured over others through the award of government funding, and those employed in the favoured agencies were more likely to develop 'cosy' relationships with statutory partners, and more likely therefore to be cut off from the grassroots membership, thereby ironically reducing rather than building social capital. Hodgson is left in little doubt that this engagement with the voluntary sector is really more about governing at a distance than building social capital.

A second thematic strand to Labour's attempts to build social capital has already been considered above. Here, the emphasis is upon engaging with community organisations and representatives to develop bridging social capital through structures of neighbourhood management, or at higher levels of abstraction, such as through LSPs. But as we have seen, the kind of participation that this entails is set low on Arnstein's (1969) ladder, and while community organisations may be connected into partnership bodies, their opportunity to produce social capital is constrained by limited opportunities to influence political decision-making (Taylor 2003). Raco (2003) suggests that community involvement tends to be used to secure legitimacy for local policy-making, since it is perceived to come with a community seal of approval. Hastings (2003) argues that community involvement has been used as a lever for improving the quality of local government services, as representatives and organisations are drawn upon as expert sources of local knowledge whose participation will inevitably result in better-informed local policy-making. One could argue, as indeed does Cooper (2006), that this is how community involvement is used by CDRPs in the strategy-setting process, and since in such instances some sources of knowledge are privileged over others (Jasper [2006], for example, points out that that the police rarely do enough to engage black and minority ethnic groups), the overall effect here could be to undermine bonding social capital and to divide communities, or at least concretise extant divisions. Finally, as Wilks-Heeg (2003) observes, community involvement generally stops short of meaningful involvement in the evaluation of urban policies, so that, paradoxically, the presumed expertise of communities in formulating policies is suddenly denied when it comes to judging the results of policy interventions. This is connectivity, but only of a highly conditional kind.

We should not rule out the possibility of more positive and meaningful community involvement, and of the building of sustainable social capital, because as Cochrane (2003) amongst others reminds us, there is a degree of co-dependence between the state and civil society, and within such co-dependence, therefore, there is space for communities to negotiate a more meaningful role for themselves in the processes of governance. Indeed, North (2003) provides us with case study examples of successful community involvement in regeneration initiatives in London, where the plans of local authorities and developers were effectively shelved because of strong community opposition which evidenced strong bonding and bridging social capital, although success was achieved more in terms of defeating unwelcome plans rather than in seeing more welcome ones reach fruition.

A third means by which Labour has sought to build social capital, and the final one that we shall be considering here, is also the most relevant for our purposes. It concerns an attempt to build social capital through crime control, and it draws upon a number of areas that we have considered elsewhere within this book. It has been a discrete objective of Home Office policy that has picked up explicitly on the personal convictions of David Blunkett, although there is a line of continuity that runs back to Jack Straw's period of office as Home Secretary, and particularly to his call for more active citizen involvement in crime control – the idea of the 'have-a-go hero'. There is an official understanding, which resonates with research findings but also with Etzioni's communitarianism, that strong social capital prevents crime by giving individuals the confidence to intervene in broken windows-style disorders, and there is also an understanding that crime and anti-social behaviour destroy social capital by generating fear, anxiety and mistrust, and by undermining the basis of informal social control. These combined understandings, it seems, have informed a view that, therefore, the best way to build social capital may be through crime control, although the logic that underpins this view also has a ring of the '2 + 2 = 5' about it.

There are a number of different threads to this attempt to build social capital through crime control. They include, for example, the continued promotion of neighbourhood watch, despite evidence that it does not work as a crime control measure, and that it is most difficult to establish in neighbourhoods that suffer the highest levels of crime and social exclusion (Bolton 2006), and that therefore generally, but by no means always, have the least social capital. They also include an array of attempts to encourage the further encroachment of 'the extended policing family' into neighbourhoods by attaching a more or less formal responsibility for crime control to more or less formal agents of social control. Under the neighbourhood policing initiative, for example, we find extended police patrolling either from regular officers, or increasingly from PCSOs, which may be expected to forge bridging social capital, while other policing bodies, including those from the private sector, can be empowered under community safety accreditation schemes with the capacity to issue FPNs, thus adding a further layer to networks of local policing. Similarly, where they are used, neighbourhood wardens extend the network further, while as Flint (2006) observes, providers and managers of social housing, which can include voluntary housing associations and community-based TMOs, are increasingly required to shift their attention from a narrow focus upon the management of a stock of housing, to a broader focus upon the management of the neighbourhood, including the adoption of clear policies and procedures for addressing anti-social behaviour at this level. The measures that social housing agencies have at their disposal can be interpreted as measures designed to induce the formation of social capital, whether that be through various kinds of tenancy contracts to induce good behaviour; the rewarding of active citizenship through 'good neighbour' schemes; alterations to the physical design of neighbourhoods that induce a sense of shared ownership and mutuality (in much the same way as Oscar Newman's [1973] principles of defensible space were intended to induce a sense of territoriality); or socially engineered changes to the social environment such as the establishment of mixed income and tenure communities (MINCs) (see Dearling *et al.* 2006), on the understanding that this tenure mix provides a basis for more stable communities, where the stock of social capital is somehow higher. Finally, one might also include some of the measures that have emerged in the wake of the Respect Action Plan in 2006, where one of the key themes is identified as strengthening communities. In this regard, the social capital implications of proposals to introduce a 'community call for action' or for senior representatives of CDRPs to hold 'face the people' sessions are manifestly obvious.

There are, then, a lot of strings to the government's bow for building social capital through crime control. But how credible is the idea of building social capital through crime control? Lessons from the past are always salutary, and while the terminology has changed, we would do well to call upon the wise words of some academic commentators of developments in community policing in the 1980s. In that decade, community policing was put forward as a means of connecting formal and informal social control mechanisms, with a view to bolstering the latter in particular. In contemporary terminology, it was about building bridging and bonding social capital, but as Smith (1987) then observed, the prospects for strengthening communities through policing are always likely to be undermined by the fact that most police activity is essentially adversarial: it is about dealing with manifest or latent conflict. As he quite rightly observes, '[t]he idea of community does not seem to provide us with a model for dealing with these conflicts. It is an idea that is best adapted to mobilising the support of the respectable majority' (1987: 63). Since Smith wrote these words thinking about communities may have moved on, and the more pluralist conception advocated by those such as Little (2002) may be more able to accommodate some such conflicts, but Smith's point is still pertinent as contemporary government policy operates within the parameters of an Etzioni-inspired single moral authoritarian community.

Smith (1987) also observed that there was often a poor fit between formal and informal social controls, and that the aspiration for community policing to be able to manipulate informal social controls remained a major issue that had yet to be resolved by proponents of community policing. So, what has changed since the 1980s? On the positive side, there may be fewer mullet haircuts in circulation, but, although community policing is now pursued more through other members of the extended policing family, the problem of how best to engage with and harness informal social control largely remains, and it may have been made more difficult because of the shadow that has been cast by the strictures of new public management, which in the case of policing existed only in embryonic form in the mid-1980s. New public management imposes expectations of performance upon the police and, as we have seen, upon CDRPs. Consequently, notwithstanding rhetorical support for using initiatives such as neighbourhood policing to help build social capital, agencies such as the police feel the weight of expectation to deliver against targets that have not been set locally, and that use measures of performance that do not necessarily accord with local perceptions – hence the existence of the reassurance gap (Lister 2006). The problem here is similar to that found in other attempts to build social capital, where formal agencies end up engaging with communities on highly instrumental terms. Communities may be 'used' to do policing on behalf of formal agencies, and this can be resented, as Bolton (2006) found in her research into neighbourhood watch groups, where members expressed frustration at the police's neglect of them. Alternatively, communities may be used for their 'expertise', which in police terms is defined as 'community intelligence', used to inform police operations rather than to determine 'what the public wants', and harking back to familiar civil libertarian critiques of community policing in the 1980s (see, for example, Gordon [1984]).

Another change between the 1980s and the present can be found in the phenomenon of plural policing. While bodies other than the police service have always been involved in aspects of policing broadly conceived, what is particularly significant in the present is one of the dynamics that drives plural policing, namely the threat of competition. The police service has responded to the threat of competition since at least the 1990 Operational Policing Review, and its attempt to develop a more consumerist service ethos. For our purposes, what this means is that the police service, as Lister (2006) observes, has sought to preserve its market advantage, particularly through the deployment of large numbers of PCSOs in neighbourhoods. The danger inherent in the police service responding to its consumers in a market-like relationship is that it ends up responding to those 'consumers' with the loudest voice, who are usually also the most visible. There is the danger here of the police being captured by popular punitive attitudes, informed in part by populist politicians and parts of the media, but also by the failure of public agencies to engage with members of the public in an alternative, more constructive and more liberal discourse (Ryan 2006). This punitiveness informs an unhealthy dose of 'othering' and scapegoating (Young 1999), that is easily directed as more marginal groups such as asylum-seekers, travellers, black and minority ethnic groups, and young people in general.

Indeed, Farrow and Prior (2006) found in their research into community involvement in initiatives to tackle anti-social behaviour that a large number of community members found it difficult to see past a perceived need for strong enforcement measures against young people. The problem is exacerbated, according to Bacon and James (2006), by the fact that while the police can connect relatively easily with the public because they operate in a neighbourhood-based spatial field of operation, the same cannot be said for other social agencies whose field of operation is more personalised and individualised, focusing upon vulnerable individuals and families, where there is strong pressure to maintain confidentiality and essentially low-profile working styles. These agencies, therefore, do not connect so well with the public, and thus, echoing Ryan's (2006) point, opportunities for seeing the other side of the coin may be lost. This does not mean that because (parts of) the public are likely to engage most easily with the police that enforcement is the only possible outcome to community engagement, because such a view neglects the progressive agendas that many police officers seeking to engage in community or neighbourhood policing aim to pursue. However, the resources that are most readily available to the police are enforcement resources, and under pressure to respond to community concerns about local crime and disorder problems, which is likely to be intensified by devices such as the 'community call for action', it is quite understandable that enforcement should become the main currency through which the police service can demonstrate that something is being done.

This brings us to the fundamental question of whether the idea of building social capital through crime control really has any credibility. Concern about crime, and the general anxieties that constitute the fear of crime, may be widespread in late-modern risk-oriented societies such as the one presently governed by New Labour, but it requires a leap of logic to presume that crime and anti-social behaviour can bind people together in a way that promotes the kinds of social capital that can turn excluded people into included people, and that can generate social cohesion. The problem, echoing Smith's (1987) simple observation, is that the object that is supposed to unite people, namely crime or anti-social behaviour, is fundamentally about matters of conflict, mistrust and suspicion (Prior 2004; Farrow and Prior 2006; Roberts 2006), and even more welfare liberal approaches to tackling it, which as we have seen the public are not generally well connected with, are premised upon the identification of risky and thus suspicious groups. Cummings makes this point well when he notes that '[w]hile the intention of community involvement is in part to foster trust, a focus on crime necessarily involves suspicion' (2006: 10–11). People may well become united in their mistrust of others, as did the residents of Paulsgrove in Portsmouth, against alleged paedophiles living in their midst, and as did the residents of some northern towns in the racialised riots of 2001, but if this generates any kind of social capital it is of a very inward-looking nature, of the kind that keeps generally excluded groups at loggerheads, and of the kind that Marxists would see as driving an ideological wedge between the proletariat.

Even if the conflict is not so manifest, the division may still be there. Cummings (2006) suggests that this even infuses the seemingly more progressive development of restorative justice, which may be less punitive, but which nevertheless entrenches surveillance and suspicion within the social fabric of communities. As Lister (2006) observes, in the case of neighbourhood policing what is entrenched is a single moral order that takes precedence over all others, and is endowed with authority because it is backed up by the threat of enforcement. These are the problems of Etzioni's moral authoritarian communitarianism coming home to roost. And as more and more public and quasi-public officials are endowed with enforcement powers of summary justice, such as the issuing of FPNs, so the threat intensifies. It is difficult to avoid the conclusion that an attempt to build social capital through crime control is anything other than a bad idea that risks making a bad situation a whole lot worse.

Faulkner makes a similar point, albeit in softer and more measured terms, when he notes that '... effective measures to prevent and reduce crime and anti-social behaviour, to repair the damage it causes, and to provide a sense of public reassurance and confidence, demand something more than and different from the criminal justice process itself' (2003: 294). Faulkner, as a former Home Office insider, is acutely aware of the limitations of criminal justice, and equally troubled by the way the primary role of the criminal justice system has been reasserted by governments since the mid-1990s. For him '... the limitations of criminal justice as a means of preventing and dealing with crime should still be acknowledged, and should be met by the development of non-criminal methods of social intervention, and not by continually expanding the scope of social intervention' (2003: 295). Yet under New Labour, the limitations that have been recognised are those not of the system, but of the due process principles that have traditionally underpinned it. Thus the system continues to expand, but in a 'rebalanced' way, which Blunkett unconvincingly tells us is not about '... reducing the rights of the defendant to a fair trial', but is about '... increasing the rights of *the community* to a fair outcome' (both 2006: 8, emphasis added). Which community would that be, then?

Faulkner (2003) contrasts this reassertion of criminal justice with an earlier period of Home Office activity in the 1980s when the limitations of criminal justice were acknowledged, and a policy of responsibilisation was pursued, drawing in part upon the resources of the voluntary and community sectors. Yet it is not the case that responsibilisation has been replaced by a reassertion of the centrality of the state's role. Rather, responsibilisation has been a constant, but its character has changed. In the 1980s critics suspected it was sometimes a thin veneer for privatisation, but in the present it is linked more fundamentally to a project of remoralisation, which is implicit in Labour's communitarian agenda, and which is fed by a MUD discourse that attributes problems of crime and anti-social behaviour to the lax morals of those living in excluded communities. Thus it is not just the offenders, but also the victims, witnesses, parents, children, and also the allegedly deficient public services operating in such areas, that all require some degree of remoralisation. Consequently, building social capital through crime control may be the stated intention, but the more likely thrust of policies, whether intended or otherwise, is a bid to remoralise, so that capacity-building is recast as an essentially coercive process (Imrie and Raco 2003), so that inclusion is performed as a kind of forced 'consensus', from which dissenting voices and those beyond the boundaries are 'othered' and excluded. Raco (2003) suggests that the turn to community in urban policy has been a necessary part of keeping the hegemonic neo-liberal project on track, in the light of the damage that it has inevitably inflicted upon social relations. If so, Labour's 'success' in its strategy of civil renewal has been to make a virtue out of this necessity, and the quote from Blunkett cited above nicely demonstrates this, because it reframes this responsibilisation as 'the rights of the community'. There's double-speak.

Labour's approach to building social capital demonstrates well that attempts by the state to influence the relatively autonomous dynamics of civil society are always likely to be vulnerable to capture by political agendas – in this case a bid for the remoralisation of excluded neighbourhoods, so that they may then be governed through. Perhaps this is why Hope and Karstedt (2003) question the capacity of state action to strengthen the fabric of civil society, although this does not mean that civil society should be left to its own devices in some dubious neo-liberal paradise. Rather, while direct state action intended to engineer civil society may be misguided (a good example of this is the way engineered MINC neighbourhoods can end up reproducing divisions along tenure lines), state action nevertheless has an important influence in providing the context in which civil society operates. Of particular importance here is the level of social inequality that state social and economic policies are prepared to tolerate. As Hope and Karstedt (2003) observe, such inequality is corrosive of social capital, and it is easy to see how, in Young's (1999) convincing but disturbing portrayal of the exclusive society. So, while New Labour's approach to building social capital may be to engage in a form of remoralisation described by Dearling et al. (2006) as 'positive nannying', perhaps what is really needed, as O'Malley (2005) suggests, is the remoralisation of government. This means having a vision, rather than no vision; playing on hopes rather than fears; and not adopting such a fatalistic approach to the apparently unstoppable forces of globalisation. It means not looking upon communities in terms of '... the therapeutic-political goals of a political class that is acutely conscious of its distance from the public ... [thus seeking] to engage them not as a public, but as anxious individuals' (Cummings 2006: 11).

A remoralised government might see 'the crime problem' in a different way. Commenting upon a speech of Tony Blair's following the 2001 election, in which he put 'persistent offenders' (identified by a common set of familiar risk factors) squarely in the sights of New Labour's second term crime control strategy, Cook notes that '[o]thers would ask, "what is the problem here"? Is it the criminal behaviours of individual persistent offenders or the conditions within which it is possible for [young] people to "slip through the net" and suffer such appalling multiple deprivations as these? Policy action – in terms of both criminal justice and social policies – is geared far more to the former than to the latter' (2005: 143). In other words, a remoralised government would put social justice before criminal justice, rather than continuing the process of criminalising the discourse of social policy, which is what happens when policy to tackle social exclusion takes on a MUD discursive form that ends up prioritising coercive social control as the principal means through which civility and neighbourhoods might be renewed. A better approach would be to tackle the social inequalities and discrimination that feed such intense degrees of relative deprivation and such strong processes of 'othering'.

Given this bigger agenda of social justice, which requires much more in the way of structural change, it is tempting to dismiss aspirations to build social capital as a diversion, a means of offloading responsibility from the government to elsewhere. Yet while in many ways this is precisely what government policy is doing (albeit then allowing it to govern through responsibilised actors at a distance), we must be careful not to dismiss concepts such as social capital out-of-hand. As Hope and Karstedt (2003) observe, older Keynesian models of government rested upon an impoverished understanding of the social that neglected the autonomy of the civil society through which 'the social' operated. Bowles and Gintis (2002) make much the same point when they suggest that modernist narratives of laissez-faire and interventionist government both rested on inflated claims about the capacity of the state, focusing upon rules of government, rather than principles of good citizenship. So, even if social capital is a slippery concept, it alludes to the role of civil society whose importance has to be acknowledged, although like government action to address social inequalities, it has to be regarded as a means to an end, rather than an end in itself (Kearns 2003).

Chapter 7

Conclusion: The road to where?

Reviewing where we have been

In this final chapter, my purpose is to review where we have been, in order to gain a better sense of where New Labour's policy of local crime control is going. Again, and this is well worth emphasising, our focus here is upon a project of local crime control that has been devised from the top, from within the New Labour political elite, and that has entailed various efforts to put it into practice as a way of governing (through a combination of crime reduction, tackling anti-social behaviour, addressing social exclusion, and building social capital) the population. In other words, this is about what in Foucauldian terms we would call biopolitics (Stenson 2005). It has involved attempts to shape the actions, and the governing mentalities, of those agencies and individuals involved in exercising governmental power over the population, and it has involved attempts to shape the conduct of the population, and particularly of those living within high-crime neighbourhoods, in governing both themselves, and their putative communities. Such a project, needless to say, is exceptionally ambitious. As noted in Chapter 1, it is limited by the power-dependence that constrains the governmental project of any sovereign ruler. There are plenty of opportunities for resistance. Local advocacy coalitions, for example, may have a very different set of priorities for action from those that the centre seeks to impose. Nevertheless, just as one should not over-exaggerate the power to rule, nor should one over-exaggerate the power to resist. But this book is not about such strategies of resistance, the empirical exploration of which remains relatively limited. The point in this book has been to acknowledge that they exist, but then to move on to centre our analysis on the New Labour project.

Another constraint that limits this ambitious governing project, which was also discussed in Chapter 1 but elaborated upon also in Chapter 2, is New Labour's accession to a globalised neo-liberal hegemony, which requires the pursuit of a particular vision of the free, responsible and entrepreneurial subject, which in turn requires not too much government, or perhaps government, but only in the right places. This self-imposed constraint – particularly conceived as a necessary response to globalisation – is presented rhetorically as an inevitability, in much the same way as the wars that justify the social order of George Orwell's dystopian vision of *1984* appear inevitable. It means that a limit is placed upon how much government can be involved in the business of local crime control, and this requires a renegotiation of the relationship between the state and the citizen that others such as Crawford (1997) have identified. But it also means that crime control, which histories of crime always show to be more about creating social order than preventing victimisation, is used to shape this neo-liberal order. Just as the criminalisation of 'vagrancy' smoothed the passage of mercantile capitalism (Chambliss 1964), therefore, local crime control smoothes the passage of neo-liberal globalisation. It may be presented as a *response* to globalisation, as one of a number of means by which 'we' may secure our readiness for, and our competitiveness in the face of, globalisation, but it is also simultaneously one of the means by which neo-liberal globalisation is constituted. It is, in other words, a cultural artefact, and one that is always contested and incomplete (Clarke 1999), which takes us back to the above point about possibilities for resistance.

In exploring New Labour's project for local crime control, we equipped ourselves, at the beginning, with two possible maps for the way ahead. One was that of crime prevention, and particularly situational crime prevention, which was how the domain of local crime control started to be shaped by the Conservatives from the 1980s to the mid-1990s, although this path, which others described as a form of risk management slanted towards 'privatised prudentialism' (O'Malley 1992), had already run into trouble before New Labour came to power in 1997. It did so because it met resistance from local practitioners whose preferred model for the local governance of crime was community safety, and it did so because, in the pursuit of a relatively naked neo-liberal agenda, such privatisation both undermined the government's claim to legitimacy as a state institution for guaranteeing security, and enhanced the insecurity of a 'fortress mentality' that it provoked (Gilling 1997).

The third way, in all honesty, never looked like it was going to embrace privatised prudentialism to any great degree, thereby ruling out crime prevention as a guide to the way ahead, and ruling out the most negative of the three possible future scenario models – that of 'privatism and exclusion' – predicted by Hughes (1998). This certainly does not mean that elements of privatised prudentialism could not be taken forward, not least because they fitted the self-imposed constraint of globalisation – not to govern too much. Consequently, we have seen strong elements of privatised prudentialism in the security-oriented activities of owners of mass private property such as shopping malls, and in the security activities of private householders, an increasing number of whom are locating themselves in the security bubbles of gated communities. Yet local crime control policy has tended to be much more about dealing with high-crime neighbourhoods where privatised prudentialism, like neighbourhood watch, is least likely to take root, and here third way rhetoric always suggested a move away from the privatisation of risk, and a move in the direction of the socialisation of risk. Two questions remain, however, namely what kind of move, and to what degree?

A second map for charting the possible way ahead was found in the concept of community safety. While it is possible to identify certain ideal typical features of community safety, as indeed we did in Chapter 1, what is lost in such an approach is a sense of the political nuance that may be lent to the concept, and to the ends to which it may be put. This nuance is sensed by Hughes (1998) again, in his portrayal of scenarios that take community safety either in a conservative moral authoritarian direction, or in a more social democratic one. So, which scenario does local crime control under New Labour most closely approximate?

Even having embarked upon the journey we have taken here, it is still difficult to characterise the shape of local crime control between 1997 and 2006. This should not be that surprising because, as different chapters to this book have hopefully shown, the New Labour project is ongoing. Office-seeking is a constant, which means a tendency from time to time to fall back on the populist punitive consensus that regrettably still characterises law and order politics in the UK; but policy changes. And policy can be repeatedly re-packaged, with the Respect Action Plan providing a good example of the way local crime control can be re-presented, taking in, for example, a slightly different mix of ingredients from education and family policy to add to those more established in the crime control domain, such as neighbourhood policing.

For me, albeit with an acknowledged selectivity that has tended to decentre the role of, for example, YOTs, local crime control is enacted primarily through the bodies of CDRPs. The problem, however, is that these CDRPs are often virtual bodies that act less in themselves, and more through the bodies of their constituent parts. These include in particular the main responsible authorities, the police and the local authorities, and this is why local crime control becomes, as we saw in Chapter 4, entwined in policing and local government, and specifically in the reform processes to which they are both subjected. In the case of both this means their attempts to connect more closely to communities and neighbourhoods. Such attempts to connect are motivated by a desire to shape the transformation of governance, for reasons such as democratic renewal and reassurance, both of which require a renegotiation of the relationship between the state and its citizens.

In these neighbourhoods the issue of anti-social behaviour has loomed large, not necessarily because it is anti-social behaviour rather than crime that is 'the problem' at this level, but rather because anti-social behaviour, by virtue of its wide-ranging nature, speaks more directly to the issue of governing conduct by and within communities. Local crime control seen in these terms is less about stopping crime and more about inducing 'free' neo-liberal individual subjects to govern themselves and their families (which means, amongst other things, respecting others' freedoms), and to participate as 'the community' in the governance of their communities. This links directly to the moral underclass discourse that can be applied to the concepts of social exclusion and building social capital, which are geared to similar ends, and which connect with crime control because of the inclusion of crime and anti-social behaviour in the 'toxic mix' of indicators of social exclusion, and because of their correlation with low social capital.

Local crime control is not only about governing the population. It is also about governing the agencies themselves, particularly in an era of governance which is often presented as a natural corollary of globalisation (because the latter 'hollows out' the nation state, thus providing the space for governance to occupy), but which is no less of a socially constructed accomplishment. Thus it is about joined-up policy, a favourite tool of New Labour's that pushes agencies into partnerships at the local neighbourhood level, as in the case of neighbourhood management, or at the authority level, as in the case of LSPs and the LAAs they are expected now to deliver. Thus the LSPs become involved in the business of local crime control, and through and alongside them flow a host of initiatives, in fields such as neighbourhood renewal, that have a significant bearing on local crime control, as we saw from Chapter 6, in the discussion of social and physical regeneration, and particularly the role of the latter in protecting the urban sites of consumption.

A cynic such as myself might be forgiven for thinking that New Labour's addiction to initiatives – its initiativitis – plays an important role, whether intended or otherwise, in generating the very complexity that accelerates and accentuates the shift from government to governance, particularly in an area such as crime control, where such initiativitis has manifested itself in the emergence of complex networks of 'plural policing', and in the shift from police to policing more generally, seen particularly in the dispersal of the responsibility for the use of enforcement powers against anti-social behaviour to a host of public, private, voluntary and even community sector bodies. Governance may well open up opportunities for non-state actors to play their parts, whether progressive or conservative, in the coordination of social life, but it does not do this necessarily by weakening the position of the centre, which can employ various steering mechanisms, such as the strictures of evidence-based policy or new public management, to govern at a distance. Rather, it does this by undermining the position of 'provider interests', against whom New Labour carries the same basic hostility that was displayed by the Conservatives. It does this because it still allows for steering mechanisms to be applied from the top (new public management, for example, is well described as the institutionalisation of mistrust [Crawford 2001]), which is why partnership working in CDRPs in practice generally falls a long way short of the horizontal trust relations that normative models of governance sometimes espouse. And it also allows for pressure to be applied from the bottom upwards, particularly from 'the community', whose prescribed role in the 'co-production' of local crime control necessarily eats into the discretion and autonomy of 'provider interests', such as the local police.

For some this may be a good thing because of the progressive potential of 'nodal governance' (Johnston and Shearing 2003). But under New Labour such potential may be more difficult to realise, because here the shift to governance is less about sharing power or enhancing democratic accountability, after which progressive visions of community safety may hanker, and more about enhancing managerial accountability, where the objectives are set from the centre, in ways that institutionalise bias in the direction of measurable features of crime and disorder reduction 'performance', particularly enforcement, and in which 'the community' is expected to play its responsibilised part. Ironically, then, while the shift to governance may be presumed to reflect its neo-liberal context of less government, this is illusory: it may allow government to govern better, *without* the irritation of 'provider interests', but *with* the co-productive effort of the community. This is a more effective biopolitics, and one that perhaps exposes a paradox of neo-liberal rule, which in its valorisation of freedom perversely requires more government to achieve.

So, does New Labour's local crime control policy come closest to following the path of community safety? As we can see from Chapters 3 and 4, the use of the term crime and disorder reduction initially introduced some ambiguity into our understanding of exactly where it was that New Labour was going, and the aspiration for localised joined-up policy – *local solutions for local problems* – initially suggested that it may be up to localities, in the shape of CDRPs, to decide the direction of local crime control. But their structural instabilities, combined with increased central government anxiety prompted by concerns about CDRP competence and *potential* rising crime, soon led to a more dirigiste approach. This endeavoured to push CDRPs down a narrow line of headline, volume crime reduction, using the tools of new public management and evidence-based policy, but in so doing it dropped local crime control into the mires of police and local government reform. Here the issues of democratic renewal, reassurance and a stronger 'neighbourhoods' orientation loomed large, and these reform projects are still running their course, and remain very much unfinished projects.

Nevertheless, a neighbourhood focus offers the *potential* for more localised, democratic approaches that really get to grips with the crime-related concerns of local people, provided, of course, that it is connected to the wider structural processes that may play a significant part in causing the problems that generate such concerns – and such a connection has so far been largely absent. However, the much greater regard given to anti-social behaviour from New Labour's second term onwards would appear to show some recognition of these local 'quality of life', fear and insecurity-generating concerns, while the linking of crime to social exclusion and the resultant strategy of neighbourhood renewal would appear to suggest *some* connection to these structural processes.

The pressure is still on CDRPs to deliver on the Home Office-imposed crime reduction targets through such measures as situational crime prevention (CCTV still looms large), law enforcement and police disruption of criminal networks identified through the application of the NIM, but these approaches have always been a part of community safety's suite of interventions. The inclusion on CDRP agendas of reassurance, a neighbourhoods approach, civil renewal, social exclusion and social capital all point to a more pan-hazard approach that is characteristic of community safety. A key moment in the transformation of local crime control may have been when David Blunkett centred civil renewal on the Home Office's agenda, and that agenda merged more with the neighbourhoods and new localism agenda that issued forth from what is now the DCLG. Interestingly, such influences may have left their mark, and while there was always a certain inconsistency in the way the Home Office spoke of crime and disorder reduction but localities spoke more of community safety, and thus both spoke past the other, it may be significant that in 2006 the government produced its first three-year *National Community Safety Plan* (Her Majesty's Government 2006), to complement the three-year National Policing Plan. The contrast with the national *Crime Reduction* Strategy launched by Jack Straw back in 1999 is significant. Community Safety has thus become lodged in government discourse, and significantly the Plan's authorship lies not with the Home Office, but with Her Majesty's Government, which communicates the impression that the joined-up policy on the ground, whether that be at the neighbourhood level or at the level of the CDRP or LSP, is supported by joined-up government at the centre. This holistic 'whole of government' approach accords very much with the principles of those who see in community safety a welcome opportunity to socialise the discourse of crime control. And this is echoed in the five thematic priorities that the Plan prioritises, which are:

1 making communities stronger and more effective;
2 further reducing crime and anti-social behaviour;
3 creating safer environments;
4 protecting the public and building confidence; and
5 improving people's lives so they are less likely to commit offences or reoffend.

Plans and strategies, of course, are all about presentation, and they are designed to look good, but it is significant nevertheless that there is an intention here to 'look good' in terms of community safety, and populist punitiveness is certainly downplayed.

Are we entering, then, the age of a new community safety consensus, bringing into being the vision that animated the authors of the 1991 Morgan Report (Home Office 1991)? We may be entering the age of community safety, but it is not necessarily a consensus. Remembering Hughes's (1998) characterisation of essentially moral authoritarian and social democratic variants of community safety as alternative future scenarios, it would appear that the present policy of community safety, if that is what it is now called, betrays the characteristics more of the former than of the latter. We can see how this is the case by exploring the way that its constituent elements have been moulded by the New Labour project.

As noted above, the strongest theme underpinning local crime control since 1997 has been crime and disorder reduction, framed largely in terms of law enforcement, targeted at crimes (such as through the Street Crime Initiative) and anti-social behaviour (deploying, for example, ASBOs and variants of zero-tolerance policing), and in terms of actuarial situational methods of crime prevention, typified but not reducible to the explosion of CCTV surveillance systems. While, as left realism acknowledges, actuarial methods have their place in the protection of deprived populations who may be more at risk of victimisation, the significant thing about policy under New Labour is that such methods have tended to be targeted not at protecting the marginal and deprived, but rather at physically excluding them from public spaces, and particularly from those spaces of consumption that are undergoing something of a renaissance, and where usually private interests demand protection, or, as the private security industry, participate in the governance of it (Coleman 2004). As other studies show, groups such as young people, homeless people and asylum-seekers may be more vulnerable to criminal victimisation than most, yet their presence on the street is unwelcome, and discourses of community safety are framed in terms of safety *from* such 'others', rather than safety *for* them. Similarly, ASBOs are issued disproportionately against young people and people with mental health and addictive problems, against whose vulnerability the ASBO stands as, itself, a remarkably anti-social response.

Turning to anti-social behaviour policy in the round, as we saw in Chapter 5, New Labour has succeeded in lumping together a range of discrete issues into the generic category of anti-social behaviour, in the process transforming social policy questions around issues of parenting, family policy, education and housing management, into community safety and crime control ones. Governing through anti-social behaviour has allowed New Labour then to pursue the 'anti-social question' primarily by means of enforcement, even against the best advice of its SEU. While the Respect Action Plan might make appropriate noises about the need to tackle the underlying causes of anti-social behaviour, the lion's share of the armoury is devoted to enforcement measures, and even when support measures are 'offered', they are offered with the threat of enforcement for non-compliance. As with the contractual nature of ASBOs, ABCs and so forth, this is a highly conditional form of inclusion. The heavy emphasis upon enforcement, and the strong whiff of populist punitiveness that emanates from central government's ASBO-mania, and which appears to be shared by certain localities such as Manchester City Council, does not match the kind of policy prescription that left realists would have had in mind when applying the square of crime to the low-level crime problems against which the fear of crime was regarded as a rational response. In fact, it is less square of crime than problem analysis triangle, with the contractual nature of the civil sanction standing as a sort of proxy 'intimate handler' for 'motivated offenders', a very literal stake in conformity.

Community safety supports methods that address the deeper social causes of crime, and New Labour has gone some way to socialise the discourse, by connecting crime and anti-social behaviour to the problem of social exclusion, which the Conservatives probably never would have done, and to the absence of social capital, which the Conservatives are perhaps more likely to have done. Yet despite this, the socialisation has been of a limited sort, which may have gone beyond the individual and into 'the community', but has not gone a long way beyond that. Consequently, particularly because of spatialised policies of neighbourhood renewal, as we saw from Chapter 6, there is little or no connection to the problem of the deeper restructuring of capital which has resulted, for example, in the decimation of some local labour markets, and the over-heating of other local housing markets, both with significant exclusionary consequences. And there is little or no connection to the neo-liberal dynamic of widening social inequalities, which feeds the relative deprivation on which problems such as crime flourish (Young 1999): if crime has become normalised in late-modern societies it is because social inequalities have too.

In place of the fully social understanding of the causes of crime that the left realist device of the square of crime is intended to deliver, New Labour's approach offers us a partially social understanding that locates the problem of crime with the problem of communities in which such crime is concentrated. The third way's communitarianism, which was discussed in Chapter 2 and again in Chapter 5 because of its particular salience for understanding the problematisation of anti-social behaviour, comes loaded with the normative expectation that 'the community', imagined as a homogenised and responsibilised entity, a collective abstraction of the responsible individuals of neo-liberal thought, will govern itself. Thus individuals – in Etzioni's understanding usually men – are 'encouraged' by 'welfare to work' schemes to find and take work, to learn the self-discipline that comes from it, and form the breadwinner role that they must assume within their families. Women and men must then work in partnership with schools to secure good discipline and good parenting for their children, as well as a good education, aided and abetted where necessary by schemes such as Sure Start. This sense of responsibility for oneself and for one's family must then be turned outward onto 'the community', generally imagined spatially, where the injunction is not so much a fraternal one of taking responsibility for one's neighbours, but rather one of ensuring that oneself and one's neighbours do not act in ways that violate the freedom of the law-abiding citizen, supported where necessary by the likes of the neighbourhood police, and more likely the PCSO, who in the future may be conjured up by the 'community call-to-action' provision in the 2006 Police and Justice Act.

This normative vision only addresses the social causes of crime as perceived from a moral authoritarian perspective, with its emphasis upon the free morally responsible neo-liberal subject. It is disconnected from structural economic causes, and it is also disconnected from a grounded understanding of community life in late-modern society. The latter is animated by a social diversity and identity group politics that defies any simple totalising vision of homogeneity, and by what Stenson (2005) refers to as a feral post-industrial masculinity, which is a delinquent solution to the market position (Taylor 1999) in which a large proportion of mainly young working-class men now find themselves. One cannot make a moral authoritarian community from these ingredients any more than one can make a silk purse from a sow's ear.

Finally, while local crime control policy under New Labour has appeared to valorise localism as a principle of such policy, from the *local solutions for local problems* rhetoric of the 1998 Crime and Disorder Act, which may well have been dropped only to be picked up again under the *new localism* of the more recent neighbourhoods approach, there are very strong grounds for questioning the extent to which such policy is really intended to produce the kind of social democratic response imagined by advocates of a progressive reading of community safety. The strength of the modernisation agenda, pursued particularly through performance management and audit, as principal tools of the new public management, has imposed an hierarchical structure of managerial rather than political accountability over localities. As Power (1997) has noted with particular regard to auditing, but with relevance also for performance management, these tools are not neutral, but have the power to 'colonise' local action, so that if such tools impose a short-term 'measurement regime' of crime reduction and enforcement, then crime reduction and enforcement in all probability will become the local stock-in-trade, to the detriment of more progressive approaches to crime control (Gilling and Barton 2004). This hierarchical structure of managerial control, which runs from the Treasury to the Home Office, to regional government offices, to LSPs and CDRPs, and down now to neighbourhoods, puts neighbourhoods not in the vanguard, but at the end of the chain of command: there to 'perform' according to the specified requirements of the centre.

This tight performance management framework appears to be at odds with the priority given to community empowerment and building social capital, which seemingly have more to do with building a capacity for local community governance. Yet as the discussion of the moral authoritarian communitarian agenda has shown, the role of communities is being imagined in ways that support and bolster the performance management agenda of the centre, rather than being an alternative to it. The abstraction of crime and disorder from other aspects of social exclusion encourages high-crime communities to address their exclusion through crime control, targeted at criminal or anti-social 'others'.

There is a moral injunction on such communities not to help address the deep-seated social causes of crime, but to co-produce crime control by governing their own conduct, but also by acting as witnesses (assisted by ASBO-related provisions for 'naming and shaming'); by identifying local crime-related problems; by putting pressure on local agencies to use their powers against anti-social behaviour, such as the dispersal order; as well as by becoming members of neighbourhood watch groups, or even acting, following Jack Straw's lead, as have-a-go heroes. Those who assist in these ways may even gain recognition in nationally-organised 'taking a stand' awards. In this way, while the centre may steer from above, 'the community' is rhetorically and practically drawn upon to help by steering from below, their 'consumer pressure' helping to ensure that local 'provider interests' are kept on track, while also connecting communities with local crime control agencies in ways that discourage an unwanted 'governance from below' (Stenson 1999), where residents take local crime control matters into their own hands. This, then, *is* community governance, but it *is not* the kind of democratic community governance the progressive adherents of community safety might have wanted to see. Communities, here, are being governed through, to assist in the co-production of social order, rather than to resolve the problems – some of which stem from the diversity of late-modern communities themselves – that such communities face at the beginning of the twenty-first century.

Understanding the New Labour project of local crime control

How, then, do we make sense of New Labour's policy of local crime control, and where is it taking us? The version of community safety being pursued by New Labour is one that comes closest to the 'high trust authoritarian communitarian society' scenario identified by Hughes (1998). Such a scenario accords most closely with third way rhetoric as it was espoused at the beginning of New Labour's period in office, and, while local crime control policy has since undergone many twists and turns, none of them has marked a substantial deviation from the set path of the third way, which may not be referred to in political discourse so frequently, but which nevertheless remains a considerable influence on the New Labour project. As noted previously, the third way, while 'sold' as a pragmatic project, is in fact no such thing, but rather seeks to achieve an accommodation between centre-left politics and a neo-liberal hegemony, in which economic globalisation is the predominant dynamic. The question that arises is whether such an accommodation is really possible: is it a 'trick' that New Labour has managed to pull off?

In practice, this accommodation is largely one-way, which means that the New Labour project is, in the main, a neo-liberal project, in which the dominant value is that of freedom. The idea of authoritarianism, used in Hughes's scenario, sits uneasily with the value of freedom, but the conundrum is solved once one recognises, as those such as Rose (1999) and O'Malley (2004) do, that the vision of freedom adopted by neo-liberalism has to be 'made' – it is a positive view of freedom, rather than a negative one, and one that requires a fair degree of 'moral engineering' (Stenson 2000a). The free individual of neo-liberal thought – as it is projected through the body of New Labour's third way – is one who is an enterprising subject, but also one who has internalised the 'norms of civility' (Rose 1999). This means taking prudential responsibility for oneself and one's family, but also, and this is where the third way twist comes in, taking responsibility for and as a part of a putative community. This is the extent to which the third way socialises risk. One is made 'free', therefore, to be 'made' responsible, or responsibilised, as individuals, families and communities.

The paradox of neo-liberalism is that it requires more government than the minimal government that is often implied in neo-liberal discourse. This is where the authoritarian bit comes in, and particularly the moral authoritarian communitarianism. Hopefully the discussion throughout the pages of this book has served to illustrate that local crime control plays an important part in a political strategy geared towards bringing about, and governing through, this particular view of freedom. While there may be many other ways of bringing about such freedom, the importance of local crime control arises from the normality of crime in late-modern societies, which renders crime control equally normal, especially as it advances, through the logic of risk management, to criminalise the once-socialised domain of social policy. Thus the moral underclass discourse of policies designed to tackle social exclusion, which has carried through to policies designed to build social capital, has basically offered those living in conditions of disadvantage an opportunity to become one of the included, through work, good parenting and community participation.

Those at risk of anti-social behaviour, meanwhile, have been offered a veritable barrage of forms of *contractual governance* (Crawford 2003), from parenting contracts to ABCs, through which to demonstrate a capacity for autonomous, responsible action, and thus for conditional inclusion. Technologies of risk management, particularly expressed through situational crime prevention and security patrolling, then bolster such conditionality by designing surveillance, and its dynamics of suspicion and mistrust, into the physical and social fabric, as typified in the now-common CCTV schemes operating in public spaces and in mass private property. Individuals are free to go about their business so long as their business is responsible freedom. And then, for those who act irresponsibly, committing crimes and indulging in acts of anti-social behaviour that curtail the freedom of others, there is enforcement-oriented crime reduction, which in the case of the ASBO offers inclusion of the last-chance saloon variety, but more usually leads in the direction of exclusionary penal sanctions.

New Labour's project of local crime control has not stopped short of deploying these exclusionary penal sanctions – the bulging prisons bear testimony to that. But for others there is conditional inclusion which, under New Labour, has reached further down into the ranks of the marginalised and excluded than it did under the Conservatives. This may be an improvement, because it does not simply abandon a putative 'underclass' to the mercies of the free market, but ultimately this hardly makes its project any less neo-liberal in orientation, because inclusion is imagined in only a weak sense, in terms of becoming part of an 'included' society of morally responsible individuals, families and communities. As those such as Young (1999) point out, in this inclusionary vision little attention is paid to the way 'the included' are stratified. Inclusion is not the same thing as social justice, and amongst 'the included' there are still considerable social inequalities that relate, to a large degree, to the very different 'market positions' that people occupy in market society (Taylor 1999), depending upon who they are and where they live. Inclusion, therefore, is all about maintaining order within the status quo.

New Labour's community safety, then, spans both inclusionary and exclusionary dynamics, for those who will be orderly, and for those who will not. As a neo-liberal project, however, it remains deeply flawed, for a number of reasons.

First, the freedom that neo-liberalism cherishes for its included numbers is a freedom that comes in concert with uncertainty (O'Malley 2004). While this uncertainty might act as the mother of invention in unleashing a much-valorised entrepreneurial spirit, it comes at the cost also of breeding a degree of insecurity. Within the context of late-modern society, where high crime is normal, this is easily translated into a fear, anxiety or concern about crime. Garland (2001), for example, argues that the cultural sensibilities of the professional middle classes have shifted away from welfarism and towards support for the culture of control; while the research of Girling *et al.* (2000) and Taylor (1996) shows how this anxiety manifests itself within 'middle England', amongst those who mostly have been net beneficiaries of the rise of neo-liberalism, whose anxiety is often projected on to 'others', whether they be 'travelling criminals' from urban sink estates, youths, New Age Travellers, or whoever.

Such anxiety may be a perverse sign of the successful implantation of the neo-liberal project of freedom. If this project is also New Labour's project, which I think it largely is, then this means that the corollary of a freedom project may be a security project, particularly if New Labour's office-seeking strategy entails responding to the concerns of this putative middle England, comprising those most likely to get the neo-liberal message. This could work rather like the self-generating dynamic of risk, that always seeks new risks to manage. Thus more freedom means more of a felt need for security: the former fans the flames of the latter. Perhaps this could explain the persistence of the 'reassurance gap' despite statistical falls in the crime rate over recent years, and perhaps it results in a lowering of the threshold of tolerance which means that, even in the face of crime control 'success', more and more 'others' will be targeted. In this regard, it is interesting to note that anti-social behaviour, which was originally conceived as a 'risk factor' for more serious crime, which needed to be 'nipped in the bud', is now a phenomenon that official discourse conceives as having its own 'risk factors' (Home Office 2006a), and so the net-widening dynamic (Cohen 1985) may continue – one can be at risk of being at risk.

The persistence of insecurity may ensure the buoyancy of local markets for security which might be met, for those who can afford it, in part by private security patrols, gated communities and the like, but it is also likely to entail the occasional show of force from sovereign strategies such as zero-tolerance policing (Stenson 2000b), that demonstrate the state's credentials as 'precinct policeman' (Bauman 2000). Such shows of force, however, are less the anachronistic response of a sovereign state enduring a sovereignty predicament (Garland 2001), and more a corollary of governing through freedom. And as Garland shows, security is not just pursued through sovereignty. The other side of the security project is one that involves the community in its own self-government, involved therefore in the co-production of social order. What is missing from such a security project is democratic engagement with diverse communities, and any serious attempt to pursue security through social rather than criminal justice.

Second, if the vision of New Labour's crime control policy is to encourage civil society to act as an assemblage of free, responsible and moral agents, deploying privatised prudentialism to protect themselves, but also acting as moral communities that insulate themselves from crime by virtue of high social capital, then this vision is likely to come unstuck when it encounters social structural reality. New Labour aims to govern through an imaginary middle England, through 'one nation', comprising 'the people', acting as 'the community', but as Stenson (2005: 267) observes, '... in unequal societies with asymmetrical power relations, local public/community safety policies claiming to represent the collective interest cannot be taken at face value', Sullivan (2001: 44), meanwhile, starkly observes that neo-liberalism '... does not transport very well into the inner cities'.

The point here is that the structural causes of social exclusion, and ultimately of much crime amongst disadvantaged people, cannot be wished away by taking 'pragmatic' responses to economic globalisation, and by making the injunctions that underpin moral authoritarian communitarianism, as if morality can be detached from its social context (Byrne 2005). As Jock Young (1999) has been at pains to point out, people living in deprived circumstances and excluded communities know that others are better placed than they are; their live out their relative deprivation knowing that this is not only material deprivation, but also a deprivation of freedom. They find themselves in communities of fate, not communities of choice (Jordan 1996). They do not have the same access to the cathedrals of consumption in urban centres, or to trendy urban villages. And picking up on Sullivan's point, they feel the force of crime control, and live the politics of enforcement, much more intensely than do the better off, whether that be from 'quality of life' policing patrols; from the suspicious gaze of CCTV schemes that penetrate residential areas; or from the policing of their personal conduct by social housing providers, who now have been responsibilised to tackle anti-social behaviour. Neo-liberalism makes such people 'free' to experience the culture of control, and offers no prospect for building social solidarity or social justice.

Third, and on a related point, the freedom that New Labour's version of neo-liberalism seeks to make is one that, in addition to neglecting inequality, also largely neglects the pluralism that characterises the UK at the beginning of the twenty-first century. Etzioni's communitarianism too often looks like the articulations of the moral majority by a different name, and too often crime control pursued in the name of the community reads simply as majoritarian control. Young's (1999) work is important here in drawing attention to the relatively neglected cultural side of the changes that have emerged amidst the exclusionary dynamics of neo-liberal market society. As a consequence of the individualisation of lifestyle that has accompanied the rise of consumerism, the growth of immigration and the commodification of culture as a consequence of globalisation, we occupy a society that is more plural and more differentiated than it was at the height of modernity. Cohesion and solidarity in such a society is problematic, and as Young points out, there is a tendency instead towards insecurity, and an urge to draw exclusionary boundaries, based on essentialised and demonised difference, and 'othering'. The problematisation of anti-social behaviour, and the identity group politics that those such as Stenson (2005) identify as

227

a key dynamic of urban social relations may be seen in such a light, reflecting the changes in levels of tolerance that are a part of what Young calls the dyadic nature of crime.

So, because the freedom to be different, in cultural terms, elicits insecurity, neo-liberalism seeks to manage this by imposing social order, which in the case of New Labour means resorting to moral authoritarian communitarianism. Yet attempting to neutralise identity politics and to achieve cohesion through the moral authority of 'the community' is not likely to succeed, but is likely to accelerate the political exclusion and disengagement of identity groups who feel unrepresented and shut out by this single moral authority, particularly those who are already socially excluded, or 'included' but economically disadvantaged, and thus with no great stake in conformity. As Young and Matthews (2003) remind us, by reference to the northern town disturbances of 2001, riot is a likely consequence of such political exclusion, although the capacity for such organisation may be beyond many of the usual suspects of moral authoritarianism, such as those vulnerable and young people who are disproportionately the focus of those enforcing measures against anti-social behaviour.

If insecurity is endemic to neo-liberalism's project of freedom, then so too will be the quest for security, but its form changes as the role of the state is reconfigured by the drift from government to governance. For state crime control agencies, crime once set the parameters of their contribution to the security project. Under welfare liberalism, crime was partly governed through social policy – hence the penal welfarism (Garland 1985) that socialised a part of the discourse of criminal justice. With the decline of the welfare consensus, this discourse was no longer socialised, but instead relied mainly on a combination of punitive sovereignty and the risk management orientation of situationalism. Those hoping that the emergence of community safety under New Labour might mark a return to the socialisation of the discourse of crime control have been largely disappointed, however. As state agencies are drawn into working with others in relations of governance, in the co-production of community safety, so the terms of the security project become more negotiable. Safety is hard to confine to legal categories. The focus switches from 'doing something about crime', to doing something about those 'problems' that generate insecurity, and in this switch there is much greater flexibility governing the 'something' that is done, and the 'problems' that are so addressed. For guardians of the urban renaissance, for example, the problems are those things that threaten urban fortunes, and particularly the sterilised consumption experience. The threat comes from the likes of street drinkers, homeless people, beggars, and youths hanging around. These problems do not require crime control, however: they simply require approaches such as physical exclusion, as a form of risk management.

Meanwhile others, especially those living in deprived neighbour-hoods, as we can tell from responses to the BCS, as well as from the contents of MP's postbags, may be more concerned about the minor disorders and incivilities that punctuate everyday life in late-modern neo-liberal societies. Again, however, these problems do not require crime control, they require anti-social behaviour control, so safety and security here are stretched to cover protection from anti-social behaviour, which defies clear legal classification, but which has been given legal meaning through its questionable manifestation in the *reaction* of 'harassment, alarm or distress'. But as Cummings (2005) astutely observes, giving a name and a conceptual framework to civil society's concerns – anti-social behaviour – does not allay such concerns, it actually amplifies them. Waiton (2005) makes the point that the problem of anti-social behaviour is not so much the problem of an increase in such behaviour, but rather it is the consequence of the atomisation of society that neo-liberalism has hastened, and the insecurity that such atomisation creates, which is easily projected onto minor issues of civility, turning them into major problems of anti-social behaviour. The controlling response to anti-social behaviour, which as we have seen is largely enforcement oriented, does not, however, solve the problem, because of its paucity of vision. This is because aiming to make people safe and secure from problems such as anti-social behaviour – which is regarded by many of the architects of New Labour as the ultimate freedom – does nothing to address the atomisation that generates the anxiety in the first place. In Waiton's (2005) understanding, this valorisation of safety, which is not the same kind of safety that progressive advocates of community safety ever had in mind, is based on an amoral political vision, a point with which Cummings (2005: 8) also concurs in attributing increased attention to anti-social behaviour to: '... the political elite's failure to develop credible progressive politics for the twenty-first century, rather than any significant increase in nuisance behaviour by young people'.

Nowhere is this lack of a credible progressive politics more visible than in New Labour's approach to social exclusion which, as we have seen, has deployed a moral underclass discourse that uses technologies of community safety to establish social order in high crime, excluded neighbourhoods. If forcing the social casualties of economic globalisation into poor jobs, and imposing parenting skills and school discipline upon them were not bad enough, the ultimate example of the paucity of New Labour's vision must be the ill-fated attempt to engineer civil renewal by building social capital through addressing fear and tackling anti-social behaviour. If all that is going to bring people together is their mutual mistrust, suspicion and hatred of 'the other', then there is no basis here for social solidarity. Indeed, because the underlying problem, namely neo-liberalism's project of atomising freedom, is not addressed, there is not even any basis for sustainable safety, regardless of how much 'reassurance' or 'neighbourhood' policing is applied to civil society.

Returning to the question of whether New Labour has managed, through its third way, to pull off the trick of accommodating neo-liberalism with centre-left politics, my answer in the case of local crime control policy would have to be a resounding no. Such policy may bear a superficial resemblance to a more progressive view of community safety, with its focus upon partnership, and its apparent incursion into a more socialised understanding of safety, but ultimately it fails to offer anything more than the maintenance of a neo-liberal social order, which is inherently insecure, and which will therefore always require a security project that tolerates questionable practices of physical exclusion and inclusionary moral regulation, backed up by the threat of punitive sovereignty.

I am sounding a bit too pessimistic here, and need to be reminded of Hughes's (2002) warning not to totalise, and not to neglect the possibility for progressive empowerment that is opened up by community governance. I do not deny this possibility, but my focus here upon the New Labour project demonstrates that such a project wraps community governance in central governmental powers that have been used to bolster neo-liberalism, rather than to supplant it. Such wrapping does not amount to a straitjacket, but it is pretty restrictive nonetheless, with tight performance management regimes to secure crime reduction; a veritable panoply of measures to tackle anti-social behaviour that can be levered in from below as well as from above; and an approach to social exclusion that is spatially confined, and that falls back too easily on moral regulation. There is space for more progressive local 'translations' (Edwards 2002) of community safety, but my point is that this space needs widening with a more progressive politics, which does not necessarily require a return to the Keynesian welfare state, not least because that operated with an impoverished view of the social that neglected the vital autonomous role of civil society (Hope and Karstedt 2003). But it is difficult to be positive about the prospects for 'nodal governance' as some are (Johnston and Shearing 2003), or for civil renewal, when it has been hijacked by a largely neo-liberal agenda, which has a distorted vision of the good society, and which imposes a project of freedom that ends up producing and reproducing insecurity.

Bibliography

ACPO (1996) *Towards 2000*. Leicester: ACPO Crime Committee Sub-Committee on Crime Prevention.

ACPO (2001) *Policing in the 21st Century*. http://www.acpo.police.uk/asp/policies/Data/blueprnt.doc

Allen, R. (1999) 'Is what works what counts? The role of evidence-based crime reduction in policy and practice', *Safer Society*, 2: 21–3.

Allen, R. (2006) 'Communities and the criminal justice system', in B. Shimshon (ed.) *Social Justice: Criminal Justice*. London: The Smith Institute.

Arnstein, S. (1969) 'A ladder of citizen participation', *JAIP*, 35 (4): 216–24.

ASBO Concern (2005) *ASBOs: An Analysis of the First 6 Years*. London: ASBO Concern/NAPO.

Atkinson, R. (2003) 'Addressing urban social exclusion through community involvement in urban regeneration', in R. Imrie and M. Raco (eds) *Urban Renaissance? New Labour, Community and Urban Policy*. Bristol: Policy Press.

Atkinson, R. and Savage, S. (2001) 'Introduction: New Labour and Blairism', in S. Savage and R. Atkinson (eds) *Public Policy Under Blair*. Basingstoke: Palgrave.

Audit Commission (1993) *Helping With Enquiries*. London: Audit Commission.

Audit Commission (1996) *Misspent Youth*. London: Audit Commission.

Audit Commission (1999) *Safety in Numbers*. London: Audit Commission.

Audit Commission (2002) *Community Safety Partnerships*. London: Audit Commission.

Bacon, N. and James, S. (2006) 'Working with communities to tackle low level disorder and anti-social behaviour', *Criminal Justice Matters*, 64: 25–6.

Barnes, M., McCabe, A. and Ross, L. (2004) 'Public participation in governance: the institutional context', in Civil Renewal Research Centre (ed.) *Researching Civil Renewal*. Birmingham: Civil Renewal Research Centre.

Barnett, A. (2000) 'Corporate populism and partyless democracy', *New Left Review*, 11 (3): 80–9.

Barrett, S. and Fudge, C. (eds) (1981) *Policy as Action*. London: Methuen.

Bauman, Z. (2000) 'Social uses of law and order', in D. Garland and R. Sparks (eds) *Criminology and Social Theory*. Oxford: Oxford University Press.

Beck, U. (1992) *Risk Society: Towards a New Modernity*. London: Sage.

Bennington, J. and Donnison, D. (1999) 'New Labour and social exclusion: the search for a Third Way, or just gilding the ghetto again?', in H. Dean and R. Woods (eds) *Social Policy Review 11*. Luton: Social Policy Association.

Blackman, T. and Palmer, A. (1999) 'Continuity or modernisation? The emergence of New Labour's welfare state', in H. Dean and R. Woods (eds) *Social Policy Review 11*. Luton: Social Policy Association.

Blair, T. (1993) 'Why crime is a socialist issue', *New Statesman and Society*, 29 (12): 27–8.

Blair, T. (1998) *The Third Way: A New Politics for A New Century*. London: Fabian Society.

Blair, T. (2001) *Speech at the Peel Institute*, 26 January.

Blunkett, D. (2003) *Civil Renewal: A New Agenda.* London: Home Office.

Blunkett, D. (2006) 'Community rights and rebalancing the system', *Criminal Justice Matters*, 64: 8–9.

Bolton, S. (2006) 'Crime prevention in the community: the case of neighbourhood watch', *Criminal Justice Matters*, 64: 40–1.

Bottoms. A. (1995) 'The philosophy and politics of punishment and sentencing', in C. Clarkson and R. Morgan (eds) *The Politics of Sentencing Reform*. Oxford: Clarendon Press.

Bottoms, A. and Wiles, P. (1996) 'Understanding crime prevention in late modern societies', in T. Bennett (ed.) *Preventing Crime and Disorder*. Cambridge: Institute of Criminology.

Bowles, S. and Gintis, H. (2002) 'Social capital and community governance', *The Economic Journal*, 112: 419–36.

Brantingham, P. and Faust, F. (1976) 'A conceptual model of crime prevention', *Crime & Delinquency*, 22 (3): 284–96.

Brown, A. (2003) 'Anti-social behaviour, crime control and social control', *Howard Journal of Criminal Justice,* 43 (2): 203–11.

Burney, E. (1999) *Crime and Banishment: Nuisance and Exclusion in Social Housing*. Winchester: Waterside Press.

Burney, E. (2004a) 'Talking tough, acting coy: what happened to the anti-social behaviour order?', *Howard Journal*, 41 (5): 469–84.

Burney, E. (2004b) 'Nuisance or crime? The changing uses of anti-social behaviour control', *Criminal Justice Matters*, 57: 4–5.

Burney, E. (2005) *Making People Behave: Anti-social Behaviour, Politics and Policy*. Cullompton: Willan Publishing.

Byrne, D. (2005) *Social Exclusion* (2nd edn). Maidenhead: Open University Press.

Campbell, B. (1993) *Goliath*. London: Methuen.

Campbell, S. (2002) *A Review of Anti-social Behaviour Orders*. London: Home Office.

Chadwick, A. and Heffernan, R. (eds) (2003) *The New Labour Reader*. Cambridge: Polity Press.

Chambliss, W. (1964) 'A sociological analysis of the law of vagrancy', *Social Problems*, 12 (1): 67–77.

Clark, T. (2002) 'New Labour's big idea: joined-up government', *Social Policy and Society*, 1 (2): 107–17.

Clarke, J. (1999) 'Coming to terms with culture', in H. Dean and R. Woods (eds) *Social Policy Review 11*. Luton: Social Policy Association.

Clarke, J. (2001) 'Globalisation and welfare states: some unsettling thoughts', in R. Sykes, B. Palier and P. Prior (eds) *Globalisation and European Welfare States*. Basingstoke: Palgrave.

Clarke, J. (2004) 'Producing transparency? Evaluation and the governance of public services', in G. Drewry, C. Greve and T. Tanquerel (eds) *Contracts, Performance Measurement and Accountability in the Public Sector*. Amsterdam: IOS Press.

Clarke, J. and Newman, J. (1997) *The Managerial State*. London: Sage.

Clarke, J., Gewirtz, S., Hughes, G. and Humphrey, J. (2000) 'The rise of audit and evaluation', in J. Clarke, S. Gewirtz and E. McLaughlin (eds) *New Managerialism, New Welfare?* London, Sage.

Clarke, R. (ed.) (1997) *Situational Crime Prevention: Successful Case Studies*. New York: Harrow and Heston.

Clarke, R. and Mayhew, P. (1980) *Design Against Crime*. Oxford: Home Office Research Unit Publications.

Cochrane, A. (1994) 'Restructuring the Local Welfare State', in R. Burrows and B. Loader (eds) *Towards a Post-Fordist Welfare State?* London: Routledge.

Cochrane, A. (2003) 'The new urban policy: towards empowerment or incorporation?', in R. Imrie and M. Raco (eds) *Urban Renaissance? New Labour, Community and Urban Policy*. Bristol: Policy Press.

Cohen, P. (1979) 'Policing the working-class city', in B. Fine, R. Kinsey, J. Lea, S. Piciotto and J. Young (eds) *Capitalism and the Rule of Law: From Deviancy Theory to Marxism*. London: Hutchinson.

Cohen, S. (1972) *Folk Devils and Moral Panics*. London: MacGibben and Kee.

Cohen, S. (1985) *Visions of Social Control: Crime, Punishment and Classification*. Cambridge: Polity Press. Cohen, S. (1988) 'Footprints in the sand: a further report in criminology and the sociology of deviance in Britain', republished in S. Cohen, *Against Criminology*. Oxford: Transaction Books.

Coleman, R. (2004) *Reclaiming the Streets: Surveillance, Social Control and the City*. Cullompton: Willan Publishing.

Coleman, R., Sim, J. and Whyte, D. (2002) 'Power, politics and partnerships: the state of crime prevention on Merseyside', in G. Hughes and A. Edwards (eds) *Crime Control and Community: The New Politics of Public Safety*. Cullompton: Willan Publishing.

Commission on Social Justice (1994) *Social Justice: Strategies for National Renewal*. London: IPPR.

Considine, M. (2005) *Making Public Policy*. Cambridge: Polity Press.

Cornish, D. and Clarke, R. (eds) (1986) *The Reasoning Criminal*. New York: Springer Verlag.

Cook, D. (1999) 'Putting crime in its place: the causes of crime and New Labour's solutions', in H. Dean and R. Woods (eds) *Social Policy Review 11*. Luton: Social Policy Association.

Cook, D. (2005) 'Crime and criminal justice policy', in H. Bochel, C. Bochel, R. Page and R. Symes (eds) *Social Policy: Issues and Developments*. London: Pearson/Prentice Hall.

Cooper, C. (2006) 'Community involvement in community safety – but whose "community" and whose "safety"?', in A. Dearling, T. Newburn and P. Somerville (eds) *Supporting Safer Communities: Housing, Crime and Neighbourhoods*. Coventry: Chartered Institute of Housing/Housing Studies.

Cramphorn, C. (1998) 'Positioning community safety strategies: a planning and process model', *Police Research and Management*, 2 (3): 3–12.

Crawford, A. (1997) *The Local Governance of Crime*. Oxford: Clarendon Press.

Crawford, A. (1998) *Crime Prevention and Community Safety: Politics, Policies and Practices*. Harlow: Longman.

Crawford, A. (2000) 'Situational crime prevention, urban governance and trust relations', in A. von Hirsch, D. Garland and A. Wakefield (eds) *Ethical and Social Perspectives on Situational Crime Prevention*. Oxford: Hart Publishing.

Crawford, A. (2001) 'Joined-up but fragmented', in R. Matthews and J. Pitts (eds) *Crime, Disorder and Community Safety*. London: Routledge.

Crawford, A. (ed.) (2002) *Crime and Insecurity: The Governance of Safety in Europe*. Cullompton: Willan Publishing.

Crawford, A. (2003) '"Contractual governance" of deviant behaviour', *Journal of Law and Society*, 30 (4): 479–505.

Crawford, A., Lister, S., Blackburn, S. and Burnett, J. (2005) *Plural Policing: The Mixed Economy of Visible Patrols in England and Wales*. Bristol: Policy Press.

Crime Concern (2002) *Tackling Anti-social Behaviour*. Swindon: Crime Concern.

Crowther, C. (2002) 'The politics and economics of disciplining an inclusive and exclusive society', in R. Sykes, C. Bochel and N. Ellison (eds) *Social Policy Review 14*. Bristol: Policy Press/Social Policy Association.

Cummings, D. (2005) 'Introduction', in C. O'Malley, S. Waiton and D. Cummings (eds) *Whop's Anti-social? New Labour and the Politics of Anti-social Behaviour*. London: Academy of Ideas.

Cummings, D. (2006) 'Communities of fear: justice or therapy?', *Criminal Justice Matters*, 64: 10–11.

Daly, G. and Davis, H. (2002) 'Partnerships for local governance: citizens, communities and accountability', in C. Glendinning, M. Powell and K. Rummery (eds) *Partnerships, New Labour and the Governance of Welfare*. Bristol: The Policy Press.

Davis, M. (1990) *City of Quartz: Excavating the Future in Los Angeles*. London: Pimlico.

Dean, H. and Woods, R. (eds) (1999) *Social Policy Review 11*. Luton: Social Policy Association.

Dearling, A., Newburn, T. and Somerville, P. (eds) (2006) *Supporting Safer Communities: Housing, Crime and Neighbourhoods*. Coventry: Chatered Institute of Housing/Housing Studies Association.

Delanty, G. (2003) *Community*. London: Routledge.

DETR (2000) *Our Towns and Cities: The Future – Delivering on Urban Renaissance*. Norwich: The Stationery Office.

DETR (2001) *Local Strategic Partnerships: Government Guidance*. London: DETR.

Dillane, J., Hill, M., Bannister, J. and Scott, S. (2001) *Evaluation of the Dundee Families Project Final Report*. Glasgow: Centre for the Child and Society, Department of Urban Studies, University of Glasgow.

Dingwall, G. and Moody, S. (eds) (1999) *Crime and Conflict in the Countryside*. Cardiff: University of Wales Press.

Dinham, A. (2005) 'Empowered or overpowered? The real experiences of local participation in the UK's New Deal for Communities', *Community Development Journal*, 40 (3): 301–12.

Downes, D. and Morgan, R. (2002) 'The skeletons in the cupboard: the politics of law and order at the turn of the millennium', in M. Maguire, R. Morgan and R. Reiner (eds) *The Oxford Handbook of Criminology* (3rd edn). Oxford: Oxford University Press.

Driver, S. and Martell, L. (2002) *Blair's Britain*. Cambridge: Polity Press.

DTLR (2001) *Strong Local Leadership – Quality Public Services*. London: DTLR.

Du Gay, P. (2000) *In Praise of Bureaucracy: Weber, Organisation, Ethics*. London: Sage.

Edwards, A. (2002) 'Learning from diversity: the strategic dilemmas of community-based crime control', in G. Hughes and A. Edwards (eds) *Crime Control and Community: The New Politics of Public Safety*. Cullompton: Willan Publishing.

Edwards, A. and Hughes, G. (2002) 'Introduction: the new community governance of crime control', in G. Hughes and A. Edwards (eds) *Crime Control and Community: The New Politics of Public Safety*. Cullompton: Willan Publishing.

Edwards, A. and Hughes, G. (2005) 'Comparing safety in Europe: a geohistorical approach', *Theoretical Criminology*, 9 (3): 345–63.

Emmel, N. (2005) 'Comments on Tackling Social Exclusion: Taking stock and looking to the future: a response'. *ESRC Research Methods Programme Working Papers*, at http://www.ccsr.ac.uk/methods/publications/documents/WP8.pdf.

Entwistle, T. and Laffin, M. (2005) 'A prehistory of the Best Value regime', *Local Government Studies*, 32 (2): 205–18.

Ericson, R.V. and Haggerty, K.D. (1997) *Policing the Risk Society*. Oxford: Clarendon Press.

Etzioni, A. (1994) *The Spirit of Community: The Reinvention of American Society*. New York: Touchstone Books.

Farrow, K. and Prior, D. (2006) '"Togetherness"? Tackling anti-social behaviour through community engagement', *Criminal Justice Matters*, 64: 4–5.

Faulkner, D. (2003) 'Taking citizenship seriously: social capital and criminal justice in a changing world', *Criminal Justice*, 3 (3): 287–315.

Faulkner, D. (2004a) *Civil Renewal, Diversity and Social Capital in a Multi-ethnic Britain*. London: Runnymede Trust.

Faulkner, D. (2004b) 'Active citizenship, crime and disorder'. Paper presented to *Active Citizenship Seminar, Thames Valley Partnership*, 16 June 2004.

Feeley, M. and Simon, J. (1992) 'The new penology: notes on the emerging strategy of corrections and its implications', *Criminology*, 30 (4): 449–74.

Feeley, M. and Simon, J. (1994) 'Actuarial justice: the emerging new criminal law', in D. Nelken (ed.) *The Futures of Criminology*. London: Sage.

Field, F. (2003) *Neighbours from Hell: The Politics of Behaviour*. London: Politico's Publishing.

Fielding, S. (2002) 'A new politics?', in P. Dunleavy, A. Gamble, R. Heffernan and I. Holliday (eds) *Developments in British Politics 6*. Basingstoke: Palgrave.

Fitzpatrick, T. (2005) *New Theories of Welfare*. Basingstoke: Palgrave Macmillan.

Fletcher, R. (2006) *The Changing Face of Crime Governance in London: An Examination of the Metropolitan Police Service Response to the Crime and Disorder Act 1998*. PhD thesis, University of Portsmouth.

Flint, J. (2006) 'Active, responsible citizens? Changing neighbourhoods, changing order', in A. Dearling, T. Newburn and P. Somerville (eds) *Supporting Safer Communities: Housing, Crime and Neighbourhoods*. Coventry: Chartered Institute of Housing/Housing Studies Association.

Foley, M. (2000) *The British Presidency*. Manchester: Manchester University Press.

Foord, M. and Young, F. (2006) 'Housing managers are from Mars, social workers are from Venus: anti-social behaviour, "Respect" and inter-professional working – reconciling the irreconcilable?', in A. Dearling, T. Newburn and P. Somerville (eds) *Supporting Safer Communities: Housing, Crime and Neighbourhoods.* Coventry: Chartered Institute of Housing/ Housing Studies Association.

Foster, J. (2002) '"People pieces": the neglected but essential elements of community crime prevention', in G. Hughes and A. Edwards (eds) *Crime Control and Community.* Cullompton: Willan Publishing.

Fox, C. (2005) 'The future of crime and disorder reduction partnerships'. *Community Safety Journal,* 4 (3): 40–3.

Franklin, B. (2000) 'The hand of history: New Labour, news management and governance', in S. Ludlam and M. Smith (eds) *New Labour, Ideology, Policy and Government.* London: Palgrave.

Freeden, M. (1999) 'The ideology of New Labour', *Political Quarterly,* 70 (1): 42–51.

Fyfe, N. (2005) 'Making space for neo-communitarianism? The third sector, state and civil society in the UK', *Antipode,* 37: 536–57.

Garland, D. (1985) *Punishment and Welfare.* Aldershot: Gower.

Garland, D. (1996) 'The limits of the sovereign state: strategies of crime control in contemporary society', *British Journal of Criminology,* 36 (4): 445–71.

Garland, D. (2001) *The Culture of Control.* Oxford: Oxford University Press.

Garland, D. and Sparks, R. (eds) (2000) *Criminology and Social Theory.* Oxford: Oxford University Press.

Garside, R. (2006) 'Criminality and social justice: challenging the assumptions', in B. Shimshon (ed.) *Social Justice: Criminal Justice.* London: The Smith Institute.

Giddens, A. (1998) *The Third Way: The Renewal of Social Democracy.* Cambridge: Polity Press.

Giddens, A. (2002) *Where Now for New Labour?* Cambridge: Polity Press.

Gilling, D. (1994) 'Multi-agency crime prevention in Britain: the problem of combining situational and social strategies', *Crime Prevention Studies,* 3: 231–48.

Gilling, D. (1997) *Crime Prevention: Theory, Policy and Politics.* London: UCL.

Gilling, D. (2003) 'The Audit Commission and the ills of local community safety: an accurate diagnosis?', *Community Safety Journal,* 2 (1): 4–11.

Gilling, D. (2005) 'Partnership and crime prevention', in N. Tilley (ed.) *Handbook of Crime Prevention and Community Safety.* Cullompton: Willan Publishing.

Gilling, D. and Barton, A. (2005) 'Dangers lurking in the deep: the transformative potential of the crime audit', *Criminal Justice,* 5 (2): 163–80.

Gilling, D. and Hughes, G. (2002) 'The community safety "profession"', *Community Safety Journal*, 1: 4–12.

Girling, E., Loader, I. and Sparks, R. (2000) *Crime and Social Change in Middle England: Questions of Order in an English Town*. London: Routledge.

Gladstone, F. (1980) *Co-ordinating Crime Prevention Efforts*. Research Study No. 62. London: Home Office.

Glass, N. (1999) 'Sure Start: the development of an early intervention programme for young children in the United Kingdom', *Children and Society*, 13: 257–64.

Glendinning, C., Powell, M. and Rummery, K. (eds) (2002) *Partnerships, New Labour and the Governance of Welfare*. Bristol: Policy Press.

Goldblatt, P. and Lewis, C. (eds) (1998) *Reducing Offending: An Assessment of Research Evidence on Ways of Dealing with Offending Behaviour*. London: Home Office.

Goodwin, M. (2004) 'The scaling or urban policy: neighbourhood, city or region', in C. Johnstone and M. Whitehead (eds) *New Horizons in British Urban Policy*. Aldershot: Ashgate.

Gordon, P. (1984) 'Community policing: towards the local police state?', *Critical Social Policy*, 10: 39–58.

Griggs, S. and Smith, M. (2004) 'Partnerships, politics and civil renewal', in Civil Renewal Research Centre (ed.) *Researching Civil Renewal*. Birmingham: Civil Renewal Research Centre.

Hall, S. (1985) 'Authoritarian populism: a reply to Jessop *et al.*', *New Left Review*, 151: 115–24.

Hall, S. (1998) 'The great moving nowhere show', *Marxism Today*, November/December: 9–14.

Hall, S. (2003) 'The "third way" revisited: "New" Labour, spatial policy and the national strategy for neighbourhood renewal', *Planning, Practice and Research*, 18 (4): 265–77.

Hall, S., Critcher, C., Jefferson, T., Clarke, J. and Roberts, B. (1978) *Policing The Crisis: Mugging, the State and Law and Order*. London: Macmillan.

Hallam, S. (2002) 'Police Performance, reform and community safety: how we came to where we are going', *Community Safety Journal*, 1 (2): 19–26.

Hancock, L. (2001) *Crime, Disorder and Community*. London: Palgrave.

Hancock, L. (2003) 'Urban regeneration and crime reduction: contradictions and dilemmas', in R. Matthews and J. Young (eds) *The New Politics of Crime and Punishment*. Cullompton: Willan Publishing.

Harvey, L., Grimshaw, P. and Pease, K. (1989) 'Crime prevention delivery: the work of CPOs', in R. Morgan and D. Smith (eds) *Coming to Terms With Policing*. London: Routledge.

Hastings, A. (2003) 'Strategic multi-level neighbourhood regeneration: an outward-looking approach at last?', in R. Imrie and M. Raco (eds) *Urban Renaissance? New Labour, Community and Urban Policy*. Bristol: Policy Press.

Hay, C. (1999) *The Political Economy of New Labour: Labouring Under False Pretences?* Manchester: Manchester University Press.

Heal, K. (1987) 'Crime prevention in the United Kingdom: from start to go', in J. Graham (ed.) *Home Office Research Bulletin 24: Special European Edition.* London: HMSO.

Hedderman, C. and Williams, C. (2001) *Making Partnerships Work: Emerging Findings from the Reducing Burglary Initiative.* PRCU Briefing Note 1/01. London: Home Office.

Heffernan, R. and Marqusee, M. (1992) *Defeat From the Jaws of Victory: Inside Kinnock's Labour Party.* London: Verso.

Hennessy, P. (2000) *The Prime Minister: The Office and its Holders Since 1945.* Basingstoke: Palgrave Macmillan.

Her Majesty's Government (2005) *National Community Safety Plan 2006–2009.* London: Community Safety and Local Government Unit, Home Office.

Higgins, P., James, P. and Roper, I. (2004) 'Best Value: is it delivering?', *Public Money and Management*, 24: 251–8.

Hill, M. (1997) *The Policy Process in the Modern State* (3rd edn). Brighton: Harvester Wheatsheaf.

Hill, M. and Hupe, P. (2002) *Implementing Public Policy.* London: Sage.

Hirst, P. (2000) 'Democracy and governance', in J. Pierre (ed.) *Debating Governance.* Oxford: Oxford University Press.

Hirst, P. and Thompson, G. (1996) *Globalization in Question.* Cambridge: Polity Press.

HMIC (1998) *Beating Crime.* London: HMIC.

HMIC (2000) *Calling Time on Crime: A Thematic Inspection of Crime and Disorder.* London: Home Office Communication Directorate.

HMIC (2001) *Open All Hours.* London: Home Office.

HMIC (2003) *Streets Ahead.* London: Home Office.

Hobbs, D. (2004) 'Memorandum'. Written evidence submitted to the *Home Affairs Committee on Anti-social Behaviour.* London: House of Commons.

Hodgson, L. (2004) 'Manufactured civil society: counting the cost', *Critical Social Policy*, 24 (2): 139–64.

Home Office (1984) *Crime Prevention: A Co-ordinated Approach. Circular 8/84.* London: Home Office.

Home Office (1991) *Safer Communities: The Local Delivery of Crime Prevention Through the Partnership Approach.* London: Home Office.

Home Office (1993) *Police Reform: A Police Service for the Twenty-first Century.* Cm 2281. London: HMSO.

Home Office (1997) *Getting to Grips with Crime: A New Framework for Local Action. A Consultation Document.* London: Home Office.

Home Office (1998) *Guidance on Statutory Crime and Disorder Partnerships.* www.homeoffice.gov.uk/cdact/cdaguide.htm.

Home Office (1999a) *The Government's Crime Reduction Strategy.* London: Home Office.

Home Office (1999b) *Statutory Partnerships: Pathfinder Sites Report*. London: Home Office.

Home Office (2000) 'Jack Straw launches new action plan to combat anti-social behaviour', *News Release*, 30 March 2000.

Home Office (2001a) *Policing a New Century*. London: Home Office.

Home Office (2001b) *Criminal Justice: The Way Ahead*. Norwich: The Stationery Office.

Home Office (2002a) *The Safer Communities Initiative. Circular 14/2002*. London: Home Office.

Home Office (2002b) *Respect and Responsibility*. London: Home Office.

Home Office (2003) *Building Safer Communities Together*. London: Home Office.

Home Office (2004a) *The Building Safer Communities Fund 2004–05. Circular 14/2004*. London: Home Office.

Home Office (2004b) *Building Communities, Beating Crime*. Cm. 6360. London: Home Office.

Home Office (2006a) *Respect Action Plan*. London: Home Office.

Home Office (2006b) *Review of the Partnership Provisions of the Crime and Disorder Act 1998 – Report of Findings*. London: Home Office.

Homel, P., Nutley, S., Webb, B. and Tilley, N. (2005) *Investing to Deliver: Reviewing the Implementation of the UK Crime Reduction Programme. Home Office Research Study 281*. London: Home Office.

Hope, T. (1995) 'Community crime prevention', in M. Tonry and D. Farrington (eds) *Building a Safer Society*. Chicago: University of Chicago Press.

Hope, T. (2004) 'Pretend it works. Evidence and governance in the evaluation of the Reducing Burglary Initiative', *Criminal Justice*, 4 (30): 287–308.

Hope, T. (2005) 'The new local governance of community safety in England and Wales', *Canadian Journal of Criminology and Criminal Justice*, 47 (2): 369–87.

Hope, T. and Karstedt, S. (2003) 'Towards a new social crime prevention', in H. Kury and J. Oberfell-Fuchs (eds) *Crime Prevention – New Approaches*. Mainz: Weisse Ring.

Hoskins, G. and Tallon, A. (2004) 'Promoting the "urban idyll": policies for city centre living', in C. Johnstone and M. Whitehead (eds) *New Horizons in British Urban Policy*. Aldershot: Ashgate.

Hough, M. (2004) 'Modernization, scientific rationalism and the Crime Reduction Programme', *Criminal Justice*, 4 (3): 239–53.

Hough, M. and Jacobson, J. (2004) 'Getting to grips with anti-social behaviour', in J. Grieve and R. Howard (eds) *Communities, Social Exclusion and Crime*. London: Centre for Crime and Justice Studies.

Hough, M. and Tilley, N. (1998) *Getting the Grease to the Squeak: Research Lessons for Crime Prevention*, Crime Detection and Prevention Series Paper 85. London: Home Office.

Hughes, G. (1996) 'Communitarianism and law and order', *Critical Social Policy*, 16 (4): 17–41.

Hughes, G. (1998) *Understanding Crime Prevention: Social Control, Risk and Late Modernity*. Buckingham: Open University Press.

Hughes, G. (2002) 'Plotting the rise of community safety: critical reflections on research, theory and politics', in G. Hughes and A. Edwards (eds) *Crime Control and Community*. Cullompton: Willan Publishing.

Hughes, G. (2006) *The Politics of Crime and Community*. Basingstoke: Palgrave Macmillan.

Hughes, G. and Edwards, A. (eds) (2002) *Crime Control and Community: The New Politics of Public Safety*. Cullompton: Willan Publishing.

Hughes, G. and Gilling, D. (2004) 'Mission Impossible: the habitus of the community safety manager and the new expertise in the local partnership governance of crime and safety', *Criminal Justice*, 4 (2): 129–49.

Hughes, G. and McLaughlin, E. (2002) 'Together we'll crack it: crime prevention and the partnership approach', in C. Glendinning, M. Powell and K. Rummery (eds) *Partnership, Welfare and New Labour*. Bristol: Policy Press.

Hughes, G., McLaughlin, E. and Muncie, J. (eds) (2002) *Crime Prevention and Community Safety: New Directions*. London: Sage.

Hughes, O. (2003) *Public Management and Administration: An Introduction* (3rd edn). Basingstoke: Palgrave.

Hunter, C. (2001) 'Anti-social behaviour and housing – can law be the answer?', in D. Cowan and A. Marsh (eds) *Two Steps Forward – Housing Policy into the New Millennium*. Bristol: Policy Press.

Hunter, C. (2003) 'Looking two ways at once: anti-social behaviour, law and social inclusion'. Paper presented to *Housing Studies Association Conference*, Bristol, September 2003.

Hunter, C. and Nixon, J. (2001) 'Social Landlords' responses to neighbour nuisance and anti-social behaviour: from the negligible to the holistic?', *Local Government Studies*, 27 (4): 89–104.

Hutton, W. (1995) *The State We're In*. London: Verso.

Imrie, R. (2004) 'Governing the cities and the urban renaissance', in C. Johnstone and M. Whitehead (eds) *New Horizons in British Urban Policy*. Aldershot: Ashgate.

Imrie, R. and Raco, M. (2003) 'Community and the changing nature of urban policy', in R. Imrie and M. Raco (eds) *Urban Renaissance? New Labour, Community and Urban Policy*. Bristol: Policy Press.

Innes, M. (2005) 'Why "soft" policing is hard: on the curious development of reassurance policing, how it became neighbourhood policing and what this signifies about the politics of police reform', *Journal of Community and Applied Social Psychology*, 15: 156–69.

Innes, M. and Sheptycki, J. (2004) 'From detection to disruption: intelligence and the changing logic of police crime control in the United Kingdom', *International Criminal Justice Review*, 14: 1–24.

Irving, B. and Bourne, D. (2002) *Enhancing performance in BCUs: The Appropriateness of the Srategic Approach Outlined in 'Policing a New Century: A Blueprint for Reform'*. Evidence to the Home Affairs Select Committee's pre-legislative scrutiny of the Police Reform Bill. London: Police Foundation.

Jasper, L. (2006) 'A call for action: engaging all communities', *Criminal Justice Matters*, 64: 12–13.

John, T. and Maguire, M. (2004) *The National Intelligence Model: Key Lessons from Early Research*. Home Office Online Report 30/04.

Johnson, L. (1992) *The Rebirth of Private Policing*. London: Routledge.

Johnston, L. and Shearing, C. (2003) *Governing Security: Explorations in Policing and Justice*. London: Routledge.

Johnstone, C. (2004) 'Crime, disorder and the urban renaissance', in C. Johnstone and M. Whitehead (eds) *New Horizons in British Urban Policy*. Aldershot: Ashgate.

Johnstone, C. and Whitehead, M. (eds) (2004) *New Horizons in British Urban Policy: Perspectives on New Labour's Urban Renaissance*. Aldershot: Ashgate.

Joint Consultative Committee (1990) *Operational Policing Review*. Surbiton: Police Federation.

Jones, T. and Newburn, T. (2004) 'The convergence of UK and US crime control policy: exploring substance and process', in T. Newburn and R. Sparks (eds) *Criminal Justice and Political Cultures: National and International Dimensions of Crime Control*. Cullompton: Willan Publishing.

Jones, M. and Ward, K. (2004) 'Neo-liberalism, crisis and the city: the political economy of New Labour's urban economy', in C. Johnstone and M. Whitehead (eds) *New Horizons in British Urban Policy*. Aldershot: Ashgate.

Jordan, B. (1996) *A Theory of Poverty and Social Exclusion*. Cambridge: Polity Press.

Kearns, A. (2003) 'Social capital, regeneration and urban policy', in R. Imrie and M. Raco (eds) *Urban Renaissance?* Bristol: Policy Press.

Keith, M. (2004) 'Knowing the city? 21st century urban policy and the introduction of local strategic partnerships', in C. Johnstone and M. Whitehead (eds) *New Horizons in Urban Policy*. Aldershot: Ashgate.

Kenny, M. and Smith, M. (2000) 'Interpreting New Labour: constraints, dilemmas and political agency', in S. Ludlam and M. Smith (eds) *New Labour in Government*. London: Macmillan.

Kirby, S. and McPherson, I. (2004) 'Integrating the National Intelligence Model with a "problem-solving approach"', *Community Safety Journal*, 3 (2): 36–46.

Labour Party (1979) *General Election Manifesto*. London: Labour Party.
Labour Party (1983) *General Election Manifesto*. London: Labour Party.
Labour Party (1987) *General Election Manifesto*. London: Labour Party.
Labour Party (1992) *General Election Manifesto*. London: Labour Party.
Labour Party (1995) *A Quiet Life: Tough Action on Criminal Neighbours*. London: Labour Party.
Labour Party (1997) *General Election Manifesto*. London: Labour Party.
Lawless, P. (2004) 'Locating and explaining area-based urban initiatives: New Deal for Communities in England', *Environment and Planning C: Government and Policy*, 22: 383–99.
Lea, J. (2002) *Crime and Modernity*. London: Sage.
Leach, S. and Davis, H. (1996) *Enabling or Disabling Local Government?* Buckingham: Open University Press
LeGrand, J. (1982) *The Strategy of Equality*. London: Allen and Unwin.
Leigh, A., Arnott, J., Clarke, G. and See, L. (2000) *Family Values: Grouping Similar Policing and Crime Reduction Areas for Comparative Purposes*. Briefing Note 3/00. London: Home Office.
Levitas, R. (2005) *The Inclusive Society. Social Exclusion and New Labour* (2nd edn). Basingstoke: Palgrave Macmillan.
LGMB (1996) *Survey of Community Safety Activities in Local Government in England and Wales*. Luton: LGMB.
Liddle, M. and Gelsthorpe, L. (1994a) *Inter-agency Crime Prevention: Organising Local Delivery*. Crime Prevention Unit Paper 52. London: Home Office.
Liddle, M. and Gelsthorpe, L. (1994b) *Crime Prevention and Inter-agency Co-operation*. Crime Prevention Unit Paper 52. London: Home Office.
Liddle, M. and Gelsthorpe, L. (1994c) *Inter-agency Crime Prevention: Further Issues*. Crime Prevention Unit Paper 52. London: Home Office.
Lipsky, M. (1980) *Street-Level Bureaucracy: The Dilemmas of the Individual in Public Services*. New York: Russell Sage Foundation.
Lister, S. (2006) 'Plural policing, local communities and the market in visible patrols', in A. Dearling, T. Newburn and P. Somerville (eds) *Supporting Safer Communities*. Coventry: Chartered Institute of Housing/Housing Studies Association.
Little, A. (2002) *The Politics of Community: Theory and Practice*. Edinburgh: Edinburgh University Press.
Local Government Association (1997) *Crime: The Local Solution. A Manifesto*. London: Local Government Association.
Loveday, B. (2005) 'The challenge of police reform in England and Wales', *Public Money and Management*, 25 (5): 275–81.
Ludlam, S. and Smith, M. (eds) *Governing as New Labour: Policy and Politics Under Blair*. Basingstoke: Palgrave.
Lupton, R. and Power, A. (2005) 'Disadvantaged by where you live? New Labour and neighbourhood renewal', in J. Hills and K. Stewart (eds) *A More Equal Society?* Bristol: Policy Press.

McLaughlin, E. (1994) *Community, Policing and Accountability*. Aldershot: Avebury.

McLaughlin, E. (2002a) 'The crisis of the social and the political materialization of community safety', in G. Hughes, E. McLaughlin and J. Muncie (eds) *Crime Prevention and Community Safety: New Directions*. London: Sage.

McLaughlin, E. (2002b) '"Same bed, different dreams": Postmodern reflection on crime prevention and community safety', in G. Hughes and A. Edwards (eds) *Crime Control and Community*. Cullompton: Willan Publishing.

McLaughlin, J., Muncie, J. and Hughes, G. (2001) 'The permanent revolution: New Labour, new public management and the modernisation of criminal justice', *Criminal Justice*, 1 (3): 301–18.

Maguire, M. (2004) 'The Crime Reduction Programme in England and Wales. Reflections on the vision and the reality', *Criminal Justice*, 4 (3): 213–37.

Martin, S. (2002) 'Best value: new public management or new direction?', in K. McLaughlin, S. Osborne and E. Ferlie (eds) *New Public Management: Current Trends and Future Prospects*. London: Routledge.

Matthews, R. and Pitts, J. (eds) (2001) *Crime, Disorder and Community Safety*. London: Routledge.

Matthews, R. and Young, J. (eds) (2003) *The New Politics of Crime and Punishment*. Cullompton: Willan Publishing.

Mills, C. Wright (1959) *The Sociological Imagination*. Oxford: Oxford University Press.

Morgan, R. (2000) 'The politics of criminological research', in R. King and E. Wincup (eds) *Doing Research on Crime and Justice*. Oxford: Oxford University Press.

Morgan, R. and Newburn, T. (1997) *The Future of Policing*. Oxford: Clarendon Press.

Moss, K. (2006) 'Crime prevention as law: rhetoric or reality?', in K. Moss and M. Stephens (eds) *Crime Reduction and the Law*. Abingdon: Routledge.

Mulholland, H. (2004) 'Q&A: comprehensive performance assessment', *The Guardian*, 16 December 2004.

Mulgan, G. (2005) *Joined-up Government: Past, Present and Future*. http://www.youngfoundation.org.uk/node/223.

Murie, A. (1998) 'Linking housing changes to crime', in C. Jones-Finer and M. Nellis (eds) *Crime and Social Exclusion*. Oxford: Blackwell.

Murray, C. (1990) *The Emerging British Underclass*. London: Institute of Economic Affairs.

Newburn, T. and Jones, T. (2002) *Consultation by Crime and Disorder Reduction Partnerships*. Police Research Series Paper 148. London: Home Office.

Newman, J. (2001) *Modernising Governance*. London: Sage.

Newman, O. (1973) *Defensible Space*. London: Architectural Press.

Niskanen, W. (1973) *Bureaucracy: Master or Servant?* London: Institute of Economic Affairs.

North, P. (2003) 'Communities at the heart? Community action and urban policy in the UK', in R. Imrie and M. Raco (eds) *Urban Renaissance? New Labour, Community and Urban Policy*. Bristol: Policy Press.

ODPM (2004) *Local Area Agreements: A Prospectus*. London: ODPM.

ODPM (2005) *Safer and Stronger Communities Fund. Taking the Agreements Forward*. London: ODPM.

ODPM/Home Office (2004) *Together: Tackling Anti-social Behaviour*. London: ODPM/Home Office (www.odpm.gov.uk).

O'Malley, C. (2005) 'From practical challenge to existential threat: crime and disorder in historical perspective', in C. O'Malley, S. Waiton and D. Cummings (eds) *Who's Anti-social? New Labour and the Politics of Anti-social Behaviour*. London: Academy of Ideas.

O'Malley, C., Waiton, S. and Cummings, D. (eds) (2005) *Who's Anti-social? New Labour and the Politics of Anti-social Behaviour*. London: Academy of Ideas.

O'Malley, P. (1992) 'Risk, power and crime prevention', *Economy and Society*, 21: 252–75.

O'Malley, P. (2000) 'Risk, crime and prudentialism revisited', in K. Stenson and R. Sullivan (eds) *Crime, Risk and Justice*. Cullompton: Willan Publishing.

O'Malley, P. (2004) *Risk, Uncertainty and Government*. London: Glass House.

Ormerod, P. (2005) 'The impact of Sure Start', *Political Quarterly*, 76 (4): 565–7.

Osborne, D. and Gaebler, T. (1992) *Reinventing Government: How the Entrepreneurial Spirit is Transforming the Public Sector*. Reading, MA: Addison-Wesley.

Papps, P. (1998) 'Anti-social behaviour strategies: individualistic or holistic?', *Housing Studies*, 13 (5): 639–56.

Parsons, W. (1995) *Public Policy*. Cheltenham: Edward Elgar.

Payne, L. (2003) 'Anti-social behaviour', *Children and Society*, 17: 321–4.

Phillips, C. (2002) 'From voluntary to statutory status: reflecting on the experience of three partnerships established under the Crime and Disorder Act 1998', in G. Hughes, E. McLaughlin and J. Muncie (eds) *Crime Prevention and Community Safety: New Directions*. London: Sage.

Phillips, C., Considine, M. and Lewis, R. (2000) *A Review of Audits and Strategies Produced by Crime and Disorder Partnerships in 1999*. Home Office Police and Reducing Crime Unit Briefing Note 8/00. London: Home Office.

Phillips, C., Jacobson, J., Prime, R., Carter, M. and Considine, M. (2002) *Crime and Disorder Reduction Partnerships: Round One Progress*. Police Research Series Paper 151. London: Home Office.

Pierre, J. and Peters, B.G. (2000) *Governance, Politics and the State*. New York: St Martin's Press.

Pitts, J. and Hope, T. (1997) 'The local politics of inclusion: the state and community safety', *Social Policy and Administration*, 31 (5): 37–58.

Pollard, C. (1997) 'Zero tolerance: short-term fix, long-term liability?', in N. Dennis (ed.) *Zero Tolerance: Policing a Free Society*. London: Institute of Economic Affairs.

Power, M. (1997) *The Audit Society*. Oxford: Oxford University Press.

Prideaux, S. (2005) *Not so New Labour: A Sociological Critique of New Labour's Policy and Practice*. Bristol: Policy Press.

Prior, D. (2004) 'Involving communities in crime control: dynamics of trust and suspicion', in Civil Renewal Research Centre (ed.) *Researching Civil Renewal*. Birmingham: Civil Renewal Research Centre.

Putnam, D. (2000) *Bowling Alone: The Collapse and Revival of an American Community*. New York: Simon & Schuster.

Raco, M. (2003) 'New Labour, community and the future of Britain's urban renaissance', in R. Imrie and M. Raco (eds) *Urban Renaissance? New Labour, Community and Urban Policy*. Bristol: Policy Press.

Raco, M. (2004) 'Urban regeneration in a growing region: the renaissance of England's average town', in C. Johnstone and M. Whitehead (eds) *New Horizons in British Urban Policy*. Aldershot: Ashgate.

Raco, M., Parker, G. and Doak, J. (2006) 'Reshaping spaces of local governance? Community strategies and the modernisation of local government in England', *Environment and Planning C: Government and Policy*, 24: 475–96.

Radzinowicz, L. (1991) 'Penal regressions', *Cambridge Law Journal*, 50: 422–44.

Randall, N. (2004) 'Three faces of New Labour: principle, pragmatism and populism in New Labour's Home Office', in S. Ludlam and M. Smith (eds) *Governing as New Labour: Policy and Politics Under Blair*. Basingstoke: Palgrave.

Rhodes, R. (1997) *Understanding Governance: Policy Networks, Governance, Reflexivity and Accountability*. Buckingham: Open University Press.

Richards, D. and Smith, M. (2004) 'The "hybrid state": Labour's response to the challenge of governance', in S. Ludlam and M. Smith (eds) *Governing as New Labour: Policy and Politics Under Blair*. Basingstoke: Palgrave.

Roberts, S. (2006) 'Communities and social justice', *Criminal Justice Matters*, 64: 6–7.

Rose, N. (1996) 'The death of the social', *Economy and Society*, 25 (3): 327–56.

Rose, N. (1999) *Powers of Freedom*. Cambridge, Cambridge University Press.

Rose, N. (2000) 'Government and control', *British Journal of Criminology*, 40 (2): 321–39.

Rose, N. and Miller, P. (1992) 'Political power beyond the state: problematics of government', in *British Journal of Sociology*, 43 (2): 173–205.

Rutherford, A. (1996) *Transforming Criminal Policy*. Winchester: Waterside Press.

Ryan, M. (2006) 'Public(s), politicians and punishment', *Criminal Justice Matters*, 64: 14–15.

Sampson, R., Raudenbush, S.W. and Earls, F. (1997) 'Neighborhoods and violent crime: a multi-level study of collective efficacy', *Science*, 277: 918–24.

Savage, S. and Charman, S. (2002) 'Toughing it out: New Labour's criminal record', in M. Powell (ed.) *Evaluating New Labour's Welfare Reforms*. Bristol: Policy Press.

Savage, S. and Nash, M. (1994) 'Yet another agenda for law and order: British criminal justice policy and the Conservatives. *International Criminal Justice Review* 4 (1): 37–51.

Scarman, Lord (1981) *The Brixton Disorders, 10–12 April 1981*. London: HMSO.

Schweinhart, L., Barnes, H. and Weikart, D. (1993). *Significant benefits: The High/Scope Perry Preschool Study through Age* 27. *(Monographs of the High/Scope Educational Research Foundation, 10.)* Ypsilanti, MI: High/Scope Press.

Scraton, P. (1985) *The State of the Police*. London: Pluto.

SEU (1998) *Bringing Britain Together: A National Strategy for Neighbourhood Renewal*. Cm 4045. London: Stationary Office.

SEU (2000) *Policy Action Team 8 Report: Anti-social Behaviour*. London: ODPM.

Shearing, C. and Stenning, P. (1984) 'From the panopticon to Disney World: the development of discipline', in A. Doob and E. Greenspen (eds) *Perspectives in Criminal Law: Essays in Honour of John H.J. Edwards*. Aurora: Canada Law Book.

Sherman, L., Gottfredson, D., McKenzie, D., Eck, J., Reuter, P. and Bushway, S. (1998) *Preventing Crime: What Works, What Doesn't, What's Promising*. Washington DC: National Institute of Justice.

Simon, J. (1997) 'Governing through crime', in G. Fisher and L. Friedman (eds) *The Crime Conundrum: Essays on Criminal Justice*. New York: Westview Press.

Skelcher, C. (2004) 'The new governance of communities', in G. Stoker and D. Wilson (eds) *British Local Government into the 21st Century*. Basingstoke: Palgrave Macmillan.

Skinns, L. (2005) *Cops, Councils and Crime and Disorder: A Critical Review of Three Community Safety Partnerships*. PhD thesis, University of Cambridge.

Smith, D. (1987) 'The police and the idea of community', in P. Willmott (ed.) *Policing and the Community*. London: Policy Studies Institute.

Smith, M. (2004) 'Conclusion: defining New Labour', in S. Ludlam and M. Smith (eds) *Governing as New Labour: Policy and Politics Under Blair*. Basingstoke: Palgrave.

Social Landlords' Crime and Nuisance Group (2005) Written evidence submitted to the *Home Affairs Committee on Anti-social Behaviour*. London: House of Commons

Somerville, P., Dearling, A. and Newburn, T. (2006) 'Conclusion', in A. Dearling, T. Newburn and P. Somerville (eds) *Supporting Safer Communities*. Coventry: Chartered Institute of Housing/Housing Studies Association.

Sparks, R. (1992) 'Reason and unreason in "left realism": some problems in the constitution in the fear of crime', in R. Matthews and J. Young (eds) *Issues in Realist Criminology*. London: Sage.

Squires, P. and Stephen, D. (2005) *Rougher Justice: Anti-social Behaviour and Young People*. Cullompton: Willan Publishing.

Stenson, K. (2000a) 'Crime control, social policy and liberalism', in G. Lewis, S. Gewirtz and J. Clarke (eds) *Rethinking Social Policy*. Sage: London.

Stenson, K. (2000b) 'Someday our prince will come: zero-tolerance policing and liberal government', in T. Hope and R. Sparks (eds) *Crime, Risk and Insecurity*. London: Routledge.

Stenson, K. (2001) 'The new politics of crime control', in K. Stenson and R.R. Sullivan (eds) *Crime, Risk and Justice: The Politics of Crime Control in Liberal Democracies*. Cullompton: Willan Publishing.

Stenson, K. (2005) 'Sovereignty, biopolitics and the local government of crime in Britain', *Theoretical Criminology*, 9 (3): 265–87.

Stenson, K. and Edwards, A. (2001) 'Rethinking crime control in advanced liberal government; the "third way" and the return to the local', in K. Stenson and R. Sullivan (eds) *Crime, Risk and Justice*. Cullompton: Willan Publishing.

Stenson, K. and Edwards, A. (2003) 'Crime control and local governance: the struggle for sovereignty in advanced liberal polities', *Contemporary Politics*, 9 (2): 203–18.

Stenson, K. and Watt, P. (1999) 'Crime, risk and governance in a southern English village', in G. Dingwall and S. Moody (eds) *Crime and Conflict in the Countryside*. Cardiff: University of Wales Press.

Stewart, J. and Clarke, M. (1997) *Tackling the Wicked Issues*. Birmingham: School of Public Policy.

Stoker, G. (1998) 'Governance as theory: five propositions', *International Social Science Journal*, 155: 17–28.

Stoker, G. (2004) *Transforming Local Governance: From Thatcherism to New Labour*. Basingstoke: Palgrave Macmillan.

Stoker, G. and Wilson, D. (eds) (2004) *British Local Government into the 21st Century*. Basingstoke: Palgrave Macmillan.

Straw, J. and Michael, A. (1996) *Tackling the Causes of Crime: Labour's Proposals to Prevent Crime and Criminality*. London: Labour Party.

Sullivan, H. (2004) 'Community governance and local government: a shoe that fits or the emperor's new clothes?', in G. Stoker and D. Wilson (eds) *British Local Government into the 21st Century*. Basingstoke: Palgrave Macmillan.

Sullivan, R. (2001) 'The schizophrenic state: neo-liberal criminal justice', in K. Stenson and R.R. Sullivan (eds) *Crime, Risk and Justice: The Politics of Crime Control in Liberal Democracies*. Cullompton: Willan Publishing.

Sutton, M. (1996) *Implementing Crime Prevention Schemes in a Multi-agency Setting: Aspects of Process in the Safer Cities Programme*. Home Office Research Study 160. London: HMSO.

Taylor, I. (1993) 'Driving the vermin off the streets'. *New Statesman and Society* (8 October), 16–18.

Taylor, I. (1996) 'Fear of crime, urban fortunes and suburban social movements: some reflections from Manchester', *Sociology*, 30 (2): 317–37.

Taylor, I. (1999) *Crime in Context*. Cambridge: Polity Press.

Taylor, M. (2003) *Public Policy in the Community*. Basingstoke: Palgrave Macmillan.

Tilley, N. (1993) 'Crime prevention and the safer cities story', *The Howard Journal*, 32 (1): 40–52.

Tilley, N. (2001) 'Evaluation and evidence-led crime reduction policy and practice', in R. Matthews and J. Pitts (eds) *Crime, Disorder and Community Safety*. London: Routledge.

Tilley, N. (2004) 'Applying theory-driven evaluation to the British Crime Reduction Programme', *Criminal Justice*, 4 (3): 255–76.

Tilley, N. (2005) *Handbook of Crime Prevention and Community Safety*. Cullompton: Willan Publishing.

Tonry, M. (2003) 'Evidence, elections and ideology in the making of criminal justice policy', in M. Tonry (ed.) *Confronting Crime: Crime Control Policy Under New Labour*. Cullompton: Willan Publishing.

Van Swaaningen, R. (2002) 'Towards a replacement discourse on community safety: lessons from the Netherlands', in G. Hughes *et al.* (eds) *Crime Prevention and Community Safety: New Directions*. London: Sage.

Waiton, S. (2005) 'The politics of anti-social behaviour', in C. O'Malley, S. Waiton and D. Cummings (eds) *Who's Anti-social? New Labour and the Politics of Anti-social Behaviour*. London: Academy of Ideas.

Walker, R. and Wiseman, M. (2003) 'Making welfare work: UK activation policies under New Labour', *International Social Security Review*, 56 (1): 3–28.

Wallace, M. (2001) 'A new approach to neighbourhood renewal in England', *Urban Studies*, 31 (120): 2163–6.

Walters, R. (2003) *Deviant Knowledge: Criminology, Politics And Policy*. Cullompton: Willan Publishing.

Waters, I. (1996) 'Quality of service: politics or paradigm shift?', in F. Leishman, B. Loveday and S. Savage (eds) *Core Issues in Policing* (1st edn). Basingstoke: Macmillan.

Watt, P. and Jacobs, K. (2000) 'Discourses of social exclusion: an analysis of bringing Britain together: a national strategy for neighbourhood renewal', *Housing, Theory and Society*, 17: 14–26.

Whitehead, M. (2004) 'The urban neighbourhood and the moral geographies of British urban policy', in C. Johnstone and M. Whitehead (eds) *New Horizons in British Urban Policy*. Aldershot: Ashgate.

Wilkinson, D. and Appelbee, E. (1999) *Implementing Holistic Government*. Bristol: Policy Press.

Wilks-Heeg, S. (2003) 'Economy, equity or empowerment? New Labour, communities and urban policy evaluation', in R. Imrie and M. Raco (eds) *Urban Renaissance? New Labour, Community and Urban Policy*. Bristol: Policy Press.

Williamson, H. (2006) 'Growing out of crime? Youth transitions, opportunity structures and social inclusion', in A. Dearling, T. Newburn and P. Somerville (eds) *Supporting Safer Communities*. Coventry: Chartered Institute of Housing/Housing Studies Association.

Wilson, D. (2004) 'New patterns of central-local government relations', in Stoker, G. and D. Wilson (eds) *British Local Government into the 21st Century*. Basingstoke: Palgrave Macmillan.

Wilson, D. and Game, C. (2002) *Local Government in the United Kingdom* (4th edn). Basingstoke: Palgrave MacMillan.

Wilson, J.Q. (1975) *Thinking About Crime*. New York: Basic Books.

Wilson, J.Q. and Kelling, G. (1982) 'Broken windows', *Atlantic Monthly*, March: 29–38.

Windlesham, Lord (1987) *Responses to Crime*. Oxford: Clarendon Press.

Young, J. (1988) 'Radical criminology in Britain: the emergence of a competing paradigm', in P. Rock (ed.) *A History of British Criminology*. Oxford: Clarendon Press.

Young, J. (1999) *The Exclusive Society*. London: Sage.

Young, J. (2001) 'Identity, community and social exclusion', in R. Matthews and J. Pitts (eds.) *Crime, Disorder and Community Safety*. London: Routledge.

Young, J. (2003) 'Winning the fight against crime? New Labour, populism and lost opportunities', in R. Matthews and J. Young (eds) *Crime, Disorder and Community Safety*. London: Routledge.

Young, J. and Matthews, R. (2003) 'New Labour, crime control and social exclusion', in R. Matthews and J. Young (eds) *Crime, Disorder and Community Safety*. London: Routledge.

Youth Justice Board (2006) *Anti-social Behaviour Orders*. London: Youth Justice Board for England and Wales.

Index